# Justice, Community and Civil Society

# Justice, Community and Civil Society

## A contested terrain

Edited by

**Joanna Shapland**

**WILLAN**
**PUBLISHING**

Published by

Willan Publishing
Culmcott House
Mill Street, Uffculme
Cullompton, Devon
EX15 3AT, UK
Tel: +44(0)1884 840337
Fax: +44(0)1884 840251
e-mail: info@willanpublishing.co.uk
website: www.willanpublishing.co.uk

Published simultaneously in the USA and Canada by

Willan Publishing
c/o ISBS, 920 NE 58th Ave, Suite 300,
Portland, Oregon 97213-3786, USA
Tel: +001(0)503 287 3093
Fax: +001(0)503 280 8832
e-mail: info@isbs.com
website: www.isbs.com

First published 2008

Hardback
ISBN: 978-1-84392-232-2

Paperback
ISBN: 978-1-84392-299-5

British Library Cataloguing-in-Publication Data

A catalogue record for this book is available from the British Library

Project managed by Deer Park Productions, Tavistock, Devon
Typeset by GCS, Leighton Buzzard, Bedfordshire
Printed and bound by T.J. International Ltd, Padstow, Cornwall

# Contents

# Notes on contributors

**Isabelle Bartkowiak** lectures in problem-oriented policing and vulnerable people legislation at the School of Policing Studies, Charles Sturt University, Australia. After obtaining her PhD in Paris, she studied restorative justice and community policing at the International Centre of Comparative Criminology, University of Montreal (Quebec), the Community Peace Programme (Cape Town, South Africa) and at the Regulatory Institutions Network, Australian National University.

**Adam Crawford** is Professor of Criminology and Criminal Justice and Director of the Centre for Criminal Justice Studies at the University of Leeds, UK. He held a Leverhulme Trust Major Research Fellowship between 2004 and 2006 which greatly facilitated the writing of the chapter in this collection. He is currently completing a book on the contractual governance of anti-social behaviour for Cambridge University Press.

**Anna Eriksson** is a graduate of Griffith University, Australia and Cambridge University, UK. She recently completed her PhD at Queen's University Belfast on the topic of Community Restorative Justice in Northern Ireland. From July 2007, she is a full-time lecturer in Criminology at Monash University, Australia.

**Axel Groenemeyer** is Professor of Theory and Research on Social Work and Social Services at the Faculty of Educational Science and Sociology, University of Dortmund, Germany. He is President of the

Section 'Social Problems and Social Control' of the German Society of Sociology. Recent publications include *Handbuch Soziale Probleme* with Günter Albrecht and Friedrich Stallberg (1999) and *Die Ethnisierung von Alltagskonflikten* with Jürgen Mansel (2003).

**Mylène Jaccoud** is a Professor at the School of Criminology of the University of Montreal, Canada. She is in charge of the research unit on conflict resolution, restorative justice and aboriginal people at the International Centre for Comparative Criminology of the University of Montreal.

**Marijke Malsch** is a senior researcher at the Netherlands Institute for the Study of Crime and Law Enforcement (NSCR) in Leiden, the Netherlands. Her current research focuses on the legitimacy of the judicial system, experts in the criminal justice system, the roles of the victim in the criminal justice system, stalking legislation and lay participation in the criminal justice systems of European countries.

**Philip A. Milburn** is Professor of Sociology at the Université de Versailles Saint-Quentin, France. His research interests focus on the study of the criminal justice system, considered in terms of public and local policies and professional competencies. He has published several books and articles in France on these topics, mainly concerning alternative judicial schemes such as victim–offender mediation and reparation programmes. The most recent survey he has published considers French public prosecutors' powers and competencies.

**Kieran McEvoy** is Director of the Institute of Criminology and Criminal Justice and Professor of Law and Transitional Justice at the School of Law, Queens University Belfast, UK. He has recently completed a major study on 'transitional justice from below' in Northern Ireland, Rwanda, Sierra Leone, Colombia and South Africa (with Harry Mika and Kirsten McConnachie), to be published as a monograph by Cambridge University Press in 2008. Recent publications include *Crime Community and Locale* with David O'Mahony, Ray Geary and John Morison (2000); *Paramilitary Imprisonment in Northern Ireland* (2001); *Criminology, Conflict Resolution and Restorative Justice* with Tim Newburn (2003); *Judges, Human Rights and Transition* with John Morison and Gordon Anthony (2007); and *Truth, Transition and Reconciliation: Dealing with the Past in Northern Ireland* (2007).

**Aogán Mulcahy** teaches in the School of Sociology at University College Dublin, Ireland. His research interests include the dynamics of police reform initiatives, policing and marginalisation, and cultural constructions of policing. His publications include *Policing and the Condition of England* with Ian Loader (2003) and *Policing Northern Ireland* (2006). In addition to recent projects on joyriding and youth culture, and ethnicity and marginalisation, his current research explores the themes of continuity and change in the development of policing in Ireland.

**Joanna Shapland** is Professor of Criminal Justice and Director of the Centre for Criminological Research, University of Sheffield, UK. She is Executive Editor of the *International Review of Victimology*. She is currently evaluating the use of restorative justice with adult offenders in England and Wales, funded by the Home Office/Ministry of Justice, and undertaking a longitudinal study of desistance from offending, funded by the ESRC.

**René van Swaaningen** is Professor of International and Comparative Criminology at the Erasmus University Rotterdam, the Netherlands. He has published mainly on criminal justice politics, comparative criminology, penology and crime prevention, and criminological and criminal justice theory. He is currently involved in research on the local governance of crime and insecurity in various European cities and on the question of how the private sector and technology have changed the 'culture of control'.

**Anne Wyvekens** is a researcher at CNRS (Centre National de la Recherche Scientifique)/CERSA, Paris, France. Previously, she was head of the research department of the Institut National des Hautes Etudes de Sécurité from 2002 to 2005. Her research interests include criminal justice, security and insecurity in towns, youth justice and local crime prevention policies. Recent publications include *Espace public et sécurité* (2007); *La magistrature sociale. Enquêtes sur les politiques locales de sécurité* with J. Donzelot (2004) and *La justice de proximité en Europe: pratiques et enjeux* with J. Faget (2001).

# Chapter 1

# Contested ideas of community and justice

*Joanna Shapland*[1]

Over the last ten years, there has been significant disquiet about the relationship between criminal justice and its publics (Hough and Roberts 1998; Mattinson and Mirrlees-Black 2000; Judicature 1997). In some countries this has been disquiet that state criminal justice has moved too far away from the concerns of ordinary people – it has become too distant, too out of touch, insufficiently reflective of different social groups in society. The unease has sometimes been directed at the judiciary and patterns of recruitment to the judiciary ('white, male, middle-aged, middle-class', as they have been termed in England and Wales). Sometimes it has been about the priorities of the police – that they have been insufficiently attentive to ethnic minorities or tackling hate crime, particularly when there has been violence on the streets, as in France, Germany and England. Sometimes it is about the perceived ineffectiveness of state-run criminal justice: that it promised that it would cope with crime, would prevent crime – but crime still continues and, unlike other elements of public services, criminal justice seems unaccountable. Sometimes unease is an expression of general insecurity – that in a climate of increased alert about attacks on our safety, from often indistinctly perceived foes, people crave reassurance and a more personal relationship with those who set themselves up as protectors of safety and justice: they look for local crime prevention strategies, community policing and localised justice.

Governments have sought to respond to these concerns throughout Europe and North America. The particular forms those responses have taken have varied, as will be seen throughout this book, but some move towards localised crime prevention, more responsive policing, restorative justice or mediation, or locally based prosecution or courts, can be seen in each country. Yet those responses, which combine reaching out towards individual members of the public or social groups, with a greater geographically localised presence, have involved challenging deeply held ideas of what justice is and what the state's role should be. Those ideas are part of the heritage of criminal justice in each country: often deeply held though subconscious, they strongly influence reactions to innovation, localisation and lay people.

The relation between criminal justice and its publics - communities or civil society[2] – is now deeply contested. Strangely, however, it has rarely been overtly examined, nor is there a strong comparative academic literature. Yet it concerns the fundamental tenet for state criminal justice: its legitimacy in the eyes of its publics. The authors of the chapters of this book, each of whom has researched the impact of innovation in criminal justice in their own country, felt themselves far more challenged when they met together to consider why the reaction was as it was – and, as a group, we began to realise how different the intrinsic cultural attitudes in relation to criminal justice are across Europe. What now is the attitude of state criminal justice to lay people, to localities and to groups in an increasingly multicultural society? Why is it reacting as it is? This is a time when states' monopoly on criminal justice is being questioned and they are being asked on what basis their legitimacy rests, challenged by both globalisation and localisation. The answers, as we shall see, show both cultural specificity and broader moves towards reaching out to citizens and associations representing citizens.

## Looking comparatively at criminal justice

The idea that criminal justice is the prerogative of the nation state has held sway for over a hundred years. The corollary – that the state should be the only arbiter of its nature and the main instrument through which it carries out its tasks – was taken for granted by governments and criminal justice professionals. In such a context, localisation and the greater involvement of lay people will be perceived as threats, not only to those who previously had defining power over criminal justice, but also to strongly held but often submerged views about what justice should be and what it should be doing. Justice is perhaps the last bulwark of the modernist state:

what this volume describes are the struggles as the justice terrain has become more contested in late modern society. Nor has there been just one battle in any country, or just one direction of travel from the centralised to the more local. As we shall see, some initiatives towards setting up localised criminal justice have been reversed, as criminal justice professionals prove unwilling to leave their citadels. It has proved sometimes easier for criminal justice to interact with other community professionals than with actual lay people – even if this means creating and funding the new breed of community professionals.

Each chapter in this book takes up the task of describing and analysing these contested domains of justice for a particular country. They are trends which have not previously often been brought together, because they involve considering simultaneously what has been happening in courts, in prosecution, in policing, in crime prevention and in new ways of dealing with offenders and victims. These have often been separate domains of criminological, criminal justice and penal law research.

Moreover, making sense of the results of the initiatives in each country involves interrogating that country's ideas about its own society and to what extent the nation state is and should be the dominant presence and ideology governing societal reactions to crime. What does 'community' or localisation mean to that country? Does it have warm connotations, which express ideas of solidarity, locality and help from others – or does it have negative connotations of the other and the alien, in the sense of groups different from one's own?

There are several different models for how to do comparative research. One is the simple and descriptive: 'in my country we do it this way', which will be familiar to many of those who have attended meetings of international bodies involved with criminal justice. This book aspires to reach well beyond this, though we hope that there is sufficient and sufficiently accurate description that native criminal justice actors will recognise the processes involved, even if they have often been hidden for practitioners within the daily political struggles of working out how to implement or change initiatives.

As Nelken (2002) describes, another model is the scientific one, which presumes an underlying common reality behind linguistic and cultural difference, so allowing the use of uniform methods across countries. Examples would be the International Crime Victimisation Study (van Dijk 2000) or the International Self-Report Delinquency Study (Junger-Tas 1994). The operation and fate of criminal justice initiatives, however, cannot conform to this model – because it is clear that deep underlying cultural and historic differences are still active for each nation state. International bodies, such as the EU or the Council of Europe, may facilitate and even mandate similar kinds of initiatives in different countries – and hard-pressed criminal justice policy-makers constantly scan the European environment for potential good ideas from other countries. The 'sideways look' has been operative in European criminal justice policy-making for well over a hundred years and criminologists have been making international comparisons for at least that long (Hood and Robert 1990). Yet though initiatives, such as the adoption of community service or restorative justice, may have the same names or look quite similar between countries, their implementation depends upon the routine practices and cultural beliefs of both criminal justice practitioners and members of the public. And so, as we shall see, countries' individual justice heritage strongly twists the forms the initiatives take and their outcomes.

Should we then retreat to a more nuanced version of the 'in my country we do it this way', which allows only in-depth case studies of one place? That might remain true to the lived experience of those involved in that place, but it obviates the influences of the larger European culture or of globalisation which are having clear effects across place. Movements such as the growing importance of victims, consumerism and the hollowing out of the state[3], and expectations of accountability and managerialism are impinging simultaneously on many countries and on many public service sectors, even if they are felt as change at slightly different times.

Our task is, therefore, the very difficult one of making transparent for each country their understandings of justice, who should administer justice and communities' relation to justice, and showing how these have developed in this way. A difficult task, but an interesting one – because it reaches out beyond the criminal justice system itself to people's deep-seated ideas about how they should be administered and what role lay people themselves should play in that governance. From that, we can proceed to consider the nature of the pressures governments have felt to implement change which involves justice reaching out to its publics and the initiatives they have launched – and their fate.

Nelken has set out three ways in which comparative work on criminal justice could be undertaken: relying on cooperation with foreign experts ('virtually there'), going abroad to interview legal officials and others ('researching there') and drawing on one's own direct experience of living and working in the country concerned ('living there') (2002: 181). Each has its drawbacks of selectivity of what is seen and lack of comprehension as to what is meant by what is seen. Foreign experts who do not meet together may not appreciate cultural differences in meanings of terms or criminal justice institutions. A comparison which seeks to look at justice/ lay interaction from crime prevention to court cannot rely on short research visits. Living in each place would be a lifetime's task.

We have, therefore, adopted a fourth way of working, bringing together those who have researched lay involvement in criminal justice from each country, with short introductory papers which set out initiatives, their political genesis and their outcomes. But we then asked the authors of the papers in this volume to continue meeting together, in a series of seminars over three years, organised under the auspices of the Groupe Européen de Recherche sur les Normativités (GERN). As they talked and refined their papers, so the differences in meaning, in cultural and political background, and in media prominence of different areas of criminal justice became clear. The contested meanings of community and of lay participation became very obvious. Participants agreed to draw out and expose what had been implicit or assumed in the criminological literature and to include this in their chapters. It is my task to bring together these analyses to show whether and how there are similarities and differences and how they illustrate the nation state's dilemmas in responding to its publics and its publics' demands for justice.

## Justice, community and civil society

Why is this book called 'Justice, Community and Civil Society'? Readers in some countries, such as the UK, will be very familiar with the term 'community' and, in the justice field, associate it with 'community policing' and 'community crime prevention', both of which are viewed positively. Local people should be involved in at least some areas of criminal justice. In other countries, however, the association of the word 'community' with 'justice' causes profound dismay or lack of comprehension. Here, 'community' means a separate community, one which is seen as setting itself up in opposition to the state, to create a separate justice system in opposition to the state.

Elsewhere, the idea of linking 'community' (meaning a group of lay people) with 'justice' would be perceived as very regressive. Justice is thought to demand competent administration, which is seen as being able to be undertaken only by professionals who are specialists in this area (the 'managerialist' ethic, which is described in its British form by Crawford (this volume)). Managerialism or 'modernisation' has been an agenda in public administration which has rolled across many countries in Europe in the last two decades – and criminal justice agencies have not been immune. It is an agenda which stresses efficient administration by salaried officials, managed to hit a basket of targets within tight time limits. Justice with a significant community element (which usually requires more time, more persuasion and may be more inefficient, though more effective) is then by definition a poorer, less competent, second choice system – one which may be promoted by administrations eager to save money but which should be resisted.

In other words, in some countries, the linking of 'justice' with 'community' challenges ideal conceptions of justice – either by association with perceived 'different' or 'separatist' groups or by being cast as less efficient or effective. Yet it is acknowledged in every country represented in this book that justice cannot be entirely isolationist. It cannot be entirely created, maintained and developed by justice professionals, divorced from everyone else. One reason is that justice is now a major political topic: justice ministers and ministers of the interior are no longer purely concerned with substantive criminal law (showing toughness, rehabilitation or educational credentials through proposed changes to sentencing law) but have found that whether they are elected – and their continuing tenure of their jobs – depends upon whether it is administered in accordance with public and media wishes. If justice professionals (police, prosecutors, those sentencing or releasing prisoners) seriously misjudge the public mood, demonstrations and marches follow. Justice is now very clearly a political matter, understood as not something which can be left purely to criminal justice professionals.

The public equally do not appreciate it when the hand of ministers rests too heavily or closely on individual justice decisions. The independence of the judiciary from the executive is still a very live political issue. It is more obvious where there is or has been greater dissent between sections of the public, in so-called divided societies or transitional societies. One social group will feel that the criminal justice system, as well as political state power, is biased against it. Unease has, however, also constantly appeared in relation to decisions to prosecute (especially if politicians are the possible offenders) and in decisions about public order and crime prevention at local level. Justice values, the public feels, are not to be the property of any one political party or social group within that country. The dialogue between justice and the public may, in some countries, not be a dialogue between justice and communities, but there should be a dialogue between justice and civil society (the lay people of that country), not just a dialogue between justice and politicians, or justice and professionals. Essentially, people are saying, justice matters.

As we shall see, the different understandings of community and civil society in different countries have worked through to influence not only the kinds of initiative undertaken to respond to these views that justice matters, but also the points in the criminal justice system at which they have occurred. Where 'community' is perceived as causing more concern or being in greater opposition to justice values, initiatives have tended to remain at the peripheries of justice decision-making or involve less serious cases. They have not affected the traditional criminal justice path of 'investigation – decision to prosecute – court – sentence', which has remained as the majority response to criminality following the detection of an offender. Where liaison with different groups or communities within that country has become seen as imperative, initiatives have approached closer to key decisions in the traditional path (decentralisation of criminal justice personnel, lay judges) or new, parallel paths have been established (mediation, restorative justice, new fora for determining sentence). The key here is often whether the parallel paths or new lay criminal justice actors have remained restricted to those groups or whether they have become more widespread within the country. If they remain restricted, as we shall see, there is the danger that this kind of justice becomes seen as second rate or becomes reabsorbed within the professionalised arena and its 'community' credentials then doubted.

These processes are best illustrated by drawing from the very rich material from the countries represented in this volume.

## Where 'community' is seen as problematic to justice and the only relation is with the civil society

Perhaps the most vehement response to the idea that justice might be associated with 'community' comes from France. As Wyvekens (this volume) states, 'The word "community" is not French at all. One could even say that French people, and French institutional personnel, *hate* the word "community". They hate it because in French culture it has almost entirely negative connotations.' She goes on to explain the deep-rooted cultural view of the French state that justice means the same response to every individual. 'Community' has resonances of difference, of social groups seeking deliberately to set themselves apart and hence in opposition to the hegemonic uniformity of French society. Similar connotations for the word 'community' arise for Germany and for the Netherlands (Groenemeyer, van Swaaningen, this volume).

Milburn (this volume) makes similar points: talking about 'community' would be interspersing an intermediate political entity between the state and the citizen, which would be entirely antithetical to French republican political and cultural philosophy. Geographically restricted collective entities within France, such as local authorities, are seen as part of the state, not as separate bodies.

Of course, cultural identity for the French is not in every sphere uniform. There is a lively appreciation of regional characteristics, culture and gastronomy. Moreover, local administration has considerable power, with the *préfet* and the local mayor being able to wield both financial and administrative clout in relation to devising plans to fight criminality and maintain social order. The Bonnemaison (Commission des Maires sur la Sécurité 1982) reforms in relation to crime prevention involved action plans at national, regional and local level – and many of the initiatives which resulted drew their energy from individual towns and smaller localities. The Police Nationale is indeed national, with most officers being trained in Paris before seeking transfers to their home region (Cassan 2005). But policing is increasingly being operationalised between different national and town police forces.

The negative reaction to the idea of 'community' seems partly to be a reaction to the concurrent consideration of justice and community. Justice is a state matter; justice should be republican. But, as both Wyvekens and Milburn point out, there has been a considerable perceived need to reach out to civil society. The response to disaffected local areas, especially when there have been riots, has been seen to be with advantage more localised. So decentralisation is fine; proximity justice is to be applauded. But recognition of difference between local areas is not a good idea. Proximity justice has in essence been a national rolling out of a more localised approach to justice. What is not permitted is accommodation of that justice to local conditions or different values.

In addition, as Milburn (this volume) describes, the state thinks citizens as well should be actively reaching out to the state – but as individuals, not forming rival associations to the state. Of course, such a view creates tensions in implementing such reaching-out policies – the state wishes to keep control, but no longer to be the direct implementer of all such action. Yet it cannot recognise local groups.

Under the rubric of proximity justice, in fact the kinds of initiatives that have been taken have been far more radical and more quickly created than in countries where there is a more positive association between justice and 'community'. Proximity justice is not one coherent masterplan, but a variety of initiatives created whenever and wherever it has been thought politically helpful or appropriate to bring justice closer to the people. Initially, it was intended to provide the courts with new responses to perceived rises in petty crime and nuisance for which the traditional route was too cumbersome. Because the areas seen as most afflicted by this were the disadvantaged urban areas, it was these areas which were given local prosecutors, working out of offices initially based in the same neighbourhoods (Wyvekens, this volume). The strategy was in fact to allow parallel modes of justice administration to function at the same time as the traditional route. In other countries, that might have been seen as a direct challenge to criminal justice judicial hegemony. But here, it was operated by criminal justice personnel and so within the system. Moreover, whenever there was a need for different, more localised components, these were set up not as criminal justice policy, but under the umbrella of general urban policy (literally, city policies). So crime prevention policy, with its necessarily different elements which had to be attuned to local characteristics to have any chance of fitting crime profiles or town priorities, could become urban policy. Indeed, as Wyvekens (this volume) comments, local criminal justice professionals did not involve themselves with the mayor's crime reduction partnerships, but instead developed their own responses separately.

The nature of those responses reflected criminal justice's own workload pressures. Minor offences clogged up the system and could not all be dropped without an outcry from residents of those areas. The answer was to propel them into a parallel system which used mediators. The ethos of that parallel system was to build on the already existing tendencies to use social and educational measures with the young and with family conflict. However, mediation was not allowed to become a separate system with its own values and a more leisurely timescale suited to neighbourhood conflict (Dignan 2000). Instead, its activities had to be administratively registered (and thus controlled) by state criminal justice. Moreover, in some areas, separately employed mediators became eclipsed by deputy prosecutors, who normally had backgrounds in state criminal justice or policing (Milburn, this volume).

Wyvekens (this volume) also describes how the radical and innovative neighbourhood justice centres (*maisons de justice*), designed initially to show the visibility of state justice in areas which felt far removed from national concerns, also morphed, through funding and policy changes, into advice centres, rather than places which themselves dealt with criminal justice cases. The change was facilitated by their structure as governed by agreements between criminal justice and local authorities, which brought workers increasingly into contact with other needs for advice. As Genn (1999; Genn and Paterson 2001) has found in England and Wales and in Scotland, those who come into contact with criminal justice often have clusters of problems, requiring advice and action across the social policy spectrum.

Meanwhile, crime prevention initiatives, involving partnerships initially set up under the Bonnemaison system, went through a series of shifts. Initially concentrated upon policing and local authorities, criminal justice agents started to participate as well, primarily the prosecutor. The new localised contracts at the level of towns provided funds to employ workers in police stations and municipalities. But the local consultation meetings tended to be between agencies, not with local people. Nor did agencies seem really to wish to involve local people. Instead, they, like the local justice centres, turned to informing local people about state services. The result has been that local justice centre workers, like the workers employed on the state contracts with towns, increasingly have a range of expertise appropriate to the locality's social problems. This may or may not be the most effective way for the state to reach out to the people, but it has certainly resulted in that reaching out no longer necessarily having a criminal justice flavour. The parallel path is now an advice path and a civil justice path – a far more heterogeneous set of activities.

This ties in with the state's dilemma in trying to implement its proximity policies. If it cannot recognise local groups, and finds it difficult to deal with local individuals, then who should it contact? The answer, as Milburn (this volume) shows, has sometimes been non-profit-making organisations which have a legal basis and are intended to gather together citizens working for the public good (note, the public good, not the local good). Sometimes it has been new forms of professionals, such as mediators or prosecutor's delegates. Both can be funded by and contracted to state agencies, which allows continuing state monitoring and control. The reaching out by the state does involve a greater range of actors than purely criminal justice ones – and a greater interdisciplinarity in social action in relation to crime – so being in the tradition of deliberative democracy in France. It allows action against crime, whether in solving disputes or preventing crime, to reflect ordinary, rather than legal, language and rationales. But it is very different from empowering groups or individual citizens to take or formulate their own action.

The use of intermediate agents (non-profit-making associations and professionals) can also allow state criminal justice to relax and go back to its previous ways. Judges and prosecutors, who never really liked being based outside regular courthouses, could stay where they preferred. But mediation has been admitted to the ranks of traditional criminal justice responses – though it is now to be administered by criminal justice actors with legal training and there is a considerable danger of net-widening (Wyvekens, this volume). So parallel paths have been created to meet concerns about isolation and centralisation of state criminal justice – but those parallel paths have then been reabsorbed into state administration. The longer-term question is whether this strategy will work and be seen as sufficient by civil society. Has the criminal justice system in France managed successfully to resist challenges to its legitimacy from the increasing multicultural nature of all Western societies, denying the need to be accountable to difference and attempting to reimpose traditional uniformity through education and advice? In other words, can uniformity remain? Can the vertical relationship between state and citizens remain the same for all citizens in a late modern society?

The view in Germany about the potential for 'community' in relation to criminal justice is very similar to that in France. 'Community', seen as localised groups with close ties and bonds, is not seen as an appropriate entity for the formulation of policy about justice, nor as an appropriate delivery mechanism, barring a few functions in relation to crime prevention (Groenemeyer, this volume). Local government is seen as an arm of the national state, not a separate entity, and there is a similar strong republican ethos that there should not be intermediate organisations between state and citizen. Nor has there been political pressure to change the widely held view that justice should be professionalised and a matter for the state. Hence the state has not needed to reach out to citizens. There is no tradition of lay people being involved in the administration of criminal justice. However, the same ideas of responsibilisation of citizens and the need for the state to discharge to others some of its duties in relation to social order and social welfare have occurred in Germany as in other countries in Europe, whatever position they hold about justice. The state wishes to roll back its duties and withdraw from some of its responsibilities. It no longer wishes to be responsible for all matters relating to crime and social order. Communities may be resisted: the pressure to modernise cannot.

As France has used non-profit-making organisations and professionals to undertake some of these burdens, so Germany has turned to existing social organisations rather than create a dialogue with localised geographical neighbourhoods (Groenemeyer, this volume). Professionals, particularly social welfare professionals, have always had a relatively powerful position in Germany compared with many other countries, with a strong voice in relation to new legislation. However, distrust of professionals, common throughout Europe through the adoption of a neo-liberal view of professional economics,[4] has led to a wider use of non-governmental organisations and self-help groups. Voluntary sector groups are cheaper and do not threaten state power. Where they have been used, the intention is to integrate them into state organisations.

Germany has seen innovations in criminal justice that are similar to other countries: increased use of mediation; alternative criminal sanctions, particularly for the young; victim support and assistance. But these have been introduced and implemented in Germany without reference to ideas of 'community', rather in the name of effectiveness, efficiency and modernised services to lay people involved with justice. It is an illustration of Crawford's (this volume) separation of the trends towards localisation and towards modernisation, both of which have been major trends in public services delivery in the last ten to twenty years across Europe.

The Netherlands has a similar view to France and Germany in relation to the need for professionalisation of criminal justice. Criminal justice should be administered by professional judges and prosecutors, with no tradition of lay involvement (Malsch, this volume). However, unlike in France and Germany, there has been political pressure against untrammelled professionalisation, particularly from the media. Some of this has been pressure to involve lay people more closely in criminal justice as individuals – not just to give them advice as to how to cope with the justice system (as in France), but to aid and assist them. It is linked to research showing that justice processes which involve citizens tend to lead to greater satisfaction, as Tyler and Huo (2002) have also argued from research in the United States.

As in France, there has also been political pressure on state criminal justice to be or to seem less isolationist: pressure for proximity justice rather than community justice. Malsch (this volume) has seen this political pressure as impinging on the legitimacy of justice institutions, affecting the wish of citizens to agree that the actions of justice institutions should be complied with. This is a step further than what seems to be the purely political imperative of doing something about disorder in particular neighbourhoods which occurred in France. Questioning legitimacy is questioning the fundamental quality of state institutions rather than just their ability to deliver. Crawford (this volume) makes similar points in relation to England and Wales. Isolationism undermines perceived legitimacy, particularly in the context of an increasingly diverse society. As Malsch argues, legitimacy is related to the expectations citizens have about the nature, as well as the effectiveness, of their criminal justice system. As a result, in the Netherlands, there are now increased attempts by justice to communicate directly with citizens, not just tell them what to do – but again still not using intermediate organisations of groups of citizens.

'Justice in the Neighbourhood' programmes in the Netherlands have involved prosecutors having their offices in local areas, though it is less clear to what extent this has increased participation by individuals from local areas (Malsch, this volume). Mediation and restorative justice conferences have been introduced, though these are organised outside the formal criminal justice system by non-profit-making organisations. The outcomes are not expected to influence state criminal justice action against the offender (such as sentences). Sometimes, however, the extent of use of these schemes, such as the Halt facility for diverting young offenders in relation to vandalism and shop theft towards community work, has grown so much that I would conclude that the parallel path (Halt) is now a major output of criminal justice systems. This may have been allowed to happen, as van Swaaningen (this volume) suggests, because it has become now primarily a way to reduce prosecutorial caseloads. Many of these initiatives are state funded – and funding has been affected by the perceived political priority for such programmes. If one were cynical, one might expect that, if political imperatives to be seen to being doing something to restore justice legitimacy die down, then the only initiatives which may continue to be substantially funded are those which prove to be cheaper and easier for state justice – even if they are a potential continuing challenge to the mainstream path of state justice.

## The exception: crime reduction

The exception to a dislike and distrust of local groups in France, Germany and the Netherlands is in the field of crime prevention, where local bodies have been created. Here the dominant rhetoric, as it is in the UK, is 'partnership' between local authorities, social service agencies and the police (and sometimes prosecutors). Crime prevention councils provide foci for the discussion of local problems, but they are normally councils with agencies or associations as members – not local groups of citizens or communities (except in the UK, where residents' groups etc. are often involved). The dominant partners are state agencies, such as the police, and local authorities (which, for France and Germany, are also seen as state administrations). However, a much wider range of statutory and voluntary sector agencies is involved in the Netherlands, as in the UK.

In France and in the Netherlands, although these are local bodies addressing local problems, their strategies have to fit within national plans for crime reduction. Local decisions are relatively limited decisions, though there is some local decision-making power (van Swaaningen, this volume). The overall framework in many continental European countries is the so-called tri-partite or triangular arrangement whereby measures to promote public order should be decided in discussions between the mayor of the city, the chief of police and the public prosecutor. It is this framework which has started to bring prosecutors in such countries, at least partially, into ideas of partnership with other bodies to deal with matters which are not solely within their own remit or that of the traditional criminal justice system.

In the UK, with a common law framework, in contrast, prosecutors (and the judiciary) have not had any statutory responsibility for public order or crime reduction and have tended to feel that they should not participate in many crime reduction partnership bodies. For some time, there have been parallel track partnership bodies for England and Wales. Local authorities and the police have discussed (and had statutory responsibility for) crime reduction; whereas prosecutors and the judiciary have confined themselves to partnerships dealing solely with criminal justice initiatives (such as more rapid processing of prosecutions and cases through the courts: Shapland *et al.* 2003). More recently, prosecutors in England and Wales have been prepared to join partnerships dealing with crime reduction in relation to specific high-profile crimes, where prosecution is one option for action, such as domestic violence, hate crimes, child abuse and human trafficking (Welsh 2003).

The impetus behind partnership has, I think, been twofold. One is the recognition that crime reduction initiatives often need to deal with several problems in local geographical areas in order to meet residents' concerns. Van Swaaningen (this volume), for example, points to Rotterdam's 18-point plan in 2001, which ranged from public transport to relocating drug addicts. Other partnership bodies, whether in disadvantaged neighbourhoods in France providing a multiplicity of different forms of advice for citizens (Wyvekens, this volume) or trying to meet the multiple needs of victims (Shapland and Hall 2007) or domestic violence survivors (Welsh 2003), have faced a similar need for a multiplicity of goals and actions.

The second impetus towards partnership could be construed as an attempt to shift responsibility – and blame. In all the countries discussed in this volume, the state has recognised that it cannot meet citizens' demands for less crime and more security. Of course, it can be argued that it is states' ramping up of the need for vigilance, for citizens to take precautions and for more wide-ranging security-related police powers, which itself has fed citizens' feelings of insecurity. The constant and obvious presence of security devices and surveillance, whether by cameras (particularly in the UK) or by security guards (for example, in Poland: Shapland 2006) reminds citizens that they may not be safe – that there may be threats around. Security devices and personnel may create insecurity and dependency. This is not necessarily a positive feedback loop for states which have already decided that they cannot meet the seemingly insatiable need for their citizens to feel more secure.

But the start of states' attempts to shift responsibility for crime and crime reduction towards partnerships precedes the more recent push towards security in many countries. States recognised their relative powerlessness over crime in the 1980s and 1990s (Robert 1991; Crawford 1997), when relative affluence combined with rising crime rates throughout Europe – and their powerlessness over perceptions of crime in the 1990s and into the new millennium, when decreases in crime rates were accompanied by continuing fear of crime. One answer to these political dilemmas was to share the burden and blame: to push responsibility from national towards more local government and out to different agencies. Rotterdam's attempts at responsibilisation of the different parts of local government and the private sector in 2001 (van Swaaningen, this volume) is a clear attempt to shift some responsibility.

Van Swaaningen (this volume) exposes a key dilemma even within this limited enthusiasm to involve local geographical areas in crime prevention. Where local people are fearful of not just crime, but of difference within their own communities and of incomers, then bringing in the community means bringing in these concerns and insecurities as well. People may have rosy views of ideal 'communities' as having high solidarity, but this may not be local people's local reaction to the instant problems of nuisance, crime or drug dealing. Ideally, residents would like to see improvements stemming from better social policies on housing, education, etc. – but when they feel insecure, then they need action by criminal justice agencies and local authorities now. And that action can be quite exclusionary in terms of removing from their locality people who are seen to cause problems. Very similar social pressures have been felt in England and Wales, leading to ASBOs (anti-social behaviour orders), which may contain agreements about what acceptable behaviour is, but which often contain geographical or time exclusion clauses (not to enter certain areas, not to approach certain people, curfews after certain hours) (Burney 2005).

Greater localisation of policy and responsibilisation of local agencies (Garland 2001) brings in its wake acceptance of some differentiation in policy-making to local needs and circumstances, even on a strong state model. This includes some differentiation of local services, as well as strategies for repression of crime and deviant social groups. The exact mix seems to reflect national cultural views about the philosophy behind crime reduction. France, for example, has continued for many years to have a strong educative, almost paternalistic, philosophy in its youth justice policies and sentences. In its initial national crime reduction strategies in the Bonnemaison period, this translated into feelings that, in disadvantaged neighbourhoods, French society had failed young people by not providing them with sufficient opportunities for training, employment and joining the world of work, etc. The answer was detached youth work (youth workers going out to work with young people on the streets), local arts projects led by young people, etc. The more recent answer has been advice centres to educate citizens on their rights and how they can work with the system (Wyvekens, this volume).

The Netherlands, in contrast, have tended to combine specific repressive policies with offering those engaged in criminality a new start. One long-term (and lasting) initiative towards young people of this kind is Halt (Malsch, this volume), as we saw above. Policy towards drug addiction has focused on harm reduction and help towards alternative lives, coupled with increasingly harsh sentencing for those who will not accept help (van Swaaningen, this volume).

In England and Wales, the tendency has been to turn towards other providers for specific local needs, often on state funding (but relatively short-term project funding). Initially, many of these providers were from the voluntary sector, including almost entirely state-funded arm's length agencies, such as NACRO and Crime Concern, which developed action plans and supported local partnerships towards crime reduction. From the 1980s onwards, they were increasingly from the private sector, as crime reduction policy turned to situational crime prevention and security agents (Crawford, this volume). As Crawford explains, there is no longer just partnership, but partnership supported by a family of policing agents (police, civilian community police support officers employed by the police, civilians employed by towns, private security firms providing manned guarding, corporate security, etc.). Yet the voluntary sector and community groups continue to play a major part, particularly in the more recent resurgence of criminality prevention through early years schemes such as Sure Start. There is, of course, still state control – but control in the UK tends to be exerted not through diktat, state agents or even national policies,[5] but through funding and resulting tender requirements and contractual accountability.

## Where decentralisation to 'community' is seen as a positive move nationally

Of the countries represented in this volume, the UK, Ireland and Canada are probably those in which decentralisation of justice to local 'communities' is most positively regarded. It is not a coincidence, I believe, that these are countries in which policing is delivered by police forces, many of which are locally based rather than being solely national forces.[6] Here, as Crawford (1997) has shown, citizens as well have been coopted into the multi-agency sphere as potential partners against crime.

Mulcahy (this volume), for example, has emphasised the way in which the police force in Ireland, *An Garda Síochána*, has, since its foundation, emphasised its local roots. It has seen itself simultaneously as representing the state and also being of and from local communities. It has derived its identity and its legitimacy from both, partly because its Irish identity stemmed from local communities and the image conveyed by policing with and in those communities, as compared with the colonial past where policing was imposed from outside. However, as urban areas, particularly, have become more multicultural recently, so that identity has become more strained. The monocultural rural identity of Ireland is no longer so appropriate in modern 'Celtic tiger' economic times. It is interesting that here, as in crime reduction initiatives, policy has shifted to emphasise partnership rather than state agent action (Mulcahy, this volume). The informalism of locally based action has had to give way to a more negotiated legitimacy, which, in terms of crime and security, now involves local authorities and not solely the police. These Joint Policing Committees involve primarily local councils and other politicians, as well as the police, with only a few seats allowed to community or voluntary representatives: an echo of the poverty of representation of lay people on similar partnerships in France and Germany.

So, even in these countries, there are tensions as to what 'community' might mean. Community is a complex concept. Peter Wilmott (1987), looking at the bonds between an individual and his or her community, developed the idea of a threefold typology. He saw there to be:

- *territorial communities* defined by geography, often referred to as 'local', or 'neighbourhoods';
- *interest communities* defined by common interests, which may be geographically more widespread (so, for example, faith communities, leisure activities such as sports teams or users of particular facilities, political parties);
- *attachment communities*, defined by their feeling of belonging to places or relationships.

Taking this away from his original context, which was to look at the relationship between the individual and the community, and applying these ideas to communities or collectivities themselves, we can see that the three are not exclusive groupings. They could be better regarded as dimensions on which any specific example might be measured. So a small residential area may have high territoriality. It may or may not consist of similarly minded people in relation to crime prevention or views on mediation. It may or may not be cohesive, feel it is a community, or care about itself and its area ('thick' or 'strong' social bonds). Similarly, if we consider the example of a mediation scheme or victim support scheme, each will vary in territoriality, but each one is likely to consist of people with vaguely similar ideologies on mediation (we hope), and so be an interest community as well. They may also be attachment communities, with strong bonds being developed between mediators/workers and between mediators/ workers and those whose disputes are being mediated or who are being supported. Or it may be organised so that mediators/workers are employed individually and rarely meet together.

There are other potential dimensions to 'community'. One is what I might call the 'social milieu' extent. At one extreme, the collectivity may be purely a collection of individuals brought together by events (such as those affected by a crime, or a disaster, or a planning application), who may then disband as soon as the activity spurred by that event has dissipated. That collectivity can be made up of people with no previous contact and with little, other than the event, in common. Alternatively, at the other end of the dimension, the collectivity may be a microcosm of the structured social milieu in which people live, complete with representatives of different organisations, already existing alliances and agreements, etc.

Another difference between different collectivities or communities is the extent to which the collectivity wields or attempts to wield political or ideological power: through the media, through traditional political routes, through mobilising so-called 'public opinion', through employing the tactics of an interest group, or even through simply standing there and protesting.

It is interesting that the key meaning of 'community' in countries where there is a positive association between the words 'justice' and 'community' has been primarily a geographic localisation. Community policing, community crime prevention and even community courts mean decentralisation of criminal justice decision-making and administration. They have not been operationalised to provide different policing or crime prevention or the administration of justice to different social groups, irrespective of place. So, in England and Wales, community has meant neighbourhood, whether or not the residents of that neighbourhood do things together or feel any bond with one another. There is clearly a hope in some initiatives that more local decision-making means tying in with shared local priorities, particularly in crime reduction initiatives, and that this will make the authorities better regarded, because they are linking with local priorities for local areas to which people feel a strong affinity.[7] But it is very rare that the extent of agreement on priorities is checked or a sense of 'community' becomes a prerequisite for the initiative. The extent to which the initiative embodies the whole social milieu also tends to be irrelevant.

Similarly, community crime reduction, the exception to a rejection of locality as determining justice policy in strong state countries, has also meant geographically defined communities. As tools for geographic plotting of problems, crime and action have developed (GIS systems), so this tendency seems to have become more pronounced (van Swaaningen, this volume).

In Northern Ireland, as well, though the community restorative justice schemes discussed by McEvoy and Eriksson (this volume) do each function within one social group which has shared affinity and a shared sense of community, their prime defining factor is their locality. Each works within a relatively small geographical area. They are not resources for the whole social group, wherever its members may live. Equally, in Canada, the initiatives taken by state criminal justice (termed 'Euro justice' by Bartkowiak and Jaccoub (this volume)) have primarily been to First Nations peoples in particular localities. They have been taken because of the cultural justice practices and views of First Nations peoples, but few are available to First Nations individuals living in the major metropolitan areas or where other cultural groups are in the majority.

For criminal justice, locality, rather than interests, attachment, affinity or being representative of the social milieu, is the key factor determining the spread of lay initiatives. However, another key element seems to be the extent to which the locality (often because of the extent of its affinity and the uniformity of its social milieu) pushes its own case. Many of these initiatives have involved prolonged political work by local community groups in order to develop, such as community restorative justice in Northern Ireland (McEvoy and Eriksson, this volume), action to reduce drug activity in Dublin (Mulcahy, this volume), better attuned justice initiatives in Canada for First Nations peoples (Bartkowiak and Jaccoub, this volume) or residents' groups involved in crime reduction in England and Wales.

Van Swaaningen (this volume) then poses the central dilemma for states and civil society who wish to responsibilise others, where those others are local groups rather than state agents. How can the state retain control, keep power and not let things run out of control politically – and yet persuade people to put time and effort into local schemes, when many are, in this late modern society, reluctant to get involved and feel the system and the national political culture no longer are susceptible to lay influence? The strong social ties and social capital of cohesive communities are now rare in most places. He points to the possibilities of using weak ties: more superficial social contacts, which, because they are numerous, may be just as powerful. It is an important thesis, but weak ties may require organisation in order to be focused. That organisation can be provided by sudden major events in the locality (spawning the single-issue groups which have the potential to worry national governments, change policies or even elect members of parliament): the collectivity dimension referred to above. But in the security, crime and justice fields, it will require local groups to feel security and crime are not just vague, worldwide threats, but here and now, local threats, to mobilise feelings that they can do something and so focus action. No wonder that the justice system has often decided that it is easier dealing with other agencies or professionals rather than local groups of residents.

## Where responding to 'community' is a response to particular groups or circumstances

In some countries, it is clear that state criminal justice has recognised that there are circumstances or particular social groups which need different justice institutions or procedures. This is exemplified in this volume in relation to *maisons de justice* in disadvantaged social neighbourhoods in France (Milburn, Wyvekens, this volume), community restorative justice in Northern Ireland (McEvoy and Eriksson, this volume) and justice responses to First Nations communities in Canada (Bartkowiak and Jaccoub, this volume). The exact circumstances and the ways in which this has occurred have varied, but in each case it is interesting that it has been the result of a political struggle in which the relevant communities have taken the initiative to put their views across. Groups, communities and individuals involved would not necessarily characterise themselves as part of a divided society, though some would clearly do so. McEvoy and Eriksson (this volume) comment that it is precisely when bridge-building is required between the state and historically estranged groups that there is a need for 'organic and bottom-up styles of partnership, a willingness from the state in particular to cede some ownership and control, and a commitment on all sides to the development of real relationships based upon trust and mutual respect'.

All the groups mentioned, though not always seeing themselves as in a divided society, would see themselves as a societal group which identifies itself as different from the rest of that society or from significant parts of it. In terms of the definition of communities in the last section, these are localised, interest communities which feel themselves to have strong attachment, and which have attempted to wield political or ideological power. Moreover, the struggle has taken place over some time. These are not fleeting alliances. In other words, the groups which have been acknowledged as 'different' from the nation state as a whole have been communities which score on every dimension of community. It has taken a lot to persuade nation state justice that there should be somewhat different forms of justice for different communities.

These are social groups which feel themselves to have a culture which is separate from that of the nation state as a whole. Hence their responses and the forms which have emerged are necessarily different from one another and reflect individual cultural traditions and histories. There is no one 'different' criminal justice procedure which mysteriously emerges, just as there is no uniform national criminal justice procedure overall. It is, however, interesting that the forms which have occurred in this (rather small) sample have the characteristics of greater local autonomy over justice processes and outcomes, and greater variability in justice processes within the community. They include different forms of restorative justice (where victims, offenders and sometimes community representatives or victim/offender supporters meet together to consider the offence, its consequences and what might be done) and the use of locally appointed leaders for justice events, together with the use of more 'lay friendly' procedures and locally attuned outcomes.

So far, these localised responses have occurred for a small number of groups in a few countries. However, localisation and difference may become a more prominent characteristic of criminal justice in the future. If the state is determined to pull back from its previous all-doing, all-determining, taking all responsibility ways in criminal justice, then it has to create and manage new forms of legitimacy. Trying to prescribe uniform national criminal justice may not be a stable solution: responsibilising others tends to make those others feel they should be able to have some power if they have to take responsibility. A more multicultural or more divided society also poses greater challenges to legitimacy: people will differ in their perceptions of what the state should be doing, where and to whom – and what the outcomes should be. Some localisation of decisions and potential outcomes may be one way forward.

Where locally appointed leaders are used for state criminal justice procedures, these have always been state-appointed individuals. The state does not give up its powers to choose judges or criminal justice personnel to local groups. As a result, tensions can emerge about the status and acceptability of these leaders. As Bartkowiak and Jaccoub (this volume) discuss in relation to First Nations initiatives in Canada, it is not clear exactly what identity these leaders are supposed to retain. State criminal justice often wants to train them according to national standards, which stress uniformity. If they then act exactly as someone would who was appointed to a mainstream tribunal, in what way are they reflecting their community? Yet it is precisely because they were seen as local leaders that they were appointed. Bartkowiak and Jaccoub cast it in terms of representativeness: are community leaders intended to be representatives of their locality or of the state? Are they intended to administer local justice or Euro-justice?

I would argue that these tensions are potentially wider than for such clearly separate initiatives. Whenever it is intended that criminal justice should be adapted to local conditions or for particular geographic communities, then they are likely to arise. Countries such as England and Wales have blurred their parameters by using centrally appointed judicial figures to administer locally aligned justice – as in Youth Referral Panels (Crawford, this volume, in which two locally appointed people sit with a Youth Offending Team professional); or the new community courts (chaired by professional judges or centrally appointed and trained lay magistrates). In these instances, the tensions are internal to the judicial figure, who has to balance local and national factors in each case – as lower level courts have always had to do. In the schemes and tribunals described by McEvoy and Eriksson and by Bartkowiak and Jaccoub, the identification of the scheme and its personnel as belonging to the local community permits no such blurring. In the history of the development of community restorative justice outlined by McEvoy and Eriksson, it might be argued that the area of tension is now in procedures, standards and regulations. What national safeguards (for example, human rights safeguards) should be ensured? What leeway is there for local variation? What standards should the scheme and facilitators embody? Similar disputes over training are considered by Bartkowiak and Jaccoub.

## The reaction of criminal justice actors and the retreat of the state

We should not presume, however, that the wider trend is or always will be towards differentiation and localisation. Another main thread running through all the chapters in this book is the political nature of discussions about justice systems. New initiatives are impelled by political necessity: left to itself, the state criminal justice system is unlikely to change. If that political necessity retreats, then initiatives are no longer promoted so strongly, criminal justice system personnel who have been made to change are likely to relax back, and trends reverse. This is not the retreat and hollowing out of the state in late modern times, but just staff finding it easier to do it in the old ways or between themselves.

One of the most difficult things that criminal justice personnel seem to experience is how to interact and work with lay people. Multi-professional contacts and inter-agency action seem to be much easier than contacts with a defined group of lay people. So, French and German crime reduction panels have only a few lay people (usually business people) on them (Milburn, Wyvekens, Groenemeyer, this volume). English youth justice measures, even though they are supposed to be acting on restorative principles, find it difficult to work with actual victims: community restorative justice (work on community projects) is much easier to do (Holdaway *et al.* 2001). The same tendencies to work with other professionals, rather than with local community representatives or lay individuals, can be seen in many other places in these chapters.

There also seems to be significant difficulty for criminal justice professionals to decentralise their ways of working: to move out from the legal environment of centralised courthouses into decentralised offices, which they may share with other professionals. Part of this unwillingness may be a generational element: it is notable that the *maisons de justice* in France and the Netherlands seem to be staffed by a much younger group of professionals. Part may be because of the tensions which Crawford (this volume) underlines between efficiency (managerialism) and outreach. Efficiency always tends to be greater if work is conducted in a uni-professional environment with common, well-known systems – even if effectiveness and legitimacy may flourish better in more diverse settings.

For all these reasons, we should not assume that the tide of criminal justice will always flow so that institutions seek to become more outward-looking and inclusive, more legitimate to their publics. If crime and justice stop producing such political headlines, then criminal justice may thankfully creep back under its comfortable state umbrella.

## Why are there similar initiatives in different countries across Europe?

This volume seeks to compare experiences of state criminal justice in its relations with and reactions to civil society and local communities. Though, deliberately, each chapter deals with one country, to allow appreciation of its own cultural criminal justice context and its own political philosophy, in this chapter I have sought to compare across countries' experiences. This is a perilous exercise, as Nelken (2002) has shown. It is clear that, as Mulcahy (this volume) demonstrates, there is no criminal justice initiative which can be considered 'an innocent policy application suitable for all contexts'. Criminal justice policies speak to national identity and local struggles, as well as to the concerns of criminal justice actors to fulfil their own ideas of the historical role and image of police, prosecutors and judges. Those roles emphasise independence from others within criminal justice (the independence of judicial actors from the police, for example, in emphasising legal, not just crime control goals), as well as independence from the executive. Is it any wonder that moves towards partnership, let alone communities, cause such tension?

Yet, clearly, criminal justice has been struggling to edge closer to its publics in recent years. It has felt the need to form partnerships, at least for crime reduction. It has become concerned about isolationism, the extent to which it is inward-looking and the formalism of its procedures. Crime reduction, restorative justice, alternative penalties, initiatives for victims and witnesses – all have become more prominent in criminal justice in each country. We might seek the answer in a simple copycat tendency, given the amount of time policy-makers now spend in international fora. But that would not explain why it is these initiatives that have occurred, which all involve reaching out towards civil society and lay people, if not towards communities.

Or we might look to macro, international trends of consumerism, the hollowing of the nation state and responsibilisation of non-nation state bodies (Garland, 2001; Bottoms and Wiles 1995). These are worldwide trends, reaching far beyond Europe. They obviously influence justice policy as they influence social policies in general and the relative influences of nation states and international business. But in many ways, justice institutions are far more insulated than other areas of social and economic policy. There is no overarching justice procedures treaty which compels one type of court or one form of criminal justice process, in the same way as GATT or GATS (the general agreements relating to trade and services) suggest for manufacturing, services or professional practice. Justice conventions tend to embody values (such as the European Convention on Human Rights), rather than prescribing procedures or content. There is, at present, no policing or prosecutorial agency for Europe with operational powers to reach across borders (Europol, Eurojust and the European Judicial Network inform, aid and occasionally coordinate *national* criminal justice personnel). There is increasing agreement about the ways in which criminal justice might be run within countries through the Council of Europe and the European Community. But it is still up to countries themselves to sign up to the conventions and agreements and to operationalise those matters within their own criminal justice tradition.

The tensions and accommodations between justice and its publics seem to me to be less a matter of international or modernising pressure from outside, and more a matter of the need within each country to readjust the balance between professionalised criminal justice and the demands of the public in each country. If the perceived legitimacy of parts of criminal justice seems to be sinking too low, or citizens are too restless about the effectiveness of the criminal justice system in dealing with crime, then there is a perceived need to readjust the justice/civil society or justice/community balance. In the last decade or so, that has been in the general direction of state criminal justice needing to reach out to its publics.

If this is correct, then the tension and the adjustments are intensely political matters. They will reflect political priorities of that nation state and the policies of those who are elected. And so, they are revealed in legislation and ministerial speeches – as we see in the chapters of this volume. The historical and cultural legacies of that state's criminal justice system will be embedded in the tension and the changes – because these are tensions mediated by perceptions, rarely proved by statistics. Moreover, the tensions and adjustments will change as politicians change. And so we have seen, within a context of increasing attention to civil society, a number of moves to increase lay participation and a few moves away from it.

This analysis suggests that the current balance of the tension between justice, civil society and community is not necessarily a stable one or an end point. There is likely to be a continuing tension and continuing movement. Justice cannot give up its hold over criminal justice to the public or to communities without the break up of the nation state. Civil society is unlikely to be prepared to let criminal justice get on with it by itself while crime and security remain of importance to citizens or the media. It is likely that the future will see the development of new forms of accommodation around communication, partnership and plural means of dealing with crime.

## Notes

1 The book arises from a series of seminars, organised by Philip Milburn and Joanna Shapland under the auspices of the Groupe Européen de Recherche sur les Normativités (GERN: see www.gern-cnrs.com/gern/index.php?id=2) over three years. The seminars were held in Buxton, Derbyshire, Paris and Dublin, in which the same participants met together to explore each country's criminological and criminal justice research experiences in relation to criminal justice, community and civil society, and to seek to understand how they had developed. The seminars were funded by GERN, the University of Sheffield, University College Dublin and the Home Office of England and Wales.

2 Civil society can be expressed as the citizens or lay people of that country, considered as individual citizens rather than local groups.

3 The tendency of the state in Western countries to withdraw from providing services to all and from the extent of its previous responsibilities, though not from its wish to continue to control policy and delivery: see Bottoms and Wiles (1995).

4 This suggests that professional organisations will seek to protect their economic position against new entrants to the market through setting up greater barriers and trying to reserve work. They are seen, in economic terms, as creating barriers to the operation of a free market and as increasing the price to consumers. In justice services, the main consumer is often the state, either through the direct purchase of services or through paying for impoverished individuals to access services. The result is that the state has tended in some countries to dilute self-regulation and collude with attempts to discredit professionalism and the need for professionally provided services, in order to drive down the price to the state (see Shapland and Sorsby 1996). In the criminal justice field, this challenge to professionalism can be argued to have contributed to an overall decline in perceptions of centralised legitimacy (Crawford, this volume).

5 The lack of reliance on national policy can be seen in, for example, the failure to insert in the Criminal Justice Act 1998 (which created a statutory duty on local authorities and the police to do local crime audits and produce crime reduction plans) any requirement for local bodies to inform the Home Office what their local policies were. The resulting analysis of what was happening over the country had to use very partial data (Phillips *et al.* 2000). It showed, however, priorities towards domestic burglary, which may reflect similar tendencies to those van Swaaningen

(this volume) has commented upon – that crime reduction reflects the fears of the middle classes while increasing surveillance of poorer areas. However, this may also reflect the continuing tendencies of policing in general (and the dominant role of the police in crime reduction) which have, since the nineteenth century, tended to protect property and use coercive policing of the street pastimes of the working classes (Storch 1975).

6 In Canada, the national Royal Canadian Mounted Police does deliver policing in several provinces, through contracts with the provinces, arising out of its original role in policing rural areas, as well as federally. More urban areas, however, have their own police forces.

7 See, for example, the ministerial statement extending community justice and community courts in England and Wales, 27 November 2006, at www.communityjustice.gov.uk/258.htm.

## References

Bottoms, A.E. and Wiles, P. (1995) 'Crime and insecurity in the city', in C. Fijnaut, J. Goethals, T. Peters and L. Walgrave (eds), *Changes in Society, Crime and Criminal Justice in Europe*. The Hague: Kluwer, vol. 1.

Burney, E. (2005) *Making People Behave: Anti-social Behaviour, Politics and Policy*. Cullompton: Willan.

Cassan, D. (2005) *An International Comparison of Police Apprenticeship and Socialisation in France and England: Gardien de la Paix and Police Constable*. PhD thesis, University of Lille, France.

Commission des Maires sur la Sécurité (1982) *Face à la Délinquance: Prévention, Répression, Solidarité*. Paris: La Documentation Française.

Crawford, A. (1997) *The Local Governance of Crime*. Oxford: Clarendon Press.

Dignan, J. (2000) *Youth Justice Pilots Evaluation: Interim Report on Reparative Work and Youth Offending Teams*. London: Home Office.

Garland, D. (2001) *The Culture of Control: Crime and Social Order in Contemporary Society*. Oxford: Clarendon.

Genn, H. (1999) *Paths to Justice*. Oxford: Hart Publishing.

Genn, H. and Paterson, A. (2001) *Paths to Justice in Scotland*. Oxford: Hart Publishing.

Holdaway, S., Davison, N., Dignan, J., Hammersley, R., Hine, J. and Marsh, P. (2001) *New Strategies to Address Youth Offending: The National Evaluation of the Pilot Youth Offending Teams*, Home Office Occasional Paper. London: Home Office.

Hood, R. (1990) 'Commentary', in G. Kaiser and H.-J. Albrecht (eds), *Crime and Criminal Policy in Europe: Proceedings of the II European Colloquium*. Freiburg: Max Planck Institute, pp. 191–204.

Hough, M. and Roberts, J. (1998) *Attitudes to Punishment: Findings from the British Crime Survey*, Home Office Research Study No. 179, London: Home Office.

Judicature (1997) Special issue on *Courts and the Community* [American Judicature Society], March–April, 80: 5.

Junger-Tas, J. (1994) *Delinquent Behaviour among Young People in the Western World*. Amsterdam: Kugler.

Mattinson, J. and Mirrlees-Black, C. (2000) *Attitudes to Crime and Criminal Justice: Findings from the 1998 British Crime Survey*, Home Office Research Study No. 200. London: Home Office.

Nelken, D. (2002) 'Comparing criminal justice', in M. Maguire, R. Morgan and R. Reiner (eds), *The Oxford Handbook of Criminology*. Oxford: Oxford University Press, pp. 175–202.

Phillips, C., Considine, M. and Lewis, R. (2000) *A Review of Audits and Strategies Produced by Crime and Disorder Partnerships in 1999*, Briefing Note 8/00. London: Home Office, at: www.homeoffice.gov.uk/rds/prgpdfs/brf800.pdf.

Robert, P. (1990) 'Commentary', in G. Kaiser and H.-J. Albrecht (eds), *Crime and Criminal Policy in Europe: Proceedings of the II European Colloquium*. Freiburg: Max Planck Institute, pp. 191–204.

Robert, P. (ed.) (1991) *Les Politiques de Prévention de la Délinquance: à l'Aune de la Recherche*. Paris: Editions Harmattan.

Shapland, J. (2006) 'Security work: citizens, employees and officials working on crime', in R. Levy, L. Mucchielli and R. Zauberman (eds), *Crime et Insecurité: un Demi-siècle de Bouleversements*. Paris: L'Harmattan, pp. 259–78.

Shapland, J. and Hall, M. (2007 forthcoming) 'What do we know about the effects of crime on victims?', *International Review of Victimology*, 14: 2.

Shapland, J. and Sorsby, A. (1996) *Professional Bodies' Communications with Members and Clients*. London: Office of Fair Trading.

Shapland, J., Johnstone, J., Sorsby, A., Stubbing, T., Hibbert, J., Howes, M., Jackson, J. and Colledge, E. (2003) *Evaluation of Statutory Time Limit Pilot Schemes in the Youth Court*, Home Office Online Report 21/03. London: Home Office, at: www.homeoffice.gov.uk/rds/pdfs2/rdsolr2103.pdf.

Storch, R. (1975) 'A plague of blue locusts: police reform and popular resistance in Northern England, 1840–57', *International Review of Social History*, 20: 61–90.

Tyler, T.R. and Huo, Y.J. (2002) *Trust in the Law: Encouraging Public Cooperation with the Police and Courts*. New York: Russell Sage Foundation.

van Dijk, J. (2000) 'Implications of the International Crime Victims Survey for a victim perspective', in A. Crawford and J. Goodey (eds), *Integrating a Victim Perspective within Criminal Justice*. Aldershot: Dartmouth, pp. 97–124.

Welsh, K. (2003) 'The disassociation between domestic violence service provision and multi-agency initiatives on domestic violence', *International Review of Victimology*, 12: 3.

Wilmott, P. (1987) *Policing and the Community*, PSI Discussion Paper 16. London: Policy Studies Institute.

# Chapter 2

# 'Proximity justice' in France: anything but 'justice and community'?

*Anne Wyvekens*[1]

The word 'community' is not French at all. One could even say that French people, and French institutional personnel, *hate* the word 'community'. They hate it because in French culture it has almost entirely negative connotations. The word 'community' refers to an *ethnic* community – which is viewed, consciously or not, as something not really civilised – but above all it refers to something the French political tradition cannot accept: highlighting and giving importance to what makes people different from each other, while the major national value is equality, republican equality. In France when someone is referring to 'community' the word that is nearly always used is *communautarisme*, as in, for example, *le repli communautaire* – withdrawal into one's own community – i.e. the exact opposite of the major value for the French: that of the Republic, which emphasises unity and equality.

However, just because the French are 'republican' and value equality does not mean that they would not have anything to say about 'justice and community'. Indeed, even if the French state distrusts communities, it tries, like every state everywhere, at least in Europe, to reach out more to, let us say, 'people'. Most of the items that were pointed out by the broad framework of this book can more or less be found in French policies. This chapter cannot deal with every aspect of the diverse policies surrounding the state reaching out to the people in relation to criminal justice matters. It will, for example, leave aside some judicial practices, internal to the operation of court procedures, such as those relating to witnesses, lay judges or how the public is informed by the judiciary. For everything relating to mediation *per se* see the chapter by Philip Milburn. This chapter will focus on policies and practices that may appear at first sight as the nearest French equivalent to the English phrase 'justice and community': *la justice de proximité*. After some hesitation I shall use the literal translation of the French words, thus 'proximity justice' rather than 'community justice'. For even if the latter sounds more English, the literal rendering corresponds more closely to the situation in France, reflecting the gap existing between the French and the 'Anglo-American' ways to reach out to communities.

In contrast to the word 'community', the term 'proximity justice' is in common use in France, so much so that it seems clear and adopted by consensus by all concerned. Yet it has several shades of meaning. Both geographically and in its evolution over time proximity justice comes in not one but many forms. Therefore, rather than defining proximity justice the best way to present its current use is to trace the history of this movement by illustrating and analysing both the context in which it has been developed and the diversity of ways in which the system has been implemented and continues to evolve (section I). Section II will then address a few more general questions in order to enhance the debate from a comparative perspective and show how 'proximity justice', although based on a real concern about moving justice closer to people, has not much to do with either reinforcing 'communities' nor with giving citizens as such an active role in criminal justice practices.

## I. From experimentation to the creation of a new jurisdiction

### The origins: fear of crime and troubled neighbourhoods

Historically, French proximity justice first took shape in the context of law enforcement. In the beginning it was intended to provide the courts with better adapted responses to the rise in petty crime and misdemeanours that generated such a strong fear of crime among the population. The French justice system sought to do this by adopting a local approach, moving closer to certain geographical areas. Consequently, in the beginning the term 'proximity justice' meant criminal justice and geographical proximity.

Why adopt a local approach? Why 'proximity'? The reason lies in the situation that, when the issue of public security began to become important in the early 1980s, it was linked to the broader issue of disadvantaged urban areas or troubled neighbourhoods. In France, unlike many countries, these neighbourhoods are not the inner cities but located far from the city or town centre, in the suburbs or on the outskirts of town (Delarue 1991; Coll 1997). In these areas, housing is often very run-down and residents are particularly disadvantaged. As far as public security was concerned, a number of French suburbs at that time were described as 'no-go areas'. Initially, use of this term described the symptom itself: the difficulties encountered by police when they attempted to answer calls or take action in these areas. But more basically, the term translated two observations: that these neighbourhoods were governed by the unwritten laws of the parallel (informal or criminal) economy and trafficking (of illegal substances or stolen or smuggled goods) rather than the laws of the French Republic and, on another level (extending beyond these troubled suburbs), a 'no-go area' also meant that the basic laws of social interaction no longer seemed to apply.

It was especially in this second context that the criminal justice system was subject to severe criticism. It did not address, or very rarely addressed, what Americans call disorders or nuisance crime (which we in France translate by *incivilités*) nor petty offences – some of which are hard to define in criminal law and all of which are seldom prosecuted. There was a whole range of behaviour that made life insufferable in these neighbourhoods and gave residents the constant feeling they were never really safe, yet the authorities appeared to be doing nothing.

At the same time, the French authorities set up a general 'urban policy' (*politique de la ville*) in these areas. This ambitious policy, which has undergone several changes over time, had several elements. It originally aimed to both remedy the material degradation of these neighbourhoods by expending considerable efforts in renovation (which has gone as far as actually tearing down housing that has deteriorated too far) and also developing a series of social and community-based measures for residents themselves (Donzelot *et al.* 2003). The defining features of this policy were its geographical dimension and its focus on improving horizontal links between agencies. The primary tool in the realm of public safety was a series of local partnerships to prevent crime through setting up local councils for crime prevention (*conseils communaux de prévention de la délinquance*), initiated on the basis of the now famous *rapport Bonnemaison,* resulting from the work of a commission of mayors of large and medium-size cities (Commission des Maires sur la Sécurité 1982).

*Mediation, real-time processing, justice and law centres*

'Proximity justice' arose from this movement. For various reasons the judicial system did not really involve itself in those local consultative bodies, rather it 'invented' its own new methods to address what it saw as the 'lawlessness' affecting the most troubled neighbourhoods. The primary aim was to fight petty crime. The courts were overloaded, at least in highly urbanised areas, so that they had reached the point where reports on a number of minor offences were simply filed away. In France, the prosecutor has the power to decide whether cases should be pursued or not. Taking these minor offenders to court seemed to be too radical a solution and in any case would have come too late in the game. It became apparent at this time, however, that although dropping cases was tolerable up to a certain point, it ended up giving the victims of these minor offences the impression that the law had abandoned them, while making the perpetrators feel they ran no risk of punishment. On the one hand, there was a danger of playing into the hands of those who made public safety a political issue, in particular the extreme right wing, and on the other hand, if insufficient action was taken, especially when dealing with youth, there was the risk of reinforcing behaviour which seemed to reflect the disappearance of even the slightest reference to rules of social interaction.

This concern to find other solutions led the justice system to look elsewhere for ways to improve its work. The fashion in western Europe at that time was alternatives to the justice system, inspired by the concept of mediation, which was seen as close to the hearts of the Anglo-American countries, but yet so 'unFrench' (Crawford 2000). Mediation was thought to be especially successful in dealing with family conflicts. It was also then extended in France to a series of petty offences, on the basis of viewing them as a symptom of social breakdown, or as a conflict between individuals (an argument particularly suited to the situation of troubled neighbourhoods, particularly in disputes among residents, and somewhat linked to the problem of domestic violence). Some innovative prosecutors decided to entrust this type of offence to mediators from civil society (who would be termed 'community mediators' in England). This offered a solution at two different levels: it addressed the qualitative problem that prosecution was ill-adapted to and too severe for these petty offences, and it also took on some of the burden of the overloaded courts.

Quite quickly, however, these procedures which started off as experimental 'alternatives to the justice system' found their way back into it. They became associated with another innovation, also an aspect of proximity justice but this time a very judicial one: real-time processing of criminal cases, which aimed to speed up the handling of petty offences. In French criminal procedure, the police transmit their reports on offences to a prosecutor who decides on the follow-up to be given. Before the real-time procedure was installed, these reports were submitted primarily in writing. Only serious cases were transmitted by phone or handled immediately. Real-time processing generalises what previously occurred only as an exception. Each time an offence is reported, no matter how minor, the person charged cannot leave the police station until the police officer has called the prosecutor about the case and the latter, on the basis of the officer's report 'in real time', has been able to recommend the follow-up that seems most appropriate. We can say that the procedure has found its way back into the judicial system because real-time processing covers all the different follow-ups that may be given to a case, from mediation to traditional criminal court procedures. It is also intended to reach a highly institutional objective – improving criminal caseload management.

Another aspect of this 'rejudicialisation' is that bit by bit responsibility for the 'criminal mediation' procedure started to shift to 'deputy prosecutors' (*délégués du procureur*). The people from outside criminal justice still involved in this form of mediation soon found themselves first under tighter control by the prosecutors and then subject to requirements for speedy processing. They were thus obliged to renounce some of the more specialised mediation facets of their practices (such as lengthy consultation between the parties). Mediation in criminal cases, therefore, often came to mean filing a case away, but subject to conditions (*classement sous condition*) which, if fulfilled by the offender, would mean the end of the prosecution. Thus, for petty crimes, proximity justice started to consist of a system drawn from mediation procedures but then transformed into a diversified method of criminal court intervention.

Locally based aspects of proximity justice – its geographic arm – mainly consist of a series of 'justice and law centres' (*maisons de justice et du droit*) set up in a number of urban areas starting in the early 1990s (Vignoble 1995; Wyvekens 1997). In these so-called 'no-go' neighbourhoods, the primary role of the justice centres, regardless almost of what they actually did, was visibility: to represent the law – put it on display – in neighbourhoods seemingly abandoned to lawlessness. Obviously, this is not to say that what the centres actually did was unimportant. Their prime activity has always been to use mediation methods on criminal offences. They were the first location of the alternatives to prosecution with which prosecutors were experimenting at the same time. Gradually a second activity gained importance, one that was not judicial but instead geared toward legal advice or counselling: assisting victims and providing access to the legal system. Indeed, bringing the law back to lawless neighbourhoods not only meant exercising legal functions, but also enabling disadvantaged residents to gain access to the legal information they were lacking.

### Justice and public safety partnership policies

Proximity justice does not only imply the judiciary reaching out – or intending to reach out – to the population. As it developed within the framework of policies based on local approaches and partnership in the 1990s, it also involved reaching out to other institutions. If the judicial institution was reluctant to enter crime prevention partnerships, this was undoubtedly partly due to the fact that such partnerships had been placed under the leadership of the mayors. Gradually, the justice system instituted its own partnerships for which it was responsible.

First were the above-mentioned justice centres. Placed under the leadership of the prosecutor, they were (and still are) created through an agreement between the local court and the municipality – which thus created a considerable investment in the functioning of these structures, and which thus became a 'partner' of the judicial system. Gradually these centres provided an opportunity for the prosecutors to meet other local partners: school officials, social services and the police (Wyvekens 1996).

Another form of partnership initiated by the justice system involved more specifically schools: the 'school reporting scheme' (*signalement scolaire*) whereby school authorities report offences that occur in their establishments simultaneously to the police, the prosecutor and the educational authority (*inspection académique*). Under this scheme events that used to be dealt with internally (in a past when schools viewed themselves as 'sanctuaries', not to be broken into by the police) but which schools feel they can no longer handle adequately on their own are reported to the police.

The most sophisticated – though short-lived – form of partnership led by the justice system was the 'local groups to deal with crime' (*groupes locaux de traitement de la délinquance*) (Donzelot and Wyvekens 2004: 13–91). These complex arrangements, also initiated by the prosecutors, target very small areas of neighbourhoods that are especially run-down. The first step of the approach consists of a fast and systematic response to disorder and crime. This aspect is linked with a partnership, led by the prosecutor, gathering together all local players (the municipality, businesses, schools, public transport and housing, social workers) in order to improve each agency's ability to enforce the law against petty and more serious offences as well as encouraging working together to prevent them.[2]

In 1997, when the word 'security' replaced the word 'prevention' as the thrust of local safety policies, the judicial system was then more than ready to participate in the local partnerships of that time: the 'local security contracts' (*contrats locaux de sécurité* – CLS). The purpose of these contracts was first to monitor the local amount of crime and fear of crime, then to draw up a set of actions intended to reduce crime and fear of crime. They could embody either one municipality or a group of municipalities. Municipalities were invited, not required, to draw up a CLS. The incentive took the form of giving the town the possibility of hiring 'assistant officers' in police stations and also 'social mediators' (*agents locaux de médiation sociale* – ALMS) (Faget 2003), partly paid for by the government. CLS are signed in each case by the mayor(s), the public prosecutor of the local court and the prefect of the department.[3]

CLS are 'contracts', but not in the traditional, legal, sense of the word. They are contracts because all the operations they involve – including analysis and action – are the result of different kinds of partnership. Quantifying the amount of crime means not only collecting police and justice data, but also collecting data from schools, public housing, transport companies, etc. Furthermore, the data collected are not only quantitative, but also qualitative, such as impressions about the times of day or the places where people do not feel safe in the neighbourhood, etc. In the same way, security 'action' programmes are supposed to be the result of cooperation between various institutions, for example new ways for public housing bodies to inform the police about instances of disorder, partnerships between the prosecutor and schools, setting up a justice centre as the result of cooperation between the city, the court and several social services, etc.

What about the community? In other words, are local people, residents and the wider community also a 'partner' in this operation? When one interviews personnel from agencies or the criminal justice system about 'participation', the most frequent answer one gets is 'working with the residents is something we cannot do'. Meetings with residents are rare, and most of the time they disappoint everybody. Only a few towns have organised meetings to include the population in the analysis of crime and disorder problems. At these meetings, it was as if neither the inhabitants nor the authorities were capable of listening to one another. While residents were asking the mayor and the police, for example, why they don't arrest the people involved in crime when the police know who they are, the police and mayor were telling the residents: 'you know them, you see them, why don't you come to the police station and give names?' On one side there were local people fearing retaliation; on the other, the police unable to reassure people about this. When the moment to implement 'action' comes, together with its evaluation, the question seems to be less 'can we deal with the people?' than 'do we really want to involve them?' In most towns, the residents do not attend the 'follow-up committees' (*comités de suivi*, which follow through the implementation of the action points decided), or when they do, they attend only half the time. Why are residents not taking part? It seems primarily to be because the agencies do not seem to want to familiarise people with how they work, which might sometimes demonstrate that they do not work too well. For an agency, whether a criminal justice agency or a municipal agency, it is hard to open themselves up in this way to their institutional partners, and definitely too much to have to expose themselves in front of the population.

The way in which CLSs try to be closer to the community is quite different from involving it as a full partner in a local security partnership. The 'mission statement' of almost every CLS mentions the fact that people feel 'abandoned' as the reason why they either withdraw from neighbourhood life or fall into crime. So what should the answer be? The answer is seen as 'proximity', getting closer to the people, but not in order to work with them. Instead CLSs propose to try to inform the local population about the services provided by the town and the different agencies through teaching them what their rights are, but also informing them of their responsibilities in order to 'restore the social bond' (*restaurer le lien social*) (Donzelot *et al.* 2003).

One example of this strategy in action involves 'mediators' (ALMS) that towns can hire with government support. Their task is sometimes to make public spaces safer by their presence, sometimes to solve conflicts between inhabitants or between customers and institutions, or sometimes merely to inform the population about all kinds of services. Another example can be found in the way justice centres, which often appear as an 'action point' in the CLS contracts, have been evolving.

## Expanding the scope of proximity justice

The other facet of the diversity of proximity justice is its evolution over the years. The initial role of community justice centres, as we have seen, was oriented towards the criminal justice system and law enforcement. Indeed when the first centres were set up, the main concern of the mayors was to address the public's fear of crime and to fight petty crime, and they counted on the judicial sector to handle this aspect in their problem neighbourhoods. Yet from the very beginning the justice centres also assumed a role which was completely different from this judicial activity. They were entrusted with what is called in France *accès au droit* – 'access to the law' – in other words a whole series of both general and specialised legal methods of giving advice to the disadvantaged populations of these neighbourhoods, who were particularly deprived in this respect (as in many others). From that point on, proximity justice developed in separate directions: the judicial 'proximity' activity retreated into traditional judicial spheres and developed within that, while the 'second generation' justice centres, those set up from the mid-1990s onward, became more focused than their predecessors on access to the law.

What is gaining ground and becoming the new thrust of geographic 'proximity' measures are activities involving legal advice on a broad range of subjects: family law, housing law, employment law, the rights of foreigners and immigration law, assistance to robbery victims, etc. The staff at these centres mirror this diversity: specialised voluntary groups, young legal experts and experienced lawyers share the work according to various modes. It also mirrors the disinvestment of the judiciary: prosecutors are no longer present, only a clerk of the court. Thus the most recent justice centres no longer revolve around judicial activities *per se*. Alternatives to criminal prosecution are usually practised only marginally, taking up no more than one or two half days a week. Likewise, reconciliation in civil conflicts, a development recommended by a Parliamentary report (Vignoble 1995), has not really made much headway.

This evolution is the result of several factors. One likely cause is that elected officials are in a sense now less preoccupied with public safety matters, especially because the problem has been at least partly addressed. Another cause is the justice system's wish not to fall foul of criticism often levelled at justice centres, citing the risk of excessive stigmatisation of the neighbourhoods where the centres were located. Two other elements play an important role and are strongly linked to one another. From the mid-1990s the new responses to the problem of petty crime have gradually been generalised, often organised from the courthouse rather than from a neighbourhood base. After the implementation of penal mediation by deputy prosecutors, still in an experimental way, this kind of 'alternative to prosecution' has been given statutory form – the *composition pénale*[4] – and introduced into the ordinary criminal procedure. It is difficult not to see a connection with the reluctance of a majority of magistrates to the idea of exercising their function in 'justice centres' located in such deprived and dangerous parts of the city, and of becoming in that way more exposed to the expectations of ordinary people.

In a way it could be said that justice centres have lost their character as specific centres. They are no longer undertaking an innovative form of judicial activity, but what now goes on within their walls could be characterised as closer to a 'public service' by the judiciary. Along these lines it has much in common with modernisation happening throughout the public service sector, from the post office and social security to welfare and health services. France has recently seen a whole new wave of 'public service centres' or 'public service platforms' (*maisons ou plates-formes de services publics*), that are also part of the CLS's actions, and whose aim is to facilitate access to various services, especially in disadvantaged neighbourhoods.

### The creation of 'proximity judges'

A recent episode in the story of proximity justice is the advent of 'proximity judges' (*juges de proximité*). Their creation was announced by candidate Jacques Chirac during the 2002 presidential election campaign. The Law Reform Bill of 9 September 2002[5] provides for the creation of a 'proximity jurisdiction' (*juridiction de proximité*) which is competent to deal with both civil (involving up to 1,500 euros in value) and minor criminal cases. The aim is reminiscent of that of the first alternatives to justice: 'a judicial dealing with little things of every day life for which no adequate response exists'. A statute dated 26 February 2003[6] is devoted to proximity judges, their status, their training, and the procedure they have to follow. They are not professional magistrates since this new jurisdiction is aimed to 'increase citizens' involvement in the judiciary'. Yet this community involvement remains limited. It is limited by the law itself, which requires proximity judges to have legal skills.[7] It is also limited above all in practice, as the creation of these judges, *because* they are not professional magistrates, has given rise to considerable resistance from a number of magistrates in a way that can be qualified as 'corporatist'. The original programme envisaged hiring 3,300 proximity judges by 2007. Less than 500 proximity judges[8] were in office at the end of 2006. Most of them are former lawyers, notaries, judges and police officers. Most of them do not have a lot of work to do. The proposal to expand their competence by raising the value of cases they might deal with from 1,500 to 4,000 euros attracted the unanimous hostility of magistrates' unions. The motion from the unions repeated the main argument of their opposition to the principle of bringing in non-professional judges: law is becoming ever more complex, even in minor cases, and the training in legal matters of these judges is too weak: 'what kind of justice do we want to build?' The law has nevertheless been passed[9] and also states that proximity judges can sit in the lower courts deciding on minor offences (*tribunal correctionnel*). In November 2005, a report was prepared for the Minister of Justice. After pondering over several problems due to lack of finance, the main question it raises is that of 'the identity of proximity justice: what should it be and how can it be closer to neighhourhoods? What is its added value? Its original aspects?' (*Rapport du Groupe de Travail sur les Juridictions de Proximité*, 2005: 87).[10]

## II. From proximity to community?

This story of French 'proximity justice', starting from observations of the inability of the penal system to deal with petty crime in deprived neighbourhoods, illustrates how the notion of proximity has gradually become part of a broader debate on the way the justice system functions as a whole. From the very beginning of the movement, 'proximity' has been a way to question at least three problematic aspects of the justice–society relation: people, geography and time. The first parliamentary report on the subject, *Propositions pour une Justice de Proximité* (Haenel and Arthuis 1994), pleaded for a justice that would be closer in these three respects, expanding its scope beyond criminal justice only in order to include civil justice. Several researchers and practitioners then developed this line of thinking, some of them adding yet further dimensions of proximity, either in a positive way by appealing to a symbolic and a social proximity (Peyrat 2000) or venomously, criticising the notion by highlighting the less consensual aspects it might acquire (Kaminski 2001).

## 'Human proximity'

The term 'human proximity' is closely linked with the origin of proximity justice, the mediation approach. It calls for a less formal way of dealing with cases, taking more into account the actual expectations of the parties and speaking a less complicated language. It also evokes, as far as minor criminal offences are concerned, a less severe way of dealing with them than using traditional criminal prosecution: a *justice douce* (soft justice), as it has been called in France (Bonafé-Schmitt 1992).

This concern can be found throughout the story of proximity justice, from the observation of the inadequate response the criminal system gives to minor offences and the introduction of the law creating proximity judges, through to the emphasis put on the need to improve people's knowledge of their rights and the development of 'access to the law' services in justice centres and houses for public services.

One objection has been raised about 'human proximity'. The concept would be deceitful: not at all a way to deal with minor cases with less severity, but actually a way to deal with *more* minor offences, those that would not be prosecuted if there was no 'proximity justice'. One can recognise here the thesis of 'penalising the social' (Mary 1997), the more sophisticated version of Wacquant's (1999) notorious denunciation of a supposed switch from the welfare state to the 'crimefare state'. However, even though deprived people certainly are more frequently picked up by criminal justice, one may deplore that ideological considerations could be an obstacle against the creation of positive change in such a conservative institution as the criminal justice system.

More interesting is the discussion about *how* and *for what reasons* the justice system may be reaching out to people through proximity justice. One has noticed the evolution of justice centres, from a new judicial way of dealing with minor offences to the stress put on 'access to the law'. Two points are interesting here. First and most importantly, the judges' reluctance to serve in the justice centres indicates their unwillingness to 'expose' themselves, both 'physically' by getting closer to the 'no-go' neighbourhoods, and above all by lack of preparedness to serve as representatives of an 'authority' supposed to be holding court hearings in places where the relationship to the population is supposed to be less formal. This observation is confirmed by the way proximity justice has been institutionalised – *inside* the existing judiciary. Secondly, and in close connection with the first point, the switch of the 'justice *and law* centres' from hearing judicial cases to a more 'access to the law' approach illustrates a more general feature of the French justice system: the French judiciary does not reach out to the inhabitants as people in front of whom it should be accountable, but only as people that have to be taught and mentored in order to better know their rights *and* their duties. In France, getting closer to the community means establishing a pedagogic relationship with that community, where the institution is the teacher, rather than putting residents on an equal footing with institutions (Donzelot and Wyvekens 2004).

With regard to involving people in dispensing justice, that has never been the purpose in justice centres. One prosecutor[11] suggested one day that a justice centre could be the place where the neighbourhood's inhabitants would come and list problems of disorder and try to solve them: she remained an exception and her idea was never implemented. As far as proximity judges are concerned, even though the rhetoric has evolved that the aim of the new jurisdiction is 'to increase citizens' involvement in the judiciary', implementation of this remains extremely limited. On the one hand, the legal requirement for legal knowledge and skills to be a proximity judge means that, so far, all proximity judges can be said to belong to the 'lawyers' family': former magistrates (8.5 per cent), barristers or former barristers (about 30 per cent), business lawyers (*juristes d'entreprise*) (about 40 per cent) (*Rapport du Groupe de Travail sur les Juridictions de Proximité* 2005: 43). On the other hand, judges remain extremely suspicious of even those professionals. Judges' corporatism and professional elitism is another expression of the French difficulty in accepting any measure that would involve the community more in judicial matters.

### 'Geographical proximity'

Likewise, the need for a geographical expression of proximity has been present throughout the history of proximity justice. So justice centres were established with the objective of making justice more visible in deprived neighbourhoods. In fact, French 'proximity' consists much more of reaching out to *places* than to *people*. The origin of proximity justice, in the broader framework of the *politique de la ville*, lies above all in a concern to deal with territories – the point is about 'local policies', not about 'communities' – in the administrative (and Republican) French way of dealing with problems. Our French *politique de la ville* itself tends much more to deal with places (i.e. to address urban and housing issues, or to take care of people *within* their neighbourhood) than to try to help them to cross the barriers existing between them and a better way of life, possibly *out of* their neighbourhood (Donzelot *et al.* 2003). This is even more obvious with the recent law on urban renovation:[12] although its aim is one of 'social mixing' the means it implements are focused first and foremost on buildings – demolition of deteriorated housing – with scant attention paid to the social aspects of its consequences.

If one considers the justice system as a whole, 'geographical proximity' raises the matter of adapting the jurisdiction map to demographic change: urbanisation has developed in such a way that the geographical competence/administrative area of most of the urban jurisdictions no longer fits with where the population are located. However, the concern for a 'geographical proximity' should not be equated with genuine change. Reform in this area still remains hypothetical. Justice centres, settled in heavily built-up areas, continue to represent a marginal branch of justice. They are not given the means to become real places of justice, whereas proximity judges are located in the *tribunaux d'instance*, most of which are located outside the more urbanised parts of the country. One could even say that 'geographical proximity' has become the sign that an innovative practice remains in the realm of experiment and has few chances to become generalised.

### 'Time proximity'

'Time proximity' is the third tier of 'proximity justice'. Justice must not only be closer to people, it also has to act more quickly. This concern appeared in the early 1990s, at the same time as the idea of making justice more human and more local. Criminal courts were congested and their decisions came too long after the crime had occurred, especially in the case of young offenders, so it was necessary to find alternatives. That field is probably the one where the judiciary has shown most change. Real-time processing has been rolled out nationwide, whereas the creation of justice centres has been left to the initiative of mayors or prosecutors. Alternatives to prosecution have also been institutionalised: the 'pretorian' practices based on mediation have not only been legally recognised[13] but also complemented by new ones like *composition pénale*, all of them playing a large part in the speeding up of criminal justice.

## Conclusion

The 'rejudicialisation' of proximity justice seems to have reached a final point. It has evolved from local experimentation in deprived neighbourhoods to the creation of a new jurisdiction whose competence is defined in statute. But it has evolved in a way that has also provided its boundaries. Concern about proximity is regularly expressed, several things change, but never really in a way that would radically change the French way of dispensing justice, nor the French vertical relationship between institutions and citizens. A strong institutional paternalism on the collective level and judges' ingrained practices and culture on the individual level combine to create an ambivalence about proximity justice, *'tantôt dénigrée, tantôt affichée, souvent récupérée en même temps que vidée de son sens'* (Peyrat 2005: 164 – 'sometimes derided, sometimes displayed, often instrumental while deprived of its meaning'). Another expression of this ambivalence (or hypocrisy?) is the following: when one visits the Ministry of Justice website, the proximity judge is described in the *dossier de presse*[14] as *'un citoyen au service de la justice'* ('a citizen at the service of justice'). But when one checks the page called *'la participation des citoyens à la justice'*[15] ('participation of citizens in the justice system') there is no trace of any proximity judge.

## Notes

1 CERSA-CNRS (National Centre for Scientific Research) and previously director of research INHES, Paris (National Institute for Advanced Studies on Security).

2 It must be stressed here that 'proximity justice' practices from the beginning have differed from one city to another, and one court to another. This is because all these schemes have resulted from individual initiatives, reflecting the dynamism and inventiveness of local players, without being the subject of a national effort to unify them and without any legal obligation (for example, like that in the United Kingdom under the Crime and Disorder Act 1988). So, depending on locality in France, there may or may not be justice centres, school information systems, local groups to deal with crime, etc.

3 Sometimes they are also signed by the person in charge of public sector education in the *département* (the *recteur d'académie*) and by the *conseil général* (departmental governing authority).

4 Loi no 99-515 du 23 juin 1999 renforçant l'efficacité de la procédure pénale, *J.O.*, 24 juin 1999. Instead of taking proceedings the prosecutor

can offer a person who admits he or she has committed a (minor) offence several options, including paying a fine or doing community work, and then drop the charges.

5 Loi no 2002–1138 du 9 septembre 2002 d'orientation et de programmation pour la justice, *J.O.*, 10 septembre 2002.

6 Loi organique no 2003–153 du 26 février 2003 relative aux juges de proximité, *J.O.*, 27 février 2003.

7 Moreover, the initial version of the project, which stated that people should have occupied functions 'in the law, administrative, economic or social field' has been censured by the Constitutional Council, arguing that the three last were not sufficient to provide the required level of legal knowledge (Décision no 2003–466 DC du 20 février 2003).

8 That is one half of the number of professional judges.

9 Loi no 2005–47 du 26 janvier 2005 relative aux compétences du tribunal d'instance, de la juridiction de proximité et du tribunal de grande instance, *J.O.*, 27 janvier 2005.

10 For more recent information about proximity jurisdiction see Wyvekens (2006).

11 Interview with a deputy prosecutor, 2000.

12 Loi no. 2003–710 du 1er août 2003 'd'orientation et de programmation pour la ville et la rénovation urbaine', *J.O.*, 8 septembre 2003.

13 Loi no 99–515 du 23 juin 1999 renforçant l'efficacité de la procédure pénale, *J.O.*, 24 juin 1999.

14 www.justice.gouv.fr/presse/conf020403a.htm

15 www.justice.gouv.fr/justorg/justorg11.htm

## References

Bonafé-Schmitt, J.-P. (1992) *La Médiation: Une Justice Douce*. Paris: Syros.

Collection (1997) *Ces Quartiers dont on Parle. En Marge de la Ville, au Cœur de la Société*. La Tour d'Aigues: éd. de l'Aube.

Commission des Maires sur la Sécurité (1982) *Face à la Délinquance: Prévention, Répression, Solidarité*. Paris: La Documentation Française.

Crawford, A. (2000) 'Justice de proximité – the growth of "houses of justice" and victim/offender mediation in France: a very un-French legal response?', *Social and Legal Studies*, 9 (1): 29–53.

Delarue, J.-M. (1991) *Banlieues en Difficulté: la Relégation*. Paris: Syros.

Donzelot, J. and Wyvekens, A. (2004) *La Magistrature Sociale. Enquêtes sur les Politiques Locales de Sécurité*. Paris: La Documentation Française.

Donzelot, J., Mével, C. and Wyvekens, A. (2003) *Faire Société. La Politique de la Ville aux Etats-Unis et en France*. Paris: Seuil.

Faget, J. (2003) *Les Agents Locaux de Médiation Sociale en Quête d'Identité*. Paris: IHESI, coll. Etudes et Recherches.

Haenel, H. and Arthuis, J. (1994) *Propositions pour une Justice de Proximité.*

Kaminski, D. (2001) 'De l'amour du prochain et de son châtiment', in A. Wyvekens and J. Faget (eds), *La Justice de Proximité en Europe. Pratiques et Enjeux.* Toulouse: Erès, pp. 131–43.

Mary, P. (1997) 'Le travail d'intérêt général et la médiation pénale face à la crise de l'Etat social: dépolitisation de la question criminelle et pénalisation du social', in *Travail d'Intérêt Général et Médiation Pénale. Socialisation du Pénal ou Pénalisation du Social?* Bruxelles: Bruylant, Coll. Travaux de l'Ecole des sciences criminologiques Léon Cornil, pp. 325–47.

Peyrat, D. (2000) 'La politique judiciaire de la ville', *Gazette du Palais*, 86–8: 8–17.

Peyrat, D. (2005) *En Manque de Civilité.* Paris: Textuel.

*Rapport du Groupe de Travail sur les Juridictions de Proximité, Septembre 2003 – Novembre 2005, Bilan et Propositions.* Novembre 2005.

Vignoble, G. (1995) *Les Maisons de Justice et du Droit.* Rapport présenté au Garde des Sceaux.

Wacquant, L. (1999) *Les Prisons de la Misère.* Paris: Editions Raisons d'Agir.

Wyvekens, A. (1996) 'Justice de proximité et proximité de la justice. Les maisons de justice et du droit', *Droit et Société*, 33: 363–88.

Wyvekens, A. (1997) 'Les maisons de justice: sous la médiation, quelle troisième voie'?, in R. Cario (ed.), *La Médiation Pénale. Entre Répression et Réparation.* Paris: L'Harmattan, coll. Logiques juridiques, pp. 61–81.

Wyvekens, A. (2006) 'La justice de proximité, rapprocher la justice des citoyens?', *Les Cahiers Français*, 334, Septembre–Octobre: 4–47.

# Chapter 3

# How civil society is on the criminal justice agenda in France

*Philip A. Milburn*

The words 'community justice' do not appear in the rhetoric of French criminal policies developed in the last few decades. Yet there are significant characteristics relating to the implementation of judicial measures by recent governments which make them quite similar to the meaning and use of this expression in English-speaking countries. The absence of an explicit reference to 'community', though, deserves a preliminary examination of why the concept or the practice thus designated does not fit the political categories of this domain in France. First, we shall look at the term 'community' and its political and sociological effects in the French context of a strongly state-centred political system.

Because there are a number of processes underpinning new criminal justice schemes in this country, it is necessary to consider what kinds of rationales are used to appeal to ideas of community within them. This will lead us to examine in detail both the principle and the implementation of several of these schemes, particularly victim-offender mediation, reparation orders, new schemes flowing from guilty pleas, and a few others. This is not a mere descriptive exercise: it provides an opportunity to comment on the way in which local civil society and its members are included in these innovative judicial processes and what kind of role they are meant to play. But the answers to these questions vary according to the political complexion of the government at the time. France has undergone considerable political change in the past ten years, during which security and crime issues have been on top of the campaign agendas. Successive governments have hence put a strong emphasis on the criminal justice schemes they have adopted once in power. Therefore, significant differences result when observing their principles and effects, especially in terms of the involvement of local people.

## Community: a controversial notion in French public action

First of all, it is useful to stress that the word 'community' seems to be almost banned from French political, legal and even professional vocabularies. It refers to something which would be denied any kind of legitimacy, since it introduces an intermediate political entity between the state and the citizen which is contrary to the Republican 'Jacobin' tradition. Ideally, in this tradition, there can be no collective reality between the citizen, seen as an individual, and the state, in its wider sense which includes local authorities.

Thus it is highly significant that local authorities are named 'local communities' (*collectivités locales*) and considered as an extension of the power of the state, since they (municipalities, departments or regions) are run by councils which are directly elected by citizens. As for the word *communauté*, it seems to refer mainly to cultural, ethnic or religious communities – which have been denied any form of acknowledgement by any state office. They may exist within what is called 'civil society', but may not be granted even the slightest kind of political substance or prerogative, since that would represent a danger to the Republican charter. This explains why the word 'community' is avoided whenever community schemes are adopted from foreign models. It is mainly replaced by the word *proximité*, especially for the new policies in the fields of public security and criminal justice.[1] The idea incorporated in this word *proximité* is that of bringing state institutions closer to citizens, so that each may benefit from the particular action or policy and not feel neglected by it, especially in some urban districts where it is thought that both social cohesion and public order[2] may be imperilled.

Citizens may even become involved in these initiatives in some way. Hence, citizens are called upon in order to contribute to improve their social and urban environment, but agencies claim dominance over the process and feel they should not be ousted or even simply lose some control over this process to local collectivities which rely on a community base, whether these be social groups or geographically organised groups. Thus some ambivalence arises between the wish to keep state control over public action and the desire to call upon civil society to perform it. Two major types of agencies have turned out to be indispensable in solving the problem: non-profit-making organisations (NPOs) and professionals. Both remain in the realm of the acceptable from the point of view of the Republican state. NPOs (*associations*) have a legal basis and are meant to gather together volunteer citizens acting in the public interest for some particular (good) cause. They can be funded by annual state subsidies which allow some form of control over their organisation and activity. As for professionals, though they may gain some autonomy of action, they are seen as being ruled by the regulations of their professional bodies and tend to be employed by the state itself or by subsidised NPOs. In other words, both these societal forms remain at least partly under state control.

These two types of bodies have played a major role in the development of community and restorative justice in France. Non-profit-organisations have been utilised since the 1980s, initially to promote and where necessary intervene within the criminal process and work done by publicly funded social agencies in the interest of victims, who seemed to have been neglected until then by the judicial system. With the aim of increasing the efficiency of criminal justice processes, the state and local authorities have called for initiatives to improve the care of victims and several small NPOs across the country responded. This activity has gradually thus grown into a whole field of action, which has of course then needed to define its own strong professional standards. Hence the action of civil society has swiftly turned into an organised professional field, which still, however, remains limited in its scope and extent of provision (Faget 1992; Steinauser 2005).

A similar process has occurred with victim-offender mediation programmes. Organised through local NPOs, backed by the local prosecutor's offices, these initiatives have solidified into two major forms. The first shows professionalisation of mediators, but has only been developed to a slight degree. The second appears as disguised agencies of the prosecutor's office, relying on former police officers or former professional magistrates, all acting as pseudo-lay magistrates in very well controlled mediation schemes (Milburn 2002). The most recent evolutions of national criminal policy on mediation have followed this second option. They have given yet further functions to 'prosecutor's delegates' with similar occupational profiles, as will be shown in the third part of this chapter.

In the meantime, another arena in which criminal justice policy has called upon civil society to participate has been put under the wing of pre-constituted professional bodies. It relates to the carrying out

49

of alternatives to custody: mainly community service or community work orders (*travail d'intérêt général*), probation orders and reparation orders. They are now undertaken by two professional state agencies placed under the authority of the Ministry for Justice: one for offenders under 18 (including an educational programme) and the other for adults, which depends on correctional authorities (probation services). Though employed by the state, these professionals (education officers and probation officers) are quite independent in the way they carry out their work. This aspect is key to the development of community justice, since restorative measures (though the word 'restorative' itself is hardly used) have become a major element within their competence, with the aim of keeping some control over their professional realm – though neo-retributive policies and rationales have tended to take over in practice.

Imported from English-speaking countries, these restorative schemes aim primarily, according to the policy that justified their implementation, at putting the offender back into the community in order to restore a state of 'peace' (order) within it, and to increase the capacity of the offender to understand the principles of life within a community and his interest in abiding by its rules. The state of order is to be restored through dialogue between the members of the community and the offender: this contact may permit them to forgive the offence and the offender can see the consequences of his misdemeanour. The professionals in charge of the implementation of these measures play a major role in giving them substance and effectiveness in many ways additional to the essential principles. Therefore how restorative justice works needs to be observed within these professional practices: the way 'community' is considered – and defined – lies within the implementation of the measures in practice, rather than in the political principles to be found in the statute or in official policy pronouncements. Any discrepancy between the two is indicative of the underlying issues and tensions.

## Community and restorative justice: civil society taking part in implementation

When in power between 1997 and 2002, the socialist government favoured a series of innovative judicial measures, with the dual aims of extending the ambit of criminal action towards minor offences and avoiding too harsh a punishment for this kind of anti-social behaviour. The reference to civil society came in with the idea that an appeal to ordinary norms and 'good sense' would contribute to bringing back the offender towards more reasonable forms of behaviour, based mainly on dialogue with citizens at the same level as the offender rather than mere law enforcement by impersonal authorities.

One of these judicial instruments is aimed at adult offenders: victim-offender mediation (VOM, named *médiation pénale*). First introduced in France in the 1980s as local and experimental schemes, it has been considered as part of national criminal policy since 1993 and has been widespread since. The second scheme I propose to examine is reparation orders, which are intended to be used with young people (*mesures de réparation pénale à l'égard des mineurs*). Their history in France is similar to that of VOM but it has been implemented in a much more professional framework, since the PJJ (*Protection judiciaire de la jeunesse*: national office for judicial action aimed at young people) is in charge of carrying out these measures and has developed educational tools and good practice guidelines for this.

### Victim-offender mediation

Victim-offender mediation is a diversionary measure ordered by the prosecutor, thus avoiding indictment and a criminal record for the offender. It is, however, commonly acknowledged by prosecutors that, without mediation, the criminal process would have been discontinued in most cases in any event. The author has carried out a major survey in 1999–2000 in order to obtain a better understanding of the manner in which VOM has been implemented in France (Milburn 2002). It looked at what magistrates invested in the scheme, the way in which it was operationalised and the precise practices of mediators. The first finding was the great variety of contexts for mediation and backgrounds of mediators: mediators could be barely trained justice auxiliaries, former police officers, volunteer mediators in an independent NPO, or well trained professional mediators employed by a large NPO concerned with childcare or educational action.[3] This is indicative of the lack of clear-cut official principles delineating mediation as a restorative and community technique. Secondly, if 'civil society' is to be involved, it is unclear just how this should occur. This seemed to be decided through personal contacts and arrangements between local personnel: prosecutors, existing NPOs or pre-defined community mediation schemes. Such uncertainty results mainly from a tension between the desires of prosecutors – who embody the dominance of the state – to keep control over mediation and the wish of some mediation agencies for independence in order to maintain their own definition of the mediation process.

In the minds of most prosecutors, mediation is a way for the offender to acknowledge the criminal aspect of his or her behaviour and to become aware of the harm suffered by the victim. Its purpose is also to request the victim's participation in the judicial process as a member of a wronged community and for the victim to witness the efficiency of public action in dealing with crime.

Those mediators who were mainly under the influence of prosecutors tended to follow this target and considered mediation as a 'dejudicialisation' process whereby the offence is taken into account by the public body, cautioning the offender and alleviating the harm done to the victim (whether immaterial or material). From this perspective, the community (or civil society) is not really involved in the process, but is simply requested by the agency to witness its action, from which the community or the victim may receive some compensation for the harm done. The victim is thus considered, more than anything else, as a citizen who benefits from a public scheme which seeks to fulfil these diverse aims.

A second approach to VOM is to be found in some places where prosecutors exert less influence on the bodies in charge of its implementation. It relates to the major ethical principles and practical guidelines of the theory of mediation. The goal is not so much to concentrate upon the offence and caution the offender, or repair the harm done to the victim, but to restore and facilitate a process of communication between the parties in order to regain mutual respect and acknowledgement (of harm on one side and of regrets on the other). In this process, parties involved in the dispute are treated as members of a community of people living together, seen in terms of a social contract, which is meant to be re-energised and regenerated through mediation.

The findings of the survey uncovered a certain number of techniques and ethical viewpoints that underpin this approach (Milburn 2002). They may be summarised in two major categories. One corresponds to the techniques of communication that aim to provide a balance between the parties and avoid increasing any inequality between the identity of being an offender and that of being a victim. The mediation process is thus dominated by a principle of equity which is meant to refer to the equal status of citizens sharing a common social world. This principle is hence constituted as a regulatory element of the community.

The same process is at work in the second ethical notion that governs the methods used by mediators: the principle here is that of personal responsibility. The solution of the problem resulting from the offence – considered as a dispute – is to be found within the resources of the parties themselves. The 'neutrality' of the mediator is important and leads to the mediator not proposing solutions or outcomes to the dispute, which are to stem from the dialogue between the parties and the initiatives of the people involved. Hence, responsibility for the consequences of the agreement lies on both parties and not on enforcement agencies. Both the decision and its execution are returned to the community which leads to the principle, in terms of responsibility (in the two meanings of accountability and capacity for action), that the community is to define its own principles for regulation.

The two types of approach (institutional or communitarian) must not be taken as clear-cut, separate schemes but rather as ideal-types which are more or less apparent in most observable local schemes. In this sense, the mobilisation of the community (or the civil society, from a French point of view) is to be considered, from the VOM example, as an ambivalent attempt by the public sphere to call upon community regulation but also to keep some control over the process.

### Reparation orders

The second type of judicial measure that clearly falls into the category of restorative justice is reparation orders aimed at those under 18. The measure is supervised by educational staff. The young offender is to perform an 'activity' of collective interest, but with an educational purpose. Like VOM orders, this kind of measure has been experimented with throughout the 1980s in a few sites and was then given statutory backing in 1993. The following conclusions are based on the results of a study on the implementation of this measure in France supervised by the author in 2000–1 (Milburn 2005).

The policy document set out by the national judicial agency for young people (PJJ), guiding the social workers implementing the measure, indicated that its main objective was not to be a penalty, judged by the harshness of the 'work' set for the young person, but to provide added value through meaningful activities meant to restore both the self-esteem of the young person and the opinion that the community has of him or her. Therefore the activity was not necessarily to be linked to the offence itself but rather to the personality of the young person. Yet the young person was to define himself or herself what would make sense for him or her to do, which would be valuable both from the young person's own point of view and from that of the community.

The choice of the right activity and the way in which it should be done relies, therefore, on a dialogue between the social worker, the young offender, his or her parents and the agency which is likely to supervise the activity. This is seen as a part of a process of 'responsibilisation' which is promoted by the educational professional: criminal responsibility linked to the offence is to be converted into *personal* responsibility in the course of sorting out and performing a significant activity. This personal responsibility is considered as the major educational tool to reintegrate the juvenile into the community and, at a more general level, into society. The principle is similar to that at work in mediation, where personal responsibility is seen as a necessary competence for involvement in community life, and therefore a major element of personal development in the educational process. In contrast with past professional criteria, educational processes are not being considered as individual and psychological in nature, but as collective and interactional.

In practice, the 'site' where the activity is performed is rarely linked to the victim. In most cases it is a charitable organisation, or a community service provider or public sector agency. Which base is chosen depends on the local authority and may sometimes be the police or the fire brigade. The person in charge of the supervision of the young offender within this agency is briefed by the social worker in order to avoid considering the activity as a penalty but rather as a valuable achievement.

These new schemes in the French criminal justice system have led to an approach to community justice which is different from the one that underpins the concept of so-called 'proximity justice'. In these schemes, 'community' is considered as a kind of abstraction relating to the social links that hold people together within a smaller or larger geographic area, rather than a bounded social group of people. Hence the mediation scheme attempts to restore the link that was broken as a consequence of the offence, and the restoration process is meant to go well beyond the original parties to the offence as defined in criminal law. Reparation orders follow a similar goal for young people, with an additional educational objective: the activity in this context is seen as having pedagogical virtues, restoring social ties via providing the opportunity for the young offender to perform valuable social actions and for some members of the community to acknowledge this.

In this sense, community justice can be analysed as a way for judicial institutions to avoid exerting their responsibility in the regulation of social (or public) order, returning it to the community (or 'civil society'), seen as a collection of responsible persons living in a particular area. From this perspective, it is the values of the community which are decisive in order to restore social links. Two major principles seem to be the guidelines for this community self-regulation: personal responsibility and mutual equity.

## 'Proximity justice': civil society and law enforcement

The national elections that took place in France in 2002 made the theme of 'insecurity' a paramount issue in the campaign. The previous socialist government had already brought out a wide range of new measures to tackle insecurity. The right-wing party (UMP) which won the elections against the National Front at the second round of the presidential poll felt compelled to put additional elements into its policy against crime. The policy favouring 'proximity police' was repudiated, considered as a kind of lenient deviation from a police force whose mission was redefined towards law and order activities. Restorative measures were also seen as lenient and it was argued criminal justice needed to acquire harsher legal means to fight the supposedly rising delinquency rate. 'Proximity judges', appearing as a major element in Chirac's candidacy programme, were soon created and, quite oddly, were assigned, until recently (2005),[4] to civil law tasks where the needs were not the most prominent. Two important reforms of criminal procedure were adopted in 2002 and 2004, creating among other elements schemes which would make judicial action less formal, so avoiding trial. *Compositions pénales* and *comparutions sur reconnaissance préalable de culpabilité*, which may be translated as 'guilty plea referrals' and 'guilty plea orders', are the most remarkable of these provisions for adults. Specific new measures addressed at under 18s were also implemented.

### Guilty plea schemes and prosecutor's delegates

The principle of a guilty plea, absent in French criminal justice before this, was obviously imported from the Anglo-American system and adapted to the French one. The *composition pénale* was first created in 1999 (under the socialist government) but mainly implemented and extended under the new government. Its principle is quite simple: if the person admits the offence, the prosecutor's proposes a sanction of a fine, driving or hunting licence revocation or work of collective interest, but not prison. If the sentence is accepted by the offender, it is certified by a judge and then implemented. In practice, the whole process is monitored by the 'prosecutor's delegates'. She or he is a member of civil society (lay person) and has no proper professional status at all for this task. All that s/he does is officially under the competence of the prosecutor. S/he receives some small sums for this activity but it cannot be considered as real wages.

These delegates have in fact, from a sociological point of view, a hybrid status. They are not real volunteers, but they are meant to be lay persons, representatives of the civil society. This is the basis of the legitimacy of their action (beyond the delegation of power from the prosecutor) in the eyes of the institution (i.e. the state and the prosecutor), but also in their own eyes. The intervention has a dual dimension: both pedagogical and legal. The first of these is prominent in ordinary cautioning referrals which were the primary function for which prosecutor's delegates were created. It has some extension in guilty plea referrals where the acceptance of the sentence is meant to follow explanation by the delegate of the moral and common-sense consequences and aspects of the illegal behaviour (Milburn *et al*. 2005).

Who are these delegates? There are no official criteria for their recruitment, in terms of status or qualification, as candidates are supposed to be lay persons representing the civil society. In reality, the profile is rather homogeneous: the vast majority of delegates are older men whose former job (they are mainly retired) included the exercise of authority: former police officers, professional magistrates, senior justices' clerks and the like. The status of delegate and that of VOM mediator have been separated in the early 2000s but very frequently the same people play the two roles.

Authority-based competence is even more necessary for guilty plea referrals where an effective sentence is given. When carrying out these referrals, the delegate meets the offender in a small office (which should not be considered as equivalent to judicial or legal 'chambers'), together with the offender's lawyer where required, and talks about the nature of the offence and the social and moral consequences that it has produced. S/he indicates the powers of the tribunal (court) in this instance, implying that the sentence offered in the guilty plea scheme is likely to be significantly lighter than what would result from a trial. S/he proposes the appropriate sentence corresponding to the offence according to a scale which has been precisely defined by the prosecutor's office in consultation with the senior judge of the tribunal. Once the offender has accepted the whole procedure and signed the forms, he or she has to carry out the sentence within a certain time limit. The delegate then acts as a probation agent (or a tax collector) as s/he controls the process and its timing, contacts the offender as necessary, and sends the case back to the tribunal if the offender fails to complete the sentence.

Hence, if prosecutor's delegates are considered as representatives of civil society, they tend to play multiple roles (representing the prosecutor, teaching the law to offenders, justices' clerk circulating forms and minutes – up to 12 documents for one file – and sentence supervisor) for a very small public cost. Yet this experience may not be extended beyond certain limits and an extension of the role of guilty pleas would require professional workers. This is taking place with guilty plea orders, which follow a similar process to guilty plea referrals, but are carried out by professional magistrates (the prosecutor proposes the sentence and a judge endorses it in a public hearing). In this case, the sentence may be imprisonment.

Both guilty plea referrals and guilty plea orders are addressed at all kinds of offences save those designated *crimes* in French law (liable to more than five years' imprisonment and heard at the higher criminal court level with a jury: *Cour d'Assises*). An empirical examination of cases dealt with by means of guilty plea referrals (*composition pénale*) shows that most offences are concerned with traffic regulations or involve first offenders (brawls, carrying a knife, shoplifting, cannabis consumption, etc.). In almost all cases, there is no victim, particularly not a personal victim.

Two principles seem to flow from a closer look at these new initiatives. First, if civil society is involved through the use of a prosecutor's delegates and if common-sense moral values are meant to be infused in this way, this does not appear to have been a major issue in the implementation process of the reforms, even though it does appear to constitute the way in which delegates legitimate their own position. Hence, the main rationale for these specific referrals is a net-widening effect, with cheap, fast and efficient sentences addressed at first-hand offenders, often ordinary citizens who have committed a minor offence. The identity of the delegate as being from civil society contributes to maintain the impression of a light sentence as opposed to one passed by a court, and hence to erect a smokescreen in front of an effective extension of the criminal justice realm.

A second rationale may be discerned through analysing the way in which these provisions have been implemented in the French judicial system. The focus on an explanation of the law suggests that reference is primarily to a centralised set of norms (those present in the law) rather than to local norms stemming from communities. Though the person representing the civil society may be contributing additional legitimacy to the institutional intervention, the set of norms he or she represents remains anchored to the Republican values associated with legal provisions. The prosecutor delegate may be preaching common-sense values when dealing with the offence and the proposed sentence, but these values are not shared within the *local* community of the victim, the offender and/or the delegate (as might occur in mediation processes), but by the *whole nation* considered as 'one and undivisable' according to the French Republic's fundamental principle.

### New provisions for minors

The issues of having a separate legal regime for young offenders and what it should be are strongly disputed in the media and in public debate whenever security seems to be at risk. This issue seems to be highly symbolic, even though minors may not necessarily be the main cause of any presumed rise in the rates of crime and delinquency. Nevertheless, each new government insists on bringing in its own set of reforms to the so-called 2 February 1945 Act (*Ordonnance de 1945*) which embodies modern juvenile justice and prioritises educational methods over punishment. Considered as too lenient towards young offenders, who are seen as becoming more and more violent and lawless, according to common sense and political discourse, the provisions of this Act have been constantly revised in the past two decades towards the idea of more 'responsibilisation' of young offenders. The introduction of reparation orders stemmed from this trend. The government, since 2002, has felt compelled to bring in more severe measures aimed at recidivist young offenders. New kinds of 'closed educational centres' have been created for this purpose.

Yet another provision aimed at young offenders deserves attention in the context of an examination of the relation between criminal justice measures and civil society. This is designed for very young offenders (mainly those under 14, a response to a supposedly dropping age of first offending) and is called a 'civic training session' (*stage de formation civique*), considered by the law as an 'educational penalty' (*sanction éducative*). Its duration is determined by the court (three to five afternoons scheduled out of school time). The session is monitored by educational staff whose mission is to urge different representative bodies from government agencies or civil society to train a small group of young offenders in the civic values they are implementing in their own work. The same kinds of partners as are involved with reparation orders are invited to collaborate in such sessions: the fire brigade, security staff from big stores and the police, but another group has also become involved, including drug prevention schemes and charity organisations.

The 'civic' dimension of this kind of scheme is addressed at the 'anti-social' state of mind in which early teenage offenders are presumed to be. Hence the norms which are conveyed in such sessions have to do with the main shared values of life in common, conformity (being law abiding) and of society as a whole. In this case, representatives of civil society offer a depiction of the mainstream social order at work: of its usefulness, of the concrete grounds for the values it involves and of how well founded it is.

But in contrast to reparation orders, where 'responsibilisation' of the juvenile is grounded in his or her personal commitment to an 'activity', in which the young person is a participant in the deliberations of the local community, these 'civic training session' have a very *didactic* conception of law enforcement education. The young person is quite passive and the training is based on the 'penalty' obligations of presence and participation. Young people may certainly ask questions and find answers, but are not urged to engage in a dialogue, an exchange of meanings and understandings, where they might express the problems they are faced with when misbehaving. In a civic training session, they are considered as mere recipients of a discourse or a demonstration.[5]

Given this, civic training sessions are significantly different from restorative schemes developed in English-speaking countries and sometimes on the European continent (Walgrave 2006), known as restorative conferencing (family group conferences), which are based on debate, exchange and deliberation between the community (victim, family, other people close to the young person) and representatives of institution(s). According to the principles driving the present French juvenile justice policies, such a 'deliberative' approach would give too much authority to the 'community', taken here not as civil society but as a set of persons having a close *personal* relationship with the juvenile (including teachers, social workers, sports coaches, etc.). In spite of the noticeable and well broadcast success of restorative conferencing methodology at the international level, it has no resonance among either policy-makers or field practitioners in youth crime prevention in France.

This indicates quite well the status given to *civil society* as an *extension* of institutional action in criminal justice policies (as in most other domains of public policy) and shows how it is distinguishable from the idea of the *community* as an *autonomous entity* with its own standards and dynamics which serve law and order enforcement, as it is the case in Britain (Crawford 1997) as well as in North American countries.

## Conclusion

Civil society appears thus as a node or relay for state action but not as a social cluster in which the (offending) citizen is involved or depends. From a French policy viewpoint, civil society is seen as the non-institutional dimension of the social seal but not as an interrelational setting for individuals ready to be empowered. Power and responsibility lie either with the individual citizen or with the state, not any intermediate body. Indeed, while family conferencing is utterly ignored, the ideas of responsibilisation and penalising parents whose offspring are misbehaving because of presumed defective parental education are well anchored in the political debate on youth crime prevention. Individual responsibility hence becomes the only instance of power and legitimacy which the state may address. Intermediate elements are seen as having no value, rather as being fertile ground for uncontrollable values, groups and activities. Churches, religions and sects are the ultimate form of this kind of threat to the republican unity, with their corollary: ethical, communal and cultural clusters.

Nor is it possible to argue that communities play a decisive role in the implementation of restorative justice schemes in the field. Professionals (social workers) and intermediate agents (such as mediators) seem to play the key role here. This can be observed in mediation and reparation, for which control of the definition of the scheme is a central issue. This has become a matter of controversy between prosecutors, who in most cases prefer a more retributive definition, and mediation organisations and educational agencies which favour the restorative way. The definition of the dominant approach thus results from a struggle taking place at various levels, particularly the legal level (the law and its provisions) and that of implementation in the field, which is quite as decisive. In this context, the community comes into play merely as an argument rather than as an active agent in the definition of the penal process.

It only plays the role that the institutional and professional agents allow it to play, in the framework of the ethical guidelines they have designed for its intervention. Institutions thus keep control over the penal process while returning accountability for its performance to the 'civil society'.

Though the notion of 'community' is excluded from French public policy phraseology, there have been attempts to call upon civil society in different forms to support criminal justice. They belong to a political trend of deliberative democracy, based on the idea of it being necessary for citizens to be involved in the implementation of policy. This appears to be more substantial than a mere rhetoric concealing the reality of an always more powerful and repressive criminal justice. Whatever the hidden agenda may be, it remains true that some dimension of participation of the 'public' (whoever this may refer to) is active in the criminal justice realm, albeit in a relatively marginal way. It gives a more flexible dimension to judicial action, the miscellaneous agents intervening in the name of civil society adding extra value to the purely legal contribution borne by judicial sentences otherwise. But legal institutions, especially through the prosecutor's office, keep tight control over this intervention by ordinary citizens.

If genuine empowerment of local communities is hardly found in innovative criminal justice schemes in France, citizens' involvement in both restorative and guilty plea processes introduces some *social meaning* into law enforcement decisions. The creation of such intermediate space brings the ability to make sense of the law, as operationalised through debates during mediation, reparation activities, acknowledgement of misbehaviour in guilty plea referrals, etc. It is populated by local, common-sense, ordinary categories, values and rationales. These, though they do not alter the mainstream of criminal justice decisions and actions, contribute to make them more adapted to local, personal or collective situations. And, through the same means, they grant additional common sense-based legitimacy to the former's institutional cogency.

## Notes

1 The expressions *police de proximité* and *justice de proximité* have been chosen by government agencies to designate the schemes they have adopted in the past ten years (see Wyvekens and Faget 2001).

2 *L'ordre public,* which has a more comprehensive meaning than the absence of what is called in English 'public disorder', and includes incivilities and modes of social interaction.

3 Most childcare and youth educational services operate within the framework of a large subsidised NPO employing numerous social workers and other similar professionals.

4 Since 2005, they have been assigned as lay magistrates supporting the professional judge in collegial ordinary criminal courts (*Tribunal correctionnel*).

5 These remarks are based on an analysis of the practice guidelines of the Department of Justice and not on an analysis of actual practice. The development and practice of civic training sessions at national level is quite recent and has not been the subject, so far, of any evaluation.

## References

Crawford, A. (1997) *The Local Governance of Crime: Appeals to Community and Partnerships.* Oxford: Oxford University Press.

Faget, J. (1992) *Justice et Travail Social. Le Rhizome Penal.* Toulouse: Erès.

Milburn, P. (2002) *La Médiation: Expériences et Compétences.* Paris: La Découverte, coll. 'Alternatives sociales'.

Milburn, P. (2005) *La Réparation Pénale à l'Egard des Mineurs.* Paris: PUF.

Milburn, P. A., Mouhanna, C. and Perrocheau, V. (2005) *Enjeux et Usages de la Composition Pénale: Controverses et Compromis dans la Mise en Place d'un Dispositif Pénal Inédit,* Survey Report. Paris: CAFI/Mission de recherche droit et justice.

Steinauser, O. (2005) 'L'aide aux victimes d'infractions pénales: quand la sécurité organise une politique de proximité', *L'Homme et la Société,* 155: 69–82.

Walgrave, L. (2006) 'Les conférences de groupe familial', *Les Cahiers de la Justice,* 1: 153–74.

Wyvekens, A. and Faget, J. (2001) *La Justice de Proximité en Europe. Pratiques et Enjeux.* Toulouse: Erès.

# Chapter 4

# Crime control in Germany: too serious to leave it to the people – the great exception?

*Axel Groenemeyer*

From a comparative perspective, the translation of central concepts is always a potential source of misunderstandings. 'Community' (*Gemeinschaft*) and 'civil society' (previously: *Bürgerliche Gesellschaft*; today: *Zivilgesellschaft*) are concepts with a long sociological, political and philosophical tradition in Germany that dates back at least to the nineteenth century and had been largely abandoned as a framework for political discourse after the experience with the establishment of a national community (*Volksgemeinschaft*) in Nazi Germany. The ideas of community and civil society have been reintroduced into sociological and political discourses only recently by adopting perspectives from the Anglo-Saxon context, very often under different labels and with special meanings that only partly reflect the discussions in the UK and the USA. So today we find in Germany political and sociological discourses that mean similar things and institutional forms that seem to be similar to policies in the UK and the USA, but without using overtly the notion of community or civil society.

## The 'significant absence' of community in Germany

In social theory, modern social development very often is characterised as a process from 'status' to 'contract' or from 'community' to 'society', where social cohesion and integration are based on more or less anonymous role relations and more on interactions or exchange with systems and organisations, less on personal relationships and social solidarity. Modernisation in this sense is connected with a decline of community.[1]

In classical sociology 'community' is associated with close ties and bonds, based on kinship, shared values, culture and morality, and feelings of belonging, which is opposed to society as a form of social relations based on interests, exchange and rationalised ties between individuals as strangers. Where communities are thought of as particularistic and exclusive social relations and bonds, society is characterised by universalistic and more or less anonymous social relations. In this view, modernisation means a process of eroding of traditional forms of social cohesion and their substitution by abstract forms of integration based on law, exchange and organisations of rationalised interests.

This decline of community has always been a prominent topic of criticism that accompanies processes of modernisation and has always provoked counter-movements from different political perspectives. The idea of community always fitted well into conservative and right-wing ideologies because of its connotations of moral community and value commitment. But it also fits well into left-wing ideologies as a means of criticising alienation through professionalism and bureaucracy in modern societies and in supporting the identity politics of social movements. In the last ten years another meaning of community has gained some prominence in political discourses in discussions of 'third way' policies, which focus on the assumed capacity of social networks in dealing with social problems as a kind of outsourcing of and responsibilisation for welfare state provisions and social services.[2] In this sense the notion of community always has an ideological or at least normative loading that evokes values of unified morality, mutuality, solidarity, belonging, care, faith, loyalty, commitment, cohesion, reciprocity and effective informal control, and which could be seen as one of the reasons for its appeal and rhetorical power in political discourses.[3]

But in fact these political discourses in Germany seldom make explicit reference to the notion of community (*Gemeinschaft*), what Lacey and Zedner (1998) called a 'significant absence'. Instead of community these discourses address specific institutional forms like families and kinship networks, voluntary associations, local protest groups (*Bürgerinitiativen*), or self-help groups, only very seldom neighbourhoods.

The local, geographical or administrative dimension of policies in which they should be sited is addressed in German discourses when community is used in the sense of locality or place (*Gemeinde*) without any reference to cultural or ideological meanings. In this perspective community only refers to the unit of local government administration. In political discourses this connotation is often used to refer to policies of decentralisation of social services to promote client-orientated administration – services that serve the needs of citizens where they live (*gemeindenahe, kundenorientierte oder bürgernahe Verwaltung*). In this context the reference to community marks a new form of governance, which also forms the core of the concept of civil society.

## Civil society between market, state and family

The concept of 'civil society' has a long tradition in European philosophy and sociology. In political and sociological discourses today the concept shares many meanings with the concept of community, or at least refers to some of its aspects as a basis for the development of civil societies. Whereas 'community' refers very often more to cultural dimensions of close and locally bounded social bonds, and stresses feelings of belonging and identity, 'civil society' nowadays refers more often to institutional dimensions of social relations and their relation to the state and the polity.

Since the Enlightenment (in Germany at least since the beginning of the nineteenth century), civil society in the meaning of *bürgerliche Gesellschaft*[4] refers, first, to a more or less autonomous sphere of the public, free citizens, bourgeois culture and the economy, as opposed to the state and the family. In this sense the term has been introduced by Marx as a means of criticising capitalism and its related forms of social relations and culture, whereas in historical texts the term has been transformed into the labelling of a social stratum and social milieu (*Bürgertum*) with special cultural orientations (e.g. bourgeois virtues) and social or political forms of engagement (e.g. charitable associations).[5] However, in later periods the term civil society only developed in left-wing political discourses as a concept related to the political struggle against capitalism, and up to the 1980s it lost any meaning and disappeared completely from German political and sociological discourses.

It has been only recently in the 1990s that the concept of civil society (*Zivilgesellschaft, Bürgergesellschaft*) has come back into German political and sociological discourses as a re-translation from the English language via discussions about the social conditions necessary for processes of democratisation in the former socialist countries of the Eastern bloc and, together with a renewed interest in communities and social capital, via the introduction of American discussions about communitarianism (Etzioni 1993; 1996). Another strand of political discourse has been the idea of multiculturalism, introduced into German political discussions in the 1980s by the Green party. But it should be noted that reference to communitarian and multicultural ideas tends always to incorporate relatively critical views about these new elements, tending to stress more liberal and universalistic perspectives on human rights and democracy. The idea of legitimating special rights on the basis of group membership has never gained prominence. The model of republican integration on the basis of universalistic rights and law has never been questioned. So multiculturalism in Germany has always been discussed only in relation to tolerance of cultural differences, but tendencies towards the development of 'ethnic communities' have always been observed with scepticism and discussed as a potentially problematic failure of integration.

Some aspects of 'governmental communitarianism', as set out by Etzioni, and ideas about the civic foundations of the polity have, however, acquired remarkable success in German political discourses and appeared in political party programmes and rhetoric.[6] In this version civil society (*Bürgergesellschaft*) refers to the activation of civil institutions as well as to civil engagement on social issues.

As a theme of political philosophy and political science, 'civil society' has been re-imported into more state-centred German political discourses bringing along, at least implicitly, an American cultural self-image, according to which modern societies consist (and should consist) of civilised communities of engaged citizens which, as distinct spheres, rest only 'civilised' insofar as citizens are engaged in their own affairs and in those of collectivities to which they belong.

In German conservative political discourses' appeals to community and civil society are based on different critiques of the welfare state. In response to fiscal crises community-based treatments and social control are seen as possibilities for reducing state responsibilities and expense. At the same time, accounts featuring a decline in traditional forms of cohesion and solidarity have always been a prominent element in conservative political discourses. This may well be revived within this discussion of community, embodying a criticism of the welfare state by seeing its interventions as a cause of the decline of community values and solidarity. In this criticism of the welfare state conservative and left-wing political views meet on the same ground.

In this version 'civil society' as well as 'community' fit well into a political programme of an 'activating welfare state', propagated by the coalition of the social democratic and Green parties in government between 1998 and 2005.[7] At the heart of this version of civil society is the activation of welfare production through voluntary associations, civic engagement and self-help groups by the state, presented as a political strategy of administration reform.

There are at least four different ideas guiding this programme of a 'new' approach to governance: a) in mobilising resources for civic self-regulation it is expected to use voluntary resources of welfare production and so accomplish *release of welfare expenditures*; (b) this kind of welfare production by voluntary associations and self-help groups is also thought to be characterised by a *higher degree of effectiveness* as it is seen to be nearer to the source of social problems than the professionalised social services, but should also accomplish an *amelioration of social service provision* when civil institutions are integrated into a partnership approach with social services; (c) because of the criticism of the professionalism and the bureaucracy of current organisations, civil institutions should also *strengthen participation and promote democracy* for welfare clients and citizens directly concerned by social problems and political decisions. The mobilisation of civil institutions in these aspects follows a strategy of responsibilisation that also should *strengthen political legitimation and acceptance* of the polity, so reducing state responsibility which has also in Germany been criticised as merely a neo-liberal project. The final target of this political programme is (d) the mobilisation of civil and network resources to strengthen *social cohesion and integration* to prevent the development of social problems.

### State-centred political culture, corporatist approaches to governance and professionalism in Germany

In fact, these political targets have remained largely on a programmatic and rhetorical level in Germany, even in the domain of social policy and social services, despite some expenditure by federal state and local government agencies to promote and support some initiatives and single projects. Stating this does not mean that policy schemes and projects discussed in Britain or the USA in the context of 'community based' or 'civil society involvement' are completely absent on the local level in Germany. But, most of these schemes, such as the involvement of non-governmental organisations or volunteers in social policy or the participation of citizens in local decision-making, have a long tradition in Germany and would never be identified as community based. As Lacey and Zedner (1998: 8) have stated: 'Indeed, paradoxically, it may be that it is the very stability of social relations in Germany, or, more particularly, the institutional strength of community, which deprives this term of rhetorical appeal.' On the other hand Germany's political culture and institutions are strongly based on faith in a republican ideal of unified law (*Rechtsstaat*) and on professionalism, with the consequence that policies serving specific communities are in fact nearly completely absent, and this is especially true for the system of criminal justice. Policies in Germany on the national as well as on the federal or local level may be formulated for specific target groups but these groups would not be interpreted as communities.[8] In Germany it is so far uncontested that security, order and social welfare are the duty of and guaranteed by the state and local government.

The relative ineffectiveness of these political discourses in Germany and Germany's relative resistance to neo-liberal policies compared with Britain could be explained by institutional and cultural traditions of governance and the political system that can be traced back to the medieval system of guilds (in some respects still of significance), to administrative and republican traditions introduced in the era of the Napoleonic occupation on which the Prussian administrative reforms in the nineteenth century were based, to the feudal system of local self-administration of towns, and finally to the experience of Nazi rule.

As a consequence German political culture and its institutional system of governance can be characterised as a state-centred, corporatist federal system that has always relied on local self-regulation and the participation of citizens, as well as on professionalised administration based on law (*Rechtsstaat*).

Faith in universalistic law-based policy-making is accompanied by strong ties to professionalism and professional organisations and associations. Even in social policy and social service provision any mobilisation of volunteers and lay persons is always regarded with suspicion. Lay people are often seen as having good intentions but as being unqualified and insufficiently skilled and 'unable or unwilling to make regular and long-term commitments' (Lacey and Zedner 1998: 14). In the context of political participation, it is suspected they will follow their own sectoral interests (*Bürgerinitiativen*, the political initiatives of citizens). Using volunteers nevertheless forms an integral part of local social policy, but it is always under the control of professional organisations and associations, and their engagement as voluntary groups or initiatives depends largely on financial support controlled by local administrations.

Yet, in the tradition of political ideas of 'subsidiarity', non-governmental associations, self-help groups and associations stemming from civil society should have priority in state and governmental policy. This political ideal, which dates back to the nineteenth century, is operationalised in Germany through giving priority in social policy to local governments (*Kommune*) and to non-governmental welfare associations (*Wohlfahrtsverbände, freie Träger*). These associations mostly have their roots in the nineteenth century and were affiliated to the Protestant and Catholic churches and to labour movement organisations. Most social services on the local level are nowadays organised by five nationally organised welfare associations. They are funded by national government, the federal states (*Länder*) and local governments (*Kommunen*), and operate by order of these local governmental bodies. In this sense the institutions of civil society and governmental civil servants form a corporatist polity model that seems to fit with American models of civil society. Even if their roots lay in faith communities and in self-help by labour organisations, these welfare associations have been transformed since the Second World War into huge professional social service enterprises and interest groups that also play a very important role in influencing social policy programmes at the national level. However, their local branches ensure, working with local government, that policies are adapted to the particular local circumstances. Only in this sense could they be labelled as 'community based'.[9] In the field of criminal justice the welfare associations have gained a growing importance since the 1980s, because they have taken on responsibility for victim-offender mediation, diversion and community work programmes for offenders.

Another important feature of German political institutions and culture is the status of local government, guaranteed a right to self-administration by the German constitution. The political institutions of local government in Germany are not seen as the lowest level of national government, but instead as autonomous bodies with authority for self-regulation of local affairs through local or municipal councils and administrations. Although often, as elsewhere in Europe, local democracy is overshadowed by national party orientations and interests, local elections allow the development of local non-party issues and success for local non-party groups. Beyond this, the city councils are supplemented by the establishment of issue-based committees (*Ausschüsse*) with the participation of so-called competent and well-informed citizens (*sachkundige Bürger*), such as local experts or interest groups. These forms of local participation and democracy are strongly supported, with citizen participation in local elections averaging between 60 and 80 per cent.

## Community and civil society in German criminal justice and social control discourses

The different meanings of community and civil society can also be found in the discourse and institutions of the criminal justice system. Sometimes the community (especially the (dis)organised community) is seen as a locality with an accumulation of social problems and so as a cause of deviance; sometimes it is seen as a promising means for preventing and treating deviance; sometimes the possibility of community action is mentioned as a substitute for costly professionalised state intervention; sometimes it is seen as a means to strengthen democracy and more humane treatment, sometimes as the inverse. There are considerable, often implicit tensions in the idea of community.

One of the prominent theories of the sociology of deviance has been the idea of social disorganisation, which directly links the decline of communities with their declining capacity for social control and increasing rates of deviant behaviour and social problems. Traditional forms of cohesion and solidarity were seen as a guarantee to prevent deviant behaviour and social problems.

After the Second World War emerging social policy ideas involving the welfare state, together with a general acceptance of rehabilitational ideas of social control, the notion of community and social disorganisation led to ever-increasing dominance and institutionalisation of professional social work and social policy. In this welfare state perspective social disorganisation of communities has been interpreted as occurring as a result of poor housing, social inequality and anomie, such that the decline of informal social control should be substituted by organised and professional intervention. The notion of community itself lost much of its former appeal for politicians as well as for social scientists (Garland 1985).

This professionalisation of social control, based on welfare state organisations, then came under attack in Germany, as in other countries, in the 1970s because of criticisms about its inefficiency and instances of inhumane treatment, especially in the fields of psychiatry and public health. Ideas of community treatment under the label of anti-psychiatry gained some momentum in political and sociological discourse. These models of integrating deviants into the community in order to improve processes of rehabilitation and to avoid stigmatisation spread to other areas of social control like prisons and criminal justice in the 1970s. Community treatment or community-based interventions became one of the main foci of social reform. In contrast to the early Chicago perspective, communities were now not discussed as a cause of social problems and deviant behaviour but as a form of efficient treatment in the process of rehabilitating deviant persons.

These developments in different areas of social control were emphasised by ideas stemming from social movements in the 1970s, which criticised technocratic and expert interventions as alienating and inhumane and tried to promote greater democracy at a grass-root level. 'The possibility that community-based developments may effectively empower formerly disempowered groups and create sites for political action less repressive than and genuinely independent of the state remains a potent attraction' (Lacey and Zedner 1995: 304).

Whereas in the area of mental illness, the ideas of the anti-psychiatry movement were widely adopted in Germany with political reforms in the 1970s being transformed into new models of decentralised institutions, discussions about criminal justice which featured similar abolitionist ideas remained limited to some circles of critical criminologists without much influence on political reforms. In Germany the abolitionist idea of 'giving conflicts back to the people' never reached the public and political agenda. Processes of partial 'decarceration' and decriminalisation had already occurred through criminal law reforms at the end of the 1960s, when short prison sentences were substituted by fines – but without any reference to 'community'.

Even where there were some references to community and civil society institutions in German political and professional discourses, they tended to be imported from international discussions and were transformed into ideas of the need to decentralise (professional) social services and to develop more local services, losing in the process the original referents to community and even civil society, except maybe for an increased attention to the family.

In the field of criminal justice research, the decline of the rehabilitational ideal, criticised for its ineffectiveness (by, for example, Martinson 1978), led to research questions about the social conditions needed for informal control in social networks and its relations to institutions of formal control. Concepts such as 'social network' and 'social capital' began to be mentioned (see Karstedt 1997). But the perception of rehabilitative prison programmes as being both ineffective and too costly did not lead towards more punitive criminal justice, but instead fostered in Germany a preparedness to consider alternative forms of criminal sanctions and social control, such as diversion or forms of restorative justice and mediation. In these discussions there was no decline in the perceived legitimacy of professionalised criminal justice institutions in Germany, which remained seen as the most trusted institutions.

However, discussions within the police led to measures that could fit under the idea of community policing. In contrast to the American situation, local government in Germany provides a strong infrastructure of social services, so the responsibility of the police at the local level has always been limited to matters of crime, disorder and conflict resolution, rather than the provision of social order in a broader sense. In this context community policing just meant intensifying police controls (stops and checks) and increasing the visibility of police officers on the streets. But the target of greater proximity of the police to the community for many Germans is suspect and carries negative connotations, and it is often seen as an unwanted encroachment of the state (Feest 1988; Lacey and Zedner 1995: 311). Even within the police, patrolling the streets is rarely seen as a crime prevention measure but rather a matter of strengthening feelings of security.

In summing up these short remarks on community, it would not be too exaggerated to say that an explicit notion of 'community' does not exist in German criminal justice (see also Lacey and Zedner 1998). Except in policies and programmes for local crime prevention, which spread in the 1990s alongside the idea of 'community crime prevention', ideas of community did not gain very much prominence in German political, public or criminological discourses, and there has never been an explicit community approach to criminal sanctions in Germany.

This may be explained by an overall reliance on professional criminal justice institutions and the police and a distrust of citizens' initiatives in this field. Criminal justice in Germany is a highly professionalised system. There are no elections of judges or police officers, and even social work agencies and probation services are highly professionalised and form an integrated part of the criminal justice system. There is neither a tradition nor any significant current use of lay people or volunteers in criminal justice.[10]

Even if there are some explicit references to community or civil society institutions in criminal justice in Germany, as, for example, in the field of crime prevention, their meaning varies. Often other terms are used that could be interpreted as an orientation towards local areas or an involvement of civil society institutions in the system of criminal justice. In the most obvious meaning of community, embodying traditional forms of social bonds and informal social control (*Gemeinschaft*), the idea has been introduced in crime prevention policy discourse, but without very much impact for practice. In German discussions this meaning of community very often also has a negative connotation which emphasises its character as exclusive and as encouraging unwanted surveillance. The decline of community and its values of self-sustained regulation and solidarity form a part of conservative political discourses, but political proposals to strengthen its use in criminal justice have always been criticised for their susceptibility to populist demands. Community is seen as more a part of the problem than its solution. As a consequence, these discourses normally rely more on the family than on community as a means to prevent crime.

Another meaning of community is connected with proximity (*Bürgernähe*), which means that state institutions should offer their services in accordance with the views of and local to citizens. We can find this meaning of community in policy initiatives to strengthen the state's image of promoting citizens' security. In this sense community-based interventions form a part of public relations to strengthen legitimacy or in terms of symbolic politics to influence feelings of security among citizens. Criminal justice system institutions in Germany enjoy the most trust among citizens and so for them this perspective for promoting legitimacy has not yet been very important in public policy terms.

A third and perhaps the most important meaning of the involvement of civil society institutions in criminal justice is integrating lay people and non-governmental organisations or associations (*freie Träger, Wohlfahrtsverbände*) into the criminal justice system or within the prosecution process. In Germany, particularly in the youth court, there has been a long tradition of integrating lay assessors (*Schöffen*) into the criminal process and also using professional social work associations to provide rehabilitative treatment measures for offenders. These services are in some cases directly integrated into the criminal justice system (such as the probation services) or they have been given responsibility for alternative measures of social control like diversion and mediation. In this sense the criminal justice system has established and institutionalised a stable network of connections between the professionalised judicial system and the equally professionalised social welfare associations.

Faith in professionalised criminal justice also functions as a barrier against too much populist punitiveness, with there being still widespread reliance on the rehabilitation ideal within criminal justice. This ideology is also supported through the integration of

73

professional social work associations into the criminal justice system – they can be seen as a major interest group that promotes ideas of alternative sanctions as part of the rehabilitative model, which remains important for their professional image.

Another aspect of professionalism in the German criminal justice system is the important role played by professional associations (of judges, probation officers, advocates and social workers within the criminal justice system) in formulating and influencing political decisions and developments on criminal law and the code of criminal procedure.[11] Their national conferences always attract not only media but also political attention and very often their discussions form the basis for subsequent political decisions. In this sense these professional associations play a decisive role in defending liberal legal principles against sometimes populist political and public views.

### The appeal of community and civil society in crime prevention

Only in the field of crime prevention do we find an explicit reference to 'community' introduced and widely discussed within the German ministries of the interior, the police and criminal justice professionals. One result of this was the setting up of 'crime prevention councils' (*Kriminalpräventive Räte*) in nearly every large town or of 'crime prevention partnership networks' at the level of regions. These institutions – mostly initiated and organised by the police – are intended to rally associations and institutions of local social workers and prosecutors, local retailers' groups and representatives of local government and service providers (and sometimes also the local media), to discuss local crime problems, to initiate crime prevention initiatives, to coordinate action and to organise campaigns to promote public awareness of crime and security issues.

One important new issue for this partnership network – beyond symbolic politics and the function of building organisational social capital – is an obligation to establish contracts with local administrations, social service agencies, the police and prosecutors for certain harm reduction services related to drug problems (such as areas where there is prostitution by drug addicts, and harm reduction services like, for example, health centres where drug addicts are allowed to take drugs under the surveillance of health staff).[12]

In relation to the police, ideas of 'community policing' have been introduced in this context as 'grass-roots policing' (*bürgernahe Polizei*), with an increase in police officers patrolling the streets and mobile police offices situated in central places in cities. 'Community policing' has also involved school programmes related to crime issues, with the participation of police officers to target youth, as well as initiatives such as 'basketball at midnight' organised by the police. These police crime prevention ideas were frequently linked with surveys often initiated by the police themselves, focusing on the image of the police and on public demand placed on the police, with the public showing overall considerable reliance on the police.

In these fields of crime prevention 'community' has two different meanings. The first, relating to crime prevention councils, refers to community as the local administrative body of towns, such as in slogans like 'bringing responsibility for security issues back to local councils' and 'security is a matter not only for the police but for the whole community'. This type of policy has not been universally popular within local administrations and most of these councils still depend on initiatives of and coordination efforts by the police. The second notion of community in crime prevention is much less clear. Particularly in initiatives and political discourse, 'community' sometimes refers to everything included within civil society (local associations and initiatives, interest groups or the public in general), sometimes to specific local areas or neighbourhoods which have considerable social problems (*soziale Brennpunkte*) and sometimes to an ideal of well functioning neighbourhoods of informal control, based on conceptions or images of small villages (*Gemeinschaft*). This ideal of community – essentially a nostalgic evocation of a pre-modern world of fixed meanings, stable identities and forms of harmonious social relations that ensure social cohesion, solidarity and smooth social control – prevails in political policies and discourse as the main objective of crime prevention (Berner and Groenemeyer 2000; Kreissl 1987).

However, city crime prevention councils in most cases consist nearly exclusively of members of the local police, the city administration and, with less participation, also representatives of department stores and shopping malls. Only in a few councils is there representation from social service institutions and professionals, or teachers or schools. Members of self-help groups or other representatives of citizens, other than already represented by political parties or professional groups, are very rarely involved.

In contrast to Britain (see Crawford 1999), the crime prevention councils in Germany tend to be exclusively initiated and guided by the police (sometimes by local administrations). There has never been any 'bottom-up' development. Nevertheless there have been a few initiatives setting up neighbourhood watch schemes, but in

Germany these ideas are not very widespread and their relevance to crime prevention policy has been marginal, even if they have found some public and criminological recognition. The legal rights of those acting on behalf of such institutions are limited to the normal rights of citizens, with no special police authority. Where they have existed, they have been perceived with suspicion by the police, who have argued that very often they have only reported minor problems or disturbances not relevant to crime or the police.

In Germany criticisms of net-widening, privatisation of social control or responsibilisation of communities also seem to be exaggerated when we look at the concrete measures the crime prevention councils have been able to manage in practice. Most of their work consists of discussions about very minor problems (for example, lack of lighting at bus stops), campaigns against minor incivilities ('Keep your towns clean') or campaigns for civic engagement (*Zivilcourage*: 'Citizens of this town are not alone, they are taking care of each other'). Research on the functioning of these councils suggests that most of the discussions turn around the question of what the duties of the council are and what crime prevention there could be that is not already the responsibility of the police or other local administrative authorities. Rather than being a new form of the local governance of crime, crime prevention councils remain limited in their responsibility to more or less symbolic forms of politics. They are not useless, but their function is more that of an institutional network of sharing information and developing a kind of institutional social capital that could be used for the everyday needs of the participating departments of the local administration and local agencies (Berner and Groenemeyer 2000).

Beside these developments at the local level, the national focus of crime policies in Germany has shifted since the 1990s to areas such as organised crime, drug trafficking, dangerous sexual offenders and violent youth, and special attention is also given to immigrant offenders and, since 2002, to prevention of terrorism. Violence, insecurity and crime are at the moment in Germany no longer political or public issues that arouse much attention. In political discourse the mood that prevails is one which emphasises decreasing crime and violence, and even if official statistics show a small increase in violent crime, they are perceived as changes in public awareness and reporting to the police[13]. Rates of fear of crime also seem to be decreasing, so that the public and the media have generally lost interest in crime issues. The new forms of crime and offenders on the political agenda do not resonate with ideas of community sanctions or community crime prevention (Albrecht 2002: 244), and with the decreasing rates of crime and insecurity, community crime prevention seems about to lose much of its appeal in Germany.

### The courts and civil society: lay persons in German criminal justice

The role of lay persons in criminal justice decision-making is strictly limited. The dominant roles of professional criminal justice and criminal justice institutions are not contested and are highly trusted by the public in Germany. The code of criminal procedure provides a role for lay assessors (*Schöffen*) only for district courts (*Amtsgericht*). The courts of lay assessors, chaired by a professional judge, are responsible for all criminal cases if the expected sanction is between one and three years' imprisonment (except for complicated cases in which special legal knowledge is necessary and which are seen to go beyond the capacity of common-sense decisions). In all other cases decisions are made by professional criminal judges. On juries lay assessors have equal weight. This practice has a very long tradition in German criminal justice and has never been contested or discussed in ongoing discussions on community-based criminal justice.

In principle any citizen could be elected as a lay assessor. The local administration proposes candidates to the district courts, who are then elected by a committee of the district court whose members are representatives of local government and administration, chaired by a professional judge. In reality contested elections are infrequent and very often only members of the local administration are proposed as candidates.

### The penal system and the development of intermediate sanctions in Germany

In the 1970s measures of diversion and some projects that could be labelled as community services, especially in the framework of juvenile criminal justice, were introduced with the idea of avoiding negative effects of criminal sanctions and fostering rehabilitation, integration and resocialisation. The development of mediation schemes and compensation in the 1980s was in line with the growing importance of victims as well as arguments of cost-reduction. Prison overcrowding has also been mentioned as an argument, but remains only marginal in Germany – but the overloading of courts has always been a strong argument for decriminalisation reforms like diversion or a policy of dismissal of minor matters. Even if discussions of criminal sanctions under the title of 'community' are not present in Germany, the main focus in discussing and developing the system of criminal sanctions has been for a long time on alternatives to imprisonment.

Criminal law reforms in 1969 and 1975 were guided by this idea of abolishing short term imprisonment or any term of imprisonment, in order to avoid the assumed negative consequences of imprisonment, especially for first-time and petty offenders. Short-term imprisonment has been substituted by fines, and between imprisonment and fines an expanded system of suspended prison sentences and probation has been established.

This is one reason for the relatively stable imprisonment rates in Germany until the 1990s. The increase in the 1990s only matched in 1998 the rate before the major reform of criminal sanctions in 1969. This increase can be attributed to an increase in migrant offenders and drug addicts. Imprisonment was thought to be an *ultimo ratio* measure only for serious recidivists. At least until the beginning of the 1980s, the penal system followed the ideal of rehabilitation, including the idea of establishing special treatment-oriented penal institutions, which in fact never really occurred. In the 1980s and 1990s the public agenda and discourses about crime moved to concentrate on organised crime, hate crimes, drug-trafficking and sexual offences. In these cases the idea of incapacitation became more prominent, the idea of rehabilitation lost support and with new types of offences and offenders being emphasised (the 'rational offender', offenders from ethnic minorities), the basic approach of the 1960s and 1970s of rehabilitation and reintegration, focusing on the individual offender, came under pressure.

For juveniles aged 14–17 and young adults aged 18–20 years a separate system of treatment has been established since 1923. In this system ideas of reintegration, community sanctions and educational measures in the community, supervised by social services, have been institutionalised. Juvenile imprisonment is available only under the condition that a considerable need for rehabilitation is thought necessary for young offenders with serious criminal backgrounds. The guiding principle of this system of youth criminal justice is explicitly not to sanction but to resocialise and rehabilitate, and it is not seen to have or be required to have any deterrent effect. Some years ago there was some public discussion on expanding the system of juvenile imprisonment, and there are some political proposals to apply the adult criminal law to young adults aged 18–20, as well as to lower the minimum age for criminal responsibility below 14 years. But in fact these discussions still continue without any significant changes in practice.

The Youth Court Law contains a special system of treatment divided into educational measures (diversion with community work, offender-victim mediation), disciplinary measures (short-term detention, restitution, fines) and youth imprisonment with a minimum of six months and a maximum of five years. Community work (*gemeinnützige Arbeit*) in juvenile justice is especially interpreted as conforming with the idea of rehabilitation or re-socialisation by the community, which here does not refer to specific local affinity or geographic communities (*Gemeinschaften*) but to organisations which can provide work for the common interest in social institutions, such as homes for the elderly or hospitals.

### Diversion and informal social control

German law excludes a number of means of diversion which are available in other countries, in particular 'police diversion'. The only possibilities for diversion lie at the levels of the public prosecutor as a dismissal of the criminal process and at the judicial level as a court decision. These forms of diversion can be conditional or unconditional dismissal. Particularly in the system of juvenile justice diversion, measures have been guided by the idea of avoiding stigmatisation by criminal justice procedures and of relying on informal control by the family.

Since the 1970s the rights of prosecutors to drop an accusation and not to bring a case to a full-blown criminal procedure have been expanded. In the 1993 reform of the Criminal Procedure Law a simplified procedure was introduced, consisting only of a written process (informing the accused in writing that the case is dismissed) if the case is concluded by the public prosecutor not to be complicated in terms of proving guilt (i.e. there is no doubt about guilt) and a fine is considered as sufficient or a suspended sentence of up to one year is proposed. The rate of cases which have been dismissed by the prosecutors has increased greatly since the 1980s. In 1997 almost 40 per cent of cases were dismissed either conditionally or unconditionally, with another 25 per cent being dealt with using simplified procedures and just 11 per cent going to a full trial. The conditions imposed by public prosecutors for dismissing the case are mostly fines (about 95 per cent) whereas community work or compensation measures, especially for adult offenders, only play a minor role. However, there are special regulations for drug offenders which allow dismissal if the offender has started treatment, which are also organised by specialised social welfare associations (*freie Träger, Wohlfahrtsverbände*).

The widespread use of dismissal, because of cost pressures, has been subject to criticism, among other things because of its unequal adoption in the German *Länder*, especially for drug offences.

## Offender-victim mediation and restitution

Offender-victim mediation or restitution for adults was inserted into the criminal law via an amendment in 1994 (*Verbrechensbekämpfungsgesetz*, Criminal Control Law). According to this, the sentencer should always consider whether reconciliation, restitution or compensation has taken place. If the offender has managed to compensate the victim or at least has seriously tried to provide for complete compensation, the court may mitigate the sentence or refrain from imposing any punishment at all.

The application of offender-victim mediation has been strongly expanded in the last few years and is used now in about 25,000 cases per year in Germany, but the application of this measure by courts and prosecutors is very uneven, not only between the *Länder* but also between regions within one *Land*. Most of the cases are violent offences (about 50 per cent), followed by damage to property (about 15 per cent) and property offences (about 5 per cent) (Kerner and Hartmann 2005). These figures indicate that victim-offender mediation seems to be widely accepted by German courts and prosecutors, even for major offences. In about 80 per cent of the cases the mediation process is accepted by the criminal justice authorities as successful, and in about 92 per cent of these the criminal case is then dismissed by the prosecutor or the judge. Evaluations of some local initiatives show that these measures also seem to be more effective in preventing repeated offences than a fine or a prison sentence (Bannenberg and Rössner 2005). The mediation process is implemented by specialised institutions of social work associations (*freie Träger, Wohlfahrtverbände*) outside the court and the criminal justice system.

## Probation and suspended prison sentences

Prison sentences of up to two years can be suspended subject to probation supervision under various conditions. A prison sentence of up to six months must be suspended and should be substituted by day fines if the rehabilitative needs of the offender do not require immediate imprisonment. A prison sentence of up to one year may be suspended if there is no considerable risk of relapse. In the 1990s the rate of suspended prison sentences was about 80 per cent for sentences up to six months, 73 per cent for sentences up to one year and 65 per cent for sentences up to two years. The use of suspended prison sentences has steadily increased in the last few years.

With a suspended sentence the offender is placed on probation for a period of between two and five years. The conditions and restrictions of probation can comprise punitive conditions and restrictions as well as supervision and treatment orders that should influence the offender's lifestyle and increase social integration. Until 1998 treatment orders required the consent of the offender, but they then became compulsory for certain types of offenders under the pressure of strong political concerns over sexual crimes and drug offences. Despite the results of some studies that probation in many cases seemed to be more effective using punitive and restrictive measures (like regular registering with police and avoiding certain places and people) than using measures involving active reintegration and treatment, a social probation service is attached to each district court (*Amtsgerichte*), staffed with professional social workers.[14] In principle, the probation services are independent in their work and subject only to those provisions related to reporting duties as regards the supervision of offenders placed on probation. But their main duty is the provision of specialised social services for guiding processes of reintegration. The probation service thus has a double function: on the one hand it is an institution of judicial control with an obligation to report any breach of the conditions to the court; on the other hand, it is a social service providing help and support.

## The demands of the community in relation to German criminal justice

The professional criminal justice institutions in Germany enjoy a high degree of trust from the public as well as in political discourse. Even if there have been some demands and also reform related to strengthening the role of victims in court, the role of the community in criminal justice, as represented by lay persons involved in criminal decision-making, can be seen as marginal. In relation to so-called community sanctions, there have always been discussions on alternatives to prison and fines. Diversion measures, always present in German criminal law since the 1920s, were hugely expanded in the period between the 1970s and today, even if their guiding ideas more recently have referred to arguments rooted in destigmatisation, cost-reduction and effectiveness rather than ideas of some kind of community responsibility and integration. Measures of restorative justice, such as offender-victim mediation and reparation/ compensation, are organised outside but in close relation to the criminal justice system by professional social service organisations and non-governmental associations, but are backed up by prosecutorial decisions as a condition for dismissal of criminal justice procedures.

The only explicit reference to the notion of 'community' can be seen in political discussion about local crime prevention. In this context community refers either to the administrative body of towns (*Kommune*) or is used as a vague concept referring to geographic local targeting of crime prevention measures.

The high reliance placed on the professional criminal justice system and the police, as well as the interconnections between the criminal justice system and social work, can be seen as one major bulwark of resistance against populist demands for citizen participation in criminal justice, which in fact hardly exist in Germany because of the high degree of acceptance of professionalism in criminal justice matters. In the case of the police there have been some demands for more visibility and accountability in some quarters, but in comparison with other countries the image of the German police always has been that of a grass-roots police. One very old slogan of public police marketing has been 'The police – your friend and helper' and this image still persists for the German public (except for those who have just been caught for a traffic or other offence).

In consequence of this diversity the cognitive map associated with 'community' and 'civil society' also bears a wide range of meanings. In the German language, for example, 'community' is very near to *Gemeinschaft*, a concept opposed to all formal organisations and formal social relations which are associated with modern society (*Gesellschaft*). In this sense, 'community' can be connected to the idea of informal control in local neighbourhoods integrated through a commitment to particular common values and norms, sometimes seen as an opposite of the universalistic perspectives institutionalised in state criminal justice. This notion is linked to communitarian perspectives sometimes explicit or implicit in discourses on crime prevention.

In a less restricted but related sense, 'community' refers to institutions outside the state and is then associated with social integration into non-deviant social networks, the labour market, civil associations, etc. The idea of community in this sense is seen as supportive of processes of rehabilitation, resocialisation and informal control of offenders. In relation to the system of criminal justice, then, the question of whether community is helpful is a question of its efficiency or effectiveness in preventing reconviction, recidivism and criminal careers. In the system of youth criminal justice in Germany, sometimes community sanctions are discussed using these ideas, but then community measures refer to work for institutions such as homes for the elderly, which is seen as work for the common interest, not as work for a community.

But 'community' could also refer to the general public and its relation with criminal justice in general, or to interest groups concerned with crime. In this sense of community issues of criminal justice could be discussed under the topic of the need of the criminal justice system for legitimacy and public support. Discussions about this topic remain very limited in Germany because the system of professionalised criminal justice enjoys a very high degree of trust.

Ideas of community in a broader and normative but less sociological sense as related to local democracy or local justice in general ('Bringing society back into criminal justice' or 'Give conflicts back to the people') still exist within some groups of critical criminologists, but they have never had very much impact on the criminal justice system in Germany. One reason for this may be the relatively active system of local government self-regulation and participation in criminal justice matters.

## Notes

1 This meaning of community in social evolution as a traditional or archaic form of social integration unifies the founders of sociology from Henry Summer Maine (1905) with his notion of 'from status to contract', Ferdinand Tönnies (1963) with his classical distinction of 'community and society', Max Weber (1978) as *Vergemeinschaftung* and *Vergesellschaftung* and Emile Durkheim (1984) with the distinction between 'mechanical and organic solidarity', even if their interpretation of this development is very different. For an overview of the concept of community in classical and modern sociology, see Delanty (2003).

2 These different meanings of community in German political discourses correspond roughly with the distinction proposed by Lacey and Zedner (1995: 303): (a) community as 'an agency *by* which social policy is pursued and upon which responsibility should be thrust'; (b) community as 'the locus *in* which policy initiatives may be sited in recognition of the local specificity of social ills'; and (c) community in the 'role of beneficiary where policies are framed *for* the community in the hope of regenerating feelings of cohesiveness, security and solidarity'.

3 The remarkable career of 'community' in political and sociological discourse is accompanied by the rise of the use of 'social capital' as a basic sociological concept and political frame of reference, forming the basis for the functioning of community and civil society (though social capital is used differently by theorists such as Bourdieu, Coleman and Putnam). But

it is very seldom that analyses of 'community' and 'social capital' refer to other than their positive functions in taking into consideration their exclusive character and their sometimes violent boundary maintenance functioning, already mentioned by Durkheim (1984). Social cohesion, faith, reciprocity, mutuality and belonging – the central features of social capital – also characterise groups involved in organised crime, religious fundamentalism, corruption and informal political power networks (see Karstedt 1997).

4 To mark the difference from the English tradition of 'civil society' translations of Marx have often used the term 'bourgeois society' for *bürgerliche Gesellschaft*.

5 In this meaning some aspects of 'civil society' also apply to the sociology of inequality, but in fact the concept always was and still today remains rather outside the mainstream of sociology. Obviously 'civil society' only means certain aspects of the 'social', which have always been analysed in sociology under different labels like the public, associations, political socialisation, social movements, religion, ethnicity and social integration.

6 Other versions, like the 'liberal communitarianism' ideas of Michael Walzer, Charles Tayler and Michael Sandel, the 'feminist communitarianism' views of Seyla Benhabib or Nancy Frazer and the 'civic communitarianism' ideas of Robert Putnam and Robert Bellah *et al.* have been translated and discussed in Germany in the 1990s, but remain in the limited circles of critical political philosophy (see, for example, Honneth 1993).

7 They established in 1999 a special government expert commission on the 'Future of civil engagement'. Its results as well as the final report have been published in 11 volumes (Enquête Kommission 'Zukunft des Bürgerschaftlichen Engagements'/Deutscher Bundestag (Hrsg.) 2002).

8 Populations of migrants may be seen as an exception, but policies targeting these groups are based on the assumption that the development of cultural segregation and 'ethnic colonies' is a problem to be avoided. The target is the ethnic communities but the aim is not to serve their cultural needs but to integrate them into society.

9 Since the 1990s there is a tendency towards privatisation of social services, using business models of contract management, with open calls for tender, with the idea of introducing a greater element of competition into the market for social services. In these forms of 'contract management' local government only defines political targets and leaves the concrete operation, organisation and management of interventions to welfare associations or to private social service enterprises.

10 There is one exception – the involvement of volunteers in victim support associations, such as the *Weißer Ring*, which has about 2,000 volunteers, and the more professionalised *Deutsche Opferhilfe*. Both provide support and counselling for crime victims.

11 Some of the most important are: *Deutscher Richterbund* (the German association of judges), *Vereinigung der Strafverteidiger* (associations of

criminal defence attorneys), *Deutscher Vereinigung für Jugendgerichte und Jugendgerichtshilfen* (German association of youth courts and youth court aid institutions).

12 These contracts between police and social service agencies are also necessary to avoid regular police proactive activity in these centres, which normally would be the case given police prosecution of drug addicts.

13 This view is justified insofar as crime surveys in Germany show a clear overall decrease in violent crime over some years.

14 Up to now the probation service, staffed by social workers, has always been an integral part of the courts. Nowadays there is a tendency in some *Länder* towards its privatisation.

# References

Albrecht, H.-J. (1992) 'Gemeinde und Kriminalität – Perspektiven Kriminologischer Forschung', in H. Kury (ed.), *Gesellschaftliche Umwälzung: Kriminalitätserfahrungen, Straffälligkeit und soziale Kontrolle*. Max Planck Institut für ausländisches und internationales Strafrecht: Freiburg im Breisgau, 33–54.

Albrecht, H.-J. (2002) 'Community sanctions in the Federal Republic of Germany', in H.-J. Albrecht and A. Van Kalmthout (eds), *Community Sanctions and Measures in Europe and North America*. Max Planck Institut für ausländisches und internationales Strafrecht: Freiburg im Breisgau: edition iuscrim, 243–70.

Bannenberg, B. and Rössner, D. (2005) *Kriminalität in Deutschland*. München: C.H. Beck.

Berner, F. and Groenemeyer, A. (2000) '"… denn sie wissen nicht, was sie tun' – Die Institutionalisierung Kommunaler Kriminalprävention im Kriminalpräventiven Rat', *Soziale Probleme*, 11 (1/2): 83–115.

Crawford, A. (1999) *The Local Governance of Crime. Appeals to Community and Partnerships*. Oxford: Oxford University Press.

Delanty, G. (2003) *Community*. London: Routledge.

Durkheim, É. (1984) *The Division of Labour in Society*. Basingstoke: Macmillan. [French original (1893) *De la division du travail social: étude sur l'organisation des sociétés supérieurs*. Paris.]

Enquête Kommission 'Zukunft des Bürgerschaftlichen Engagements'/ Deutscher Bundestag (Hrsg.) (2002) *Bürgerschaftliches Engagement und Zivilgesellschaft*. Opladen: Leske & Budrich.

Etzioni, A. (1993) *The Spirit of Community. Rights, Responsibilities and the Communitarian Agenda*. New York: Crown Publishers. [German translation (1995) *Die Entdeckung des Gemeinwesens. Ansprüche, Verantwortlichkeiten und das Programm des Kommunitarismus*. Stuttgart: Schäffer-Poeschel.]

Etzioni, A. (1996) *The New Golden Rule. Community and Morality in a Democratic Society*. New York: Basic Books. [German translation (1997)

*Die Verantwortungsgesellschaft. Individualismus und Moral in der heutigen Demokratie.* Frankfurt am Main: Campus.]

Feest, J. (1988) '"Bürgernähe" – ein Spekulatives Konzept', *Kriminalistik*, 3: 128–31.

Garland, D. (1985) *Punishment and Welfare: A History of Penal Strategies.* Aldershot: Gower.

Honneth, A. (ed.) (1993) *Kommunitarismus. Eine Debatte über die Moralischen Grundlagen Moderner Gesellschaften.* Frankfurt am Main: Campus.

Karstedt, S. (1997) 'Recht und Soziales Kapital im Wohlfahrtsstaat', *Soziale Probleme*, 8 (2): 104–37.

Kerner, H.-J. and Hartmann, A. (2005) *Täter-Opfer-Ausgleich in der Entwicklung. Auswertung der Bundesweiten Täter-Opfer-Ausgleichs-Statistik für den Zehnjahreszeitraum 1993 bis 2002.* Berlin: Bundesministerium der Justiz.

Kreissl, R. (1987) 'Die Simulation Sozialer Ordnung. Gemeindenahe Kriminalitätsbekämpfung', *Kriminologisches Journal*, 19 (4): 269–84.

Lacey, N. and Zedner, L. (1995) 'Discourses of community in criminal justice', *Journal of Law and Society*, 23 (3): 301–25.

Lacey, N. and Zedner, L. (1998) 'Community in German criminal justice: a significant absence?', *Social and Legal Studies*, 7 (1).

Maine, H. S. (1905) *Ancient Law. Its Connection with Early History of Society and Its Relation to Modern Times*, 10th edn (orig. 1861). London: Murray.

Martinson, R. (1978) 'What works? Questions and answers about prison reform', in N. Johnson and L.D. Savitz (eds), *Justice and Corrections* (orig. 1975). New York: Wiley & Sons, 778–810.

Tönnies, F. (1963) *Community and Society.* New York: Harper & Row. [German orig. (1887) *Gemeinschaft und Gesellschaft. Grundbegriffe der reinen Soziologie.* Leipzig.]

Weber, M. (1978) *Economy and Society: An Outline of Interpretive Sociology.* Berkeley, CA: University of California Press. [German orig. (1922) *Wirtschaft und Gesellschaft. Grundriss der verstehenden Soziologie.* Tübingen.]

## Chapter 5

# Sweeping the street: civil society and community safety in Rotterdam

*René van Swaaningen*

### Introduction

In the Dutch newspaper *NRC Handelsblad* of 25 October 2004 we see two apparently contradictory front-page headlines: 'People fear harsh society' and 'Cohen [the mayor of Amsterdam, *RvS*] wants banning order against nuisance'. The first article is on the biannual *Social and Cultural Report 2004*, in which over two thousand people were interviewed about their wishes and expectations for the Netherlands in 2020. According to this report, there is a disparity between what people wish and what they actually expect of the future. They *would like* a more communitarian society with more solidarity, but they *fear* that society will become still more competitive and that the social climate will continue to toughen.[1] The second article is about a group of Moroccan boys who 'terrorised' a particular (middle-class) neighbourhood in Amsterdam, which resulted in one family who felt forced to move and a number of gay men who felt threatened by these boys. The mayor was answering the demands of the inhabitants that these rowdy boys should be treated harshly. If the estimated twenty habitual offenders among them, against whom an injunction prohibiting them entering that particular neighbourhood, were to be seen there once more they could count on a prison sentence of up to two years in a special 'no frills' regime.[2]

What is the role of civil society in the development of local crime and safety politics? That is the question I would like to address in this chapter. The two articles mentioned above show a rather contradictory picture. On the one hand, people are in favour of stiffer sanctions, and on the other hand they claim not to like the fact that society is developing in that direction. The people's desire for more community and more solidarity is notably *not* reflected in their reactions to crime and nuisance.

Though over the last ten years only a small percentage of the population reported feeling frequently unsafe in a general sense, a relatively large number of people feared that the problems we will be confronted with in 2020 are bigger than those of today – (Islamist) terrorism and random street violence were mentioned the most frequently. People said that currently they were most afraid of youth groups (most of all Moroccans and people from the Antilles) who are noisily hanging around, vandalising their neighbourhoods and intimidating the inhabitants.

Most people interviewed by the Social and Cultural Planning Bureau thought that the growing competitiveness of society, decreasing informal social control and globalisation were the major causes of crime and nuisance, but the solutions put forward were not connected to these developments. Because decreasing competitiveness and pushing back globalisation (in particular) were seen to be impossible, they proposed further infringements of people's privacy (mainly by increasing camera surveillance and the establishment of a general DNA database to identify the culprits) and more private security firms who could assist the police. And though local authorities in particular have implemented many efforts to support informal social control, there was close to 100 per cent popular support for stiffer penalties – especially for violent crime – and at best a reserved attitude to informal social control. It is remarkable that most citizens also wanted the authorities to pay more attention to the social prevention of crime and incivilities, but they were not so optimistic about their effectiveness. Most of them (83 per cent) expected that safety in their neighbourhood would increasingly become their own responsibility, but 40 per cent found this an undesirable development and felt left alone by the authorities.

The responsibilisation of a wide range of penal, administrative and welfare agencies is still the leading policy/philosophy on community safety in the Netherlands, but actual developments are moving in a rather different direction. Ideas on community policing have in fact already been replaced by notions of the police as 'gatekeepers' who keep 'undesirable elements' outside. 'Community justice' (*Justitie in de Buurt*) is being redefined as a means to reduce prosecutorial caseloads. Mediation projects dealing with neighbour(hood) disputes are said to be important, but they have only barely been funded. The

'Communities that Care' projects, imported from the US in the late 1990s, have only been implemented in four localities, because they were felt to be too expensive, given that the result of this considerable investment could not be quickly measured.[3] Neighbourhood mediation projects and other initiatives with respect to restorative justice may be flourishing, but their organisation and structure is not funded and by and large they depend on volunteers. In general, lay input in the criminal justice system is remarkably low in the Netherlands (see Malsch, this volume).

It is hardly an exaggeration to say that the new metaphor for community safety is 'sweeping the streets' – as if we are speaking of dirt (van Swaaningen, 2005). Many people will probably *agree* that real improvements in the safety situation are only to be expected from improvements in housing, social cohesion, education, properly equal participation of ethnic minorities in society, etc. but … such community, social and cultural solutions are seen as something for the long term, whereas people feel we need to solve today's problems now. People seem to have lost faith in a 'makeable' society, and sadly conclude that repression is the only solution that is left.

The results from the *Social and Cultural Report 2004* may be critical of the current neo-liberal breaking up of the welfare state, but they are completely in line with the government's plans for a safer society. This dilemma and paradox is most pressing at a community level. People's opinions on crime and punishment are – next to what they hear and see in the media – primarily informed by problems they experience themselves on the street. But their desire for more community and more social control is oriented at that very same level. This implies that the criminologist has good reasons to focus on the community level.

## The local dimension of safety

In fact, the often-used English word 'community' makes little sense in Dutch debates on safety. In Dutch, the word 'community' (*gemeenschap*) mainly refers to a cultural or religious (minority) group, rather than to any socio-geographic entity. Before the secularisation processes of the 1960s, we spoke of the Protestant and Roman Catholic communities. Today we still speak of the Jewish community, of the Muslim community and indeed of the Moroccan or Somali community. These 'communities' are, however, rarely mobilised in the politics of public safety. The English understanding of 'community' would in Dutch rather be referred to as 'neighbourhood' (*buurt*). In this chapter I will use the word 'community' in the English way.

In their book *Crime Control and Community*, Gordon Hughes and Adam Edwards (2002) argue that the local dimension offers a more fruitful field for comparative research on community safety than does the national level. This also fits the Dutch case, even though in the Netherlands the general contours of safety politics are set out in *national* policy plans. Safety problems emerge at a neighbourhood or borough level, but what can be done on a borough level has to 'fit' within the safety plans of the local authorities. What the city plans has to fit in with national plans and decisions on what initiatives are funded and which are not.[4] The state's policies are increasingly determined by European regulations, and these are ultimately steered by global developments. On all these levels there are decisions that can be taken relatively autonomously, and conditions that are actually determined at a higher level. To give a concrete example of the implications of this development: it is becoming increasingly questionable to what extent the Netherlands can maintain its 'deviant' approach on the consumption of drugs – for which there is quite a lot of support at a national level.

With respect to safety and the community, there is, however, something strange at stake. There are two parallel developments that seemingly point in quite different directions. On the one hand, there is clear globalisation of the ideology of the 'free market model', but on the other we can also observe a return to the local and the national. The present conservative Dutch government has a neo-liberal orientation on the economy and the welfare state, but it is inspired by communitarianism in its push towards mobilisation of the community and a renewed focus on national norms and values.

Within certain limits, local authorities in the Netherlands have quite a lot of freedom to develop their own plans which are intended to respond to specific problems in their municipality or borough. Legally, matters of public order – which form an important part of safety problems as they are currently defined – are decided on the local level, in the so-called triangular consultation (*driehoeksoverleg*) between the mayor of the biggest city in a police region, the chief of police and the chief prosecutor.[5] If we are to analyse the local governance of safety in the Netherlands, there are good reasons to consider Rotterdam.

Rotterdam is the Netherlands' second largest city, and has always played a pioneering role in the development of new experiments in the field of crime control. Sometimes these new experiments have been seen as 'progressive' - like the first Halt-project for juvenile offenders in 1981 – and sometimes as 'reactionary' – like its stop and search (*preventief fouilleren*) practices in certain problematic neighbourhoods or its attempts to prevent recently arrived 'poor people' from settling in such districts. Through these policies, and with its extremely interventionist policies on 'problematic' families, Rotterdam continuously explores the 'limits of the law'. Rotterdam is also the only Dutch city that has experimented with Anti-Social Behaviour Orders, called 'Act Normal' (*Doe Normaal*) (Klok 2006). But Rotterdam also remains an experimental field for innovative urban planning and policing. The latest example is the sale of houses in some problematic neighbourhoods for very low prices, under the condition that the new inhabitant takes care of the renovation of the house. This is a possible means to attract a new – i.e. wealthier and better-educated - 'type' of inhabitant to problematic neighbourhoods and to encourage a more diverse composition of these districts. Though there is quite a lot of interest from potential buyers, it is too soon to say something sensible about the success of this project.

## The specific case of Rotterdam

In Rotterdam, the populist right has been, since the 2002 local elections, the largest party in the city council and this party of the late Pim Fortuyn has put a firm mark on the city's safety politics (van Swaaningen 2005). Though after the 2006 local elections Rotterdam changed back again to a Labour local government, the populist right remains popular and has, at the time of writing, currently 30 per cent of the votes. This has much to do with Rotterdam's specific history and with the composition of its population. Large parts of the city (mainly the centre and the new west districts) were bombed severely by the Nazis in 1940 and (mistakenly) by the allied forces in 1942. This has resulted in a city that is very different from other Dutch cities, with many quickly built 1940s and 1950s housing blocks of rather poor quality, new prestigious high-rise buildings from the last ten or fifteen years, motorways right through the city, and no real 'heart'. It has more of a 'big city' atmosphere than, for example, Amsterdam or Utrecht; it is not a city in which many people can be seen walking about, with all the consequences for social control this implies.

Second, Rotterdam has the largest port in the world and is an ideal route for transport (over the rivers Rhine and Meuse), to Germany and France. This has always attracted a considerable workforce to the city, first from the southern provinces in the Netherlands, later from Mediterranean countries and still later with the arrival of immigrants (many of whom were 'illegal' immigrants) (Bouman and Bouman 1952; Fijnaut *et al.* 1991; Burgers and Engbersen 1998). All the Rotterdam boroughs south of the river were originally built for harbour workers. Today, the importance of this huge port with respect to safety problems lies predominantly in the fact that the city is also the centre for the distribution of many illegal goods – notably drugs. These two phenomena offer a particularly good breeding-ground for rack-renters and (drugs-related) street crime (van der Torre 2004). It is remarkable that the present-day problems are concentrated in the neighbourhoods mentioned above, with their particular history: the centre and the new west and southern districts.

The stereotype of Rotterdam is that of an industrial, dominantly working-class city, where shirts are sold with the sleeves already rolled up. The Netherlands would, following this same cliché, have three capitals: one where the money is earned (Rotterdam), one where it is distributed (The Hague) and one where it is spent (Amsterdam). And even though Rotterdam is in the post-Fordist era no longer the motor of the Dutch economy, it is still true that the level of education of the Rotterdam population is below the national average and the city attracts more than its share of the 'disadvantaged underclasses' from all over the world. It would be worthwhile for comparative criminologists to compare Rotterdam with other large port cities in Europe, such as Antwerp, Bilbao, Hamburg, Liverpool or Marseille, where the shipping industry has also largely disappeared and many industrial jobs were lost, and where it has also been necessary to look for other employment. Rotterdam now tries to attract a richer and better-educated population. Larger and nicer houses have been built and the cultural climate has also improved. But, despite the fact that Rotterdam has already become a far more attractive city than, let us say, some fifteen years ago, it still sees the richest segments of the population leaving rather than coming. This fact is quite important if we are to understand the city's safety politics.

Rotterdam has always been a stronghold of the Labour party (PvdA). From the 1990s on, Labour was, however, firmly and continuously criticised for having lost all contact with the population. The Labour local government was said to act like arrogant regents who could not listen and who played down public concerns about street crime, ethnic tensions and impoverishment. To cut a long story short: people were fed up with Labour and wanted to teach them a lesson.

Fourteen years ago, one could already predict the rise of a right-wing populist party. At the same time the right-wing extremist Flemish Block (*Vlaams Blok*) had its major success in Antwerp. In 1991, the Rotterdam electorate for the Dutch extreme right was also the highest in the Netherlands. It was just waiting for a charismatic leader. When our department presented its research findings on the deterioration of one particular neighbourhood in the southern Rotterdam borough of Feyenoord in the late 1980s, all the ingredients Fortuyn built his political programme about safety on were already present (Fijnaut *et al.* 1991). We were then already describing the situation, the toxic mix of ethnic tensions, nuisance and fear of crime, as smouldering (Beijerse and van Swaaningen 1993: 293).

Improving public safety was the most important task this new party set itself. Consequently, the safety issue started to play an even more dominant role in politics in Rotterdam than in any other Dutch city. In 2002, the mayor (Ivo Opstelten, from the liberal-conservative party VVD) even described it as his primary task to make Rotterdam safer. A special alderman for safety (from the Fortuyn party) was introduced, a large programme office for safety issues was established, producing the elaborate 'safety indexes' on a local and borough level in the whole country, and so-called 'urban marines' (high-level civil servants with a mandate to responsibilise various agencies to take up their tasks towards the improvement of the local safety situation) were introduced. There is also no other Dutch city in which the new 'revanchist urbanism' that until recently we only knew about from American cities is so clearly visible as in Rotterdam (Uitermark and Duyvendak 2004). No other city in the country has put so much energy into the fight against the insecurity of its population – and indeed into the fight against the urban poor.

## Safety in a Liveable Rotterdam

In a flyer distributed among the population the Rotterdam local authorities argued in 2001:

> Safety is our top priority and a common task for everybody. Not only for law enforcement and the police. They are – and remain – important partners in what we call the 'safety chain', but there are many others. Such as the various municipal services, the local transport company RET, the municipal offices for urban planning and housing and for welfare and employment, the

city's sanitation department ROTEB, the municipal office for education, private enterprise and social organisations. Safety must also be their top priority. All activities of municipal services, organisations and institutions that influence safety and liveability and safety should reinforce one another. Concerting and attuning actions are necessary, under strict coordination. Borough councils are those primarily responsible for this coordinating task. They are pivotal in this approach, since they are the closest to the inhabitants. Borough councils will, together with the inhabitants and all others who have a role to play with respect to safety, work on safe neighbourhoods and therewith on a safer Rotterdam.[6]

This quote echoes David Garland's (2001) thesis of responsibilisation strategies and Adam Crawford's (1997) analyses of the local governance of crime. But in Rotterdam the role of private enterprise and citizens' initiatives is less than in the UK, and the role of municipal services larger (van Swaaningen 2004). A second striking element of Rotterdam's safety politics is the action- and output-oriented tone. The word 'plan' is carefully avoided. According to 'Liveable Rotterdam' the past was characterised by too many plans and too little action.

In a debate on Rotterdam's safety politics in September 2004 at the Erasmus University, mayor Ivo Opstelten once more confirmed that if you win the elections, you have to take responsibility. He also argued that the city's drastic safety policy was born from a sense of urgency, and that he would certainly suffer the political consequences if the targets of a safer Rotterdam were not be met after 2006, when the city's 'five year action programme on safety' should be fully implemented. The question whether this is merely roaring rhetoric or that the Rotterdam safety programme actually 'works' cannot be answered unequivocally. The local authorities annually publish a 'safety index', that does show that things are actually getting a bit better. This safety index (see below) consists, however, of so many subjective indexes that can be easily manipulated that it is difficult to call it objective information. In an interesting, rather critical evaluation, the Rotterdam auditor's office concluded that the effects of the new policy on the actual safety situation and on feelings of insecurity cannot really be measured, because 'objective' data and subjective opinions are fused into one 'report mark' in the local safety index.[7]

There is also a lot of continuity in Rotterdam's safety politics. From the early 1980s, Dutch crime prevention policies have been characterised by a mixed package of situational and social prevention, increasing different forms of surveillance, a so-called 'integral', multi-agency approach towards insecurity and a major accent on specific urban problems (van Swaaningen 2002). All these elements can still be recognised in today's safety policy. The *tone* may well be the thing that differs the most from the past. The main criticism of previous safety policies was not so much to do with their content, but with the way they were (not) carried out. There was too much paperwork and too many meetings and plans but too little action, and it was never clear what the actual results of certain interventions were. Therefore the new action programme speaks of 'clear priorities and choices' and of 'concrete and visible results' and 'measurable output' (Gemeente Rotterdam 2002a: 5). There is no real break from previous safety initiatives, nor can one maintain that the city has ceased using social crime prevention. It is better to refer to new *complementary* strategies.

One of these strategies is a clear actuarial orientation towards geographic crime profiling: patterns of offending and 'hot spots' are systematically mapped. A second complementary strategy can be characterised as 'civilising the urban poor' (Uitermark and Duyvendak 2004). This latter strategy has become the most visible in the fight against so-called incivilities, with a strong accent on the need for ethnic minorities to fully 'integrate' into Dutch society (learning the language, respecting the customs, etc.) and on forcing 'drug addicts avoiding care' and street prostitutes into a more 'respectable' lifestyle. Justus Uitermark and Jan Willem Duyvendak (2004) characterise these social and, at the same time, repressive policy lines as 'a combination of carrot and stick interventions with two striking elements: it celebrates and promotes the construction of diverse neighbourhood communities while it at the same time sees cultural differences as a root cause of urban problems'.

Justus Uitermark (2006) concludes that Amsterdam 'sells' its safety policies as something more social than they actually are, whereas Rotterdam advertises its policies as 'tougher' than they actually are, but the result is not fundamentally different. In a report to the Scientific Council for Government Policy (WRR), Rotterdam sociologists Godfried Engbersen, Erik Snel and Afke Weltevrede (2005) conclude that, despite all the differences between Amsterdam and Rotterdam – socio-economically and politically – both cities' safety policies can be characterised as a politics of 'social reconquest'. It is quite likely that the excessively 'tough' tone of the Rotterdam policies is responding to the 'demands of the electorate' of the Liveable Rotterdam party, whereas people are realistic enough to see that social provisions are necessary in order to make the policies work. Though politicians argue their 'get tough' approach has been introduced because 'the citizens of Rotterdam are fed up with soft measures', the traditional Labour agenda on these issues is, albeit in silence, carried out as well.

Key words in the 2001 Rotterdam action programme are: (a) nuisance (mainly seen as caused by drug addicts, youth groups, street prostitutes and beggars), (b) dirt and deterioration (the slogan 'sweeping the street' in its literal sense) and (c) zero tolerance (sweeping the streets in a metaphorical sense). With respect to the first policy element, penal and welfare approaches are no longer contrasted; the only relevant question is what works best to improve the safety situation. 'Problematic groups' who cause nuisance on a regular basis are both locked up and placed under welfare supervision. The second policy line is inspired by the 'broken windows' philosophy. The implied political buzz of 'zero tolerance policing' reaches pretty far in Rotterdam: homeless people have been fined for causing so-called 'visual nuisance' (*sic!*), simply because they were sleeping on a bench or sought shelter against the rain in a tram stop. It has to be stressed, however, that zero tolerance is also aimed at rack-renters who facilitate drug dealing, who exploit immigrants of illegal status and who have really operated as 'block busters' – i.e. chasing law-abiding citizens away by renting houses to large numbers of very problematic people (mainly drug addicts and foreigners without valid papers), or allowed illegal brothels or illegal drugs factories to operate and then bought their houses for a very low price. Though it is legally rather difficult, Rotterdam tries to expropriate the dwellings from owners if it can be proved that they knew what was happening in their houses.

## The five year action programme and its priorities for Rotterdam

The 2001 Rotterdam action programme on safety contains no less than 18 priorities, all targets that have to be realised within five years. The most important of these is that the so-called 'safety index' of the eight most problematic neighbourhoods needs to be improved. This safety index is based on (a) so-called 'objective factors' based on police recorded crime figures; (b) so-called 'subjective factors' based on victimisation figures, collected by the police as well; and (c) so-called 'context-figures' on ethnic composition, welfare dependency, house values, frequency of moving, etc. On this basis every borough is given a report mark – the current average is a meagre pass. Though it is definitely the most elaborate and systematic measurement of safety on a borough level in the country, there are very few reflections on undesired side effects of the safety index (e.g. stigmatisation of certain groups or neighbourhoods), the reliability of the data, the extra investment needed to improve the safety level or the fact that street crime is not the only source of anxiety.[8]

A second priority is to tackle the major 'hot spots' of crime. The location of these hot spots is mentioned with an exactness corresponding to a particular block of houses at a particular junction. Most such places are called 'hot spots' because there are too many inhabitants per house, or a suspicion of illegal production or sale of drugs or of illegal brothels. The solution to these problems varies from closing and tearing down these houses, renovation and gentrification, to assisting residents with respect to work, debt control and housing. What will happen to the people who cause nuisance at these hot spots remains by and large unclear. For the 700 anti-social 'louts' (*hufters*) it is, however, quite clear: they are to be removed from the street and, if possible, locked up in new institutions for habitual offenders – with a special facility for drug addicts. Foreigners without valid papers who have committed an offence are to be deported, but in practice this is not so easy – mainly because their country of origin is unknown, or the country does not want them back. Drug addicts and (mostly also drugs-related) prostitutes who can 'prove' that they can improve their lifestyles will receive financial support and a house. For them a more civilising offensive is being applied.

A third priority is the Rotterdam Central Station. The results of the intensive policing of this railway station are often put forward as the city's success story. For many years it has been a meeting point for drug addicts. The station acquired a special status as a 'war zone', where the police were given particular powers to control different public transport lines (trains, metro, tram and bus) and to disperse any gathering of people belonging to a so-called 'risk category'. There are currently fewer junkies at the railway station than before. But, after the closure of the 'free zone' (where shooting up was tolerated) at the so-called 'Platform Zero' near the station (in 1994), the junkies moved to already vulnerable areas in the new west of the city (Spangen), where street prostitution was concentrated as well, and then later moved to the south (Millinxbuurt) (van der Torre 2004).

Summarising all the other 15 priorities set out in the action programme would add little to this general picture, since they all point in the same direction.[9] They have included the closure of the area where the authorities have condoned (illegal) street prostitution – at the Keileweg. Most of the women without valid documents working here were to be deported to their country of origin, while some were to be assisted to have a 'normal' (i.e. drugs-free) life again. Many have moved their activities to other places such as Utrecht which still has a more liberal policy. The remainder have been treated just like all the other junkies and 'louts': i.e. they live on the street and are locked away every now and then. Interestingly enough, the local authorities present putting up more CCTV cameras as a target in itself rather than a possible means to reach a target.

As well as including all the repressive measures mentioned above, urban planning has also been put forward as a means to improve the safety situation in Rotterdam. Unlike the American practice of separation and segregation of the underclass, Rotterdam aims, as we have seen above, towards a policy of mingling them with the rest of the population. A civilising offensive for the 'undeserving poor', zero tolerance towards rack-renters (whose expropriated houses are distributed) and a politics of social mixing have been going hand in hand with the most controversial element of Rotterdam's safety politics: stopping new immigrants from moving into the city. This plan aroused a lot of protest, but after the term 'immigrants' was rephrased as 'disadvantaged households' it was introduced nonetheless. Rotterdam has been given consent by the national government to prevent anybody with an income of less than 120 per cent of the legal minimum income to register as a resident of Rotterdam. Uitermark and Duyvendak (2004) comment in this respect:

> The effects of this proposal are probably limited ... but it is nevertheless significant that the central government approves of a measure that contradicts some basic rights ... While all these proposals have a xenophobic or reactionary undertone, it cannot be said that they are primarily meant to turn the city into a middle-class or upper-class area ... The reasons for promoting social mixing have more to do with the management of marginalised groups than with strengthening the tax-base.

This is quite understandable, since the costs of the presence of marginalised groups are by and large paid by the state, but the *management* of these groups is the responsibility of the local authorities.[10] Rotterdam argues, however, that they already have more than their share of problematic groups and is effectively asking for other towns to take their share too.

With respect to the role of civil society in the way community safety initiatives are given shape, we can, however, observe a considerable influence of the middle classes. They are listened to while at the same time the underclass is more or less put under permanent surveillance. The fact that the control of the underclass has been generalised as control of ethnic minorities is one of the most likely reasons why the Liveable Rotterdam party did not win the 2006 local elections. In 2002, most ethnic minorities did not vote. In 2006 they *did* and voted Labour.

## Collaboration and commitment as preconditions for a multi-agency approach

One of the key problems of safety policies is that various agencies who are supposed to work together focus so much on reaching the internal 'targets' set by their own institutions that actual multi-agency cooperation often becomes a farce. Peter Goris's (2000) study on professional actors in the safety sphere in four Flemish cities shows furthermore that, next to this managerial issue, the success of a multi-agency approach is also to a large extent determined by the political question of who sets the agenda. In the Amsterdam case mentioned in the introduction, the situation in that particular neighbourhood could have got out of hand because complaints from the inhabitants were not taken seriously, communication between different professional groups failed (itself a far cry from them collaborating) and there was no commitment to actually do something that could have prevented the neighbourhood disputes escalating. Housing corporations, the police and the town authorities were all reluctant to use the powers they had to stop the youth groups. The vandalising of cars and houses and the intimidation some people reported was not felt to be serious enough. Others argue the authorities were afraid of being accused of racism, because all the boys involved were of Moroccan descent. Policemen on the beat claimed they often *wanted* to intervene, but were told not to do so by their chiefs, because either the prosecutor (to whom the Dutch police are accountable) would first check in detail whether the facts and circumstances were sufficient for a justified legal suspicion of a punishable act, or because it was not a matter for the criminal justice system, or because it would imply unjustified infringements of people's privacy, etc. (Tomlow 2004).[11] In order to avoid such formalistic 'obstruction', complaints procedures and much paperwork if they were to intervene, the police often decided to do nothing.

The Rotterdam police and local authorities seemed to mind less about legal 'formalism' than their colleagues in Amsterdam – the mayor has explicitly argued he will continue to explore the limits of the law. Does this mean that the Rotterdam police are less lax and uncommitted than their colleagues in the capital? A similar question can be posed with respect to the 'civil inattention' of the other actors in the Amsterdam case: the housing corporation, the town authorities, the youth and community workers and the other, non-affected inhabitants. Would that be any different in Rotterdam? Given the fact that avoiding rather than addressing problems and the 'civil inattention' that accompanies it seemed to be a product of an era (or culture?) of individualisation, that appears to be highly unlikely. The Rotterdam authorities have developed an initiative that puts at least some more force on the collaboration of the different actors in the safety policy.

Six so-called 'urban marines' have been made responsible for a particular problem area in Rotterdam – yet another initiative copied from New York's former mayor Rudolph Giuliani. The first association the word 'urban marine' provokes is probably a Rambo-like figure, but actually it is a high-ranking civil servant given a coordinating task to realise the 18 priorities of the Rotterdam safety programme in 'his' area. The urban marines are immediately under the 'safety steering group' that consists of the mayor, the chief prosecutor, the chief of police and the alderman for public order and safety. The city's safety office feeds the urban marines with data and offers logistic support. The main task of the urban marine is to encourage the commitment of the different parties to close a so-called 'achievement contract', in which they promise to do their share with respect to the improvement of urban safety. The success of the urban marines will probably largely depend on their communication skills and analytic capacities to determine what is the core of the problem, who is responsible and how it can be solved. After 2006 one expects that all 'partners in the safety chain' will have internalised their responsibilities and that the urban marines will no longer be necessary. But as yet they still function as a crowbar – in a strictly metaphorical sense of course.

## Some conclusions and suggestions for further research

The least one can say about Rotterdam's policy on public safety is that it is interesting. For legal scholars, the local authorities' creative explorations of the limits of the law (with respect to stop and search, police custody for mere incivilities, denying low-income groups the right to live in the city, etc.) offer a true Eden for research. The new policies on urban planning and housing, the 'rule of the middle-class' and the civilising offensive towards the – often undocumented or 'illegal' – underclass bring us to the heartland of sociological research.

The most interesting question for criminologists is probably to what extent the governance of safety has become an issue of *us*, law-abiding citizens, *against them*, the homeless, drug users, street prostitutes, youth gangs and notably the (Muslim) ethnic minorities, and what the possible consequences are of this tendency. When authors like Malcolm Feely and Jonathan Simon (1994) or Mike Davis (1998) predicted *intifada*-like social conflicts, partly as a consequence of taking a strongly situational approach to public safety, Dutch criminologists mainly argued 'we do not live in Los Angeles' South Central district and the situation in the Netherlands will not become that extreme either'. Today, after '9/11', the murder of a potential prime minister in 2002 and a second political murder of a film director in 2004, people are no longer so sure about this (van Swaaningen 2005).

On a concrete level, Rotterdam's safety policy is neither as revolutionary nor as successful as the local authorities would like us to believe. Ultimately, it is based on the pattern that was set out in the national 1985 White Paper *Society and Crime* and the 'Integral Safety Report' of 1993 (van Swaaningen 2002). An alderman of Fortuyn's Liveable Rotterdam party, Marco Pastors, admits this:

> The Labour party says: 'you are implementing the policy we have thought out.' That is true. And they have developed a good policy indeed, for example with respect to housing: no more affordable rental housing, only expensive and medium priced owner-occupied dwellings. They just did not communicate that policy. It was not done to say 'of course to build expensive houses', with the result that the policy did not really take off.[12]

The language in which policy proposals are currently formulated has definitely changed. Nuances and scientific foundation have been replaced by proclamations about 'zero tolerance', 'louts', 'marines' and such like, together with roaring rhetoric of the simplistic 'us against them' kind. The key question for research is to what extent these changes on the discursive level are reflected in actual practice. The main developments Garland analyses as a 'culture of control' are clearly reflected in the Dutch case – and most notably in Rotterdam (van Swaaningen 2004).

We have seen numerous examples of responsibilisation – and of the dilemmas and difficulties of this strategy. An important problem is the 'culture of aloofness' and 'civil inattention' that contradicts the government's attempts to responsibilise the citizenry and professional actors. Another key problem is that the present safety policy makes it probably very difficult to get all those groups that are currently excluded from society to a point that they will feel once more committed to society. Yet this is exactly the task the (immigrant) electorate gave Rotterdam's local authorities in 2006. The interest groups representing the most excluded people – junkies, foreigners without valid papers and street prostitutes – are, however, barely listened to.

If society is to become less competitive and show more solidarity, as a majority of the Dutch population seems to wish according to the Social and Cultural Planning Bureau, we need to seek dialogue and participatory democracy. This would require some fundamental rethinking in the present Dutch political culture. The Netherlands has always been an expert-led democracy in which lay influences play a rather limited role. Representatives of the criminal justice system have treated lay influences (such as juries and lay magistrates) with suspicion and have stuck to a strictly professional system (see Malsch, this volume). How can it be possible to mobilise civic initiatives with respect to urban safety if we know that many people are reluctant to get involved, that 'the system' is not open to lay influences and that society is fragmented? We could start answering this question with a thorough rereading of Granovetter's (1973) essay on 'the strength of weak ties'. Such 'weak ties', consisting of loose and rather superficial social contacts, have replaced the 'strong ties' of religious denominations or lifetime positions. The point is that these 'weak ties', though they may imply less social cohesion, do not necessarily provide less social control. Weak ties may be looser and less demanding, but they bring the possibility of having a larger number of bonds and connections. Strong ties, on the other hand, are oriented at an in-group, and contacts with 'out-groups' are relatively rare. From this perspective, the often criticised individualism need not be that worrying.

Lastly, I want to point to some interesting research themes with respect to social and public administration. The 'governance' thesis is the first to come to mind. Most of the academic literature on this subject criticises the new 'entrepreneurial' style of administration for its democratic deficits, but at present it seems more exciting to see whether there might be *positive* points to be discovered. One often hears from progressive civil servants in Rotterdam that they actually *prefer* the 'everything is possible' style from the populist Right over the 'iron cage' that Labour has constructed in the past. They claim there is currently more openness and less paperwork, and that serious attempts are being undertaken to solve the problem of the permissive, only slightly engaged structure of the earlier safety policies with respect to the practice of cooperation between agencies. This seems to be an important lesson the new Labour authorities in Rotterdam should take very much to heart.

When I first entered the field of community safety, I thought it was one of the most boring areas of criminology: it was concerned with minor problems based on bureaucratic and ill-informed plans, and seemed to have little content or action. Nowhere had I seen so many tedious, repetitive, instrumentalist and intellectually unexciting studies on the costs and effects of intervention X, Y or Z in neighbourhood A, B and C. It took me some time to discover how interesting this field of research actually is. It touches upon all the big questions of sociology and makes them very concrete on a practical, local level. And that is exactly what brought me to criminology in the first place. I furthermore think there are few cities that offer a more interesting research field than Rotterdam ... even though I am sometimes quite sceptical, if not anxious, about where the new politics will take us.

## Notes

1 Online at: www.scp.nl/publicaties/boeken/9037701590.shtml. A report of the National Institute of Public Health and the Environment (RIVM) – *Verkenning van Duurzaamheid* – that appeared one week earlier than the above-mentioned SCP report shows a similar orientation.
2 This is made possible by the new Act on Institutions for Habitual Offenders (ISD), effective from 1 October 2004 – the new articles 38m–38u of the Dutch Code of Penal Procedures (WvSv). It is called the watered-down Dutch version of the American 'three strikes and you're out' legislation.

3 With respect to community justice (JiB) we can point to the fact that some offices have been closed down (e.g. that in Haarlem) and others have explicitly claimed that they no longer invest in contacts with the neighbourhood, prioritising instead a fast case flow (Amsterdam West). The budget reserved for Communities that Care is 2.3 million euros for the whole province of Zuid-Holland (including large cities such as Rotterdam, The Hague, Dordrecht and Leiden) whereas the safety budget of the city of Rotterdam alone is 100 million euros – the costs for 'normal' criminal justice interventions excluded. Most crime prevention projects have been initiated by agencies related to the Ministries of Justice and of Internal Affairs, while Communities that Care is mainly organised by the Ministry of Welfare and Public Health's research institute NIZW (see de Vries 2004).

4 Municipalities receive about 80 per cent of their money from the national government. Over the last ten years, however, there has been a tendency for people to expect *more* of local authorities, but they are given *less* means.

5 They have been given this political power by statute: article 14 of the Police Act (*Politiewet*) and articles 219–221 of Law on the Municipalities (*Gemeentewet*).

6 Text from a brochure on Rotterdam's 'five year action programme Safe' (*Vijfjarenactieprogramma Veilig*), entitled *Werken aan een veiliger Rotterdam; geen woorden maar daden*, December 2001 (own translation).

7 Online at: www.rekenkamer.rotterdam.nl/?/Rekenkamer_Home/Onderzoek/Rapporten?mode=view&itemID=37.

8 In this respect the Amsterdam policy is different: no report marks are given and the fight against organised crime plays a far more important role.

9 They are: (4) improving safety on public transport; (5) closing the centre to (illegal but condoned) street prostitution; (6) 700 'care avoiding addicts' to be moved off the streets; (7) juvenile offenders to be moved off the streets; (8) 'criminal' foreigners without valid papers to be moved off the streets; (9) more surveillance; (10) more CCTV; (11) the establishment of one service to which citizens can go with all their complaints about safety; (12) closing soft-drugs coffee shops that break the rules or cause a nuisance; (13) closing brothels that break the rules or cause a nuisance; (14) dismantling apartments that are known as meeting places for drug-users; (15) stricter control of, for example, health and safety regulations; (16) structural examination of people's integrity when licences or subsidies are given out; (17) stricter plans and protocols for crisis management; and (18) cleaner streets and functioning facilities (street lights, telephone booths, etc.).

10 The amount of money central government pays to local government depends on the number of inhabitants, not the amount of tax they pay.

11 The author is a defence lawyer, specialising in acting in cases of

evictions of 'anti-social' inhabitants – mostly representing the housing corporation.

12 Interview in de *Volkskrant*, 17 January 2004; translation from Uitermark and Duyvendak (2004).

## References

Beijerse, J. and van Swaaningen, R. (1993) 'Social control as a policy: pragmatic moralism with a structural deficit', *Social and Legal Studies*, 2: 281–302.

Bouman, P. J. and. Bouman, W. H. (1952) *De Groei van de Grote Werkstad: een Studie over de Bevolking van Rotterdam*. Assen: Van Gorcum.

Burgers, J. and Engbersen, G. (eds) (1998) *De Ongekende Stad 1: Illegale Vreemdelingen in Rotterdam*. Amsterdam: Boom.

Crawford, A. (1997) *The Local Governance of Crime: Appeals to Community and Partnerships*. Oxford: Clarendon Press.

Davis, M. (1998) *Ecology of Fear: Los Angeles and the Imagination of Disaster*. New York: Holt & Co.

Engbersen, G., Snel, E. and Weltevrede, A. (2005) *Sociale Herovering in Amsterdam en Rotterdam: een Verhaal over Twee Wijken*. Amsterdam: Amsterdam University Press/WRR.

Feely, M. and Simon, J. (1994) 'Actuarial justice: the emerging new criminal law', in D. Nelken (ed.), *The Futures of Criminology*. London: Sage, 173–201.

Fijnaut, C., Moerland, H. and uit Beijerse, J. (1991) *Een Winkelboulevard in Problemen: Samenleving en Criminaliteit in Twee Rotterdamse Buurten*. Arnhem: Gouda Quint.

Garland, D. (2001) *The Culture of Control: Crime and Social Order in Contemporary Society*. New York: Oxford University Press.

Gemeente Rotterdam (2002a) *Vijfjarenactieprogramma Veiligheid Rotterdam*. Rotterdam: Programmabureau Veilig.

Gemeente Rotterdam (2002b) *Het Nieuwe Elan van Rotterdam ... en zo gaan we dat doen*. Rotterdam: College van B&W.

Goris, P. (2000) 'Op Zoek naar de Krijtlijnen van een Sociaal Rechtvaardige Veiligheidszorg: Analyse van Relaties Tussen Professionele Actoren in het Kader van een Geïntegreerde Oreventieve Aanpak van Veiligheidsproblemen in Achtergestelde Woonbuurten'. Unpublished PhD thesis, Katholieke Universiteit Leuven.

Granovetter, M. (1973) 'The strength of weak ties', *American Journal of Sociology*, 78: 1360–80.

Hughes, G. and Edwards, A. (eds) (2002) *Crime Control and Community: The New Politics of Public Safety*. Cullompton: Willan.

Klok, T. (2006) 'ASBO: Fighting Smoke'. Unpublished Masters thesis in criminology, Erasmus University, Rotterdam.

Swaaningen, R. van (2002) 'Towards a replacement discourse on community safety: lessons from the Netherlands', in G. Hughes, E. McLaughlin and J. Muncie (eds), *Crime Prevention and Community Safety: New Directions.* London: Sage, pp. 260–78.

Swaaningen, R. van (2004) 'Veiligheid in Nederland en Europa: een sociologische beschouwing aan de hand van David Garland', *Justitiële Verkenningen,* 30 (7): 9–23.

Swaaningen, R. van (2005) 'Public safety and the management of fear', *Theoretical Criminology,* 9 (3): 289–306.

Tomlow, B. (2004) 'Cohen mag Burgers niet Laten Verjagen; Probleem bij Aanpak van Overlast is dat Leiderschap en Gezag Ontbreekt', *NRC Handelsblad,* 26 October 2004.

Torre, E. van der (2004) 'Rotterdamse drugsscenes: het kostbare gelijk van de straat', in E. Muller (ed.), *Veiligheid: Studies over Iinhoud, Organisatie en Maatregelen.* Alphen aan den Rijn: Kluwer, 253–78.

Uitermark, J. (2006) 'Grootstedelijke Cijferpolitiek: Rotterdam na vier jaar niet leefbaarder dan Amsterdam', *Tijdschrift voor de Sociale Sector,* March: 34–9.

Uitermark, J. and Duyvendak, J. W. (2004) *Civilizing the European City: Revanchist Urbanism in Rotterdam, the Netherlands.* Paper presented at the annual meeting of the American Sociological Association, 14–17 August, San Francisco.

Vries, I. de (2004) *Communities that Care: An Evidence-based Strategy of Preventing Juvenile Problem Behaviour; on the Role of Municipalities in Dealing with Juvenile Criminal Behaviour in the Netherlands and How the Strategy of Communities that Care Offers Tools for Well Administrating a Preventive Youth Policy.* Paper presented at the annual conference of the European Society of Criminology, 25–28 August, Amsterdam. Online at: www.esc-eurocrim. org/files/paper ctc.doc.

## Chapter 6

# Lay elements in the criminal justice system of the Netherlands

*Marijke Malsch*

## Introduction

The central issue of the GERN series of seminars on 'Justice and Community' concerns the relation between the 'community' and the criminal justice system. A number of characteristics of, and initiatives undertaken in, the Netherlands criminal justice system seem relevant in this respect. One of the most conspicuous characteristics of the Dutch criminal justice system is its professional nature. This chapter pays attention to typical features of the Dutch legal system. Among the programmes undertaken in the Netherlands to bridge the gap with the community as well as with individual civilians are *Justice in the Neighbourhood* (JiB) – an initiative in which prosecutors have their office in neighbourhoods where they can be easily reached by people living there; *Eigen Kracht* conferences in which defendants meet their victim and a conference takes place; a still growing number of alternative sanctions; and various procedures to obtain compensation for victims who suffer damage as a consequence of crime.

Some of the initiatives that are presented in this paper can be clearly characterised as 'community involvement', such as *JiB* and the *Eigen Kracht* conferences, in which neighbours and/or family members and other relatives participate. In other programmes or initiatives, civilians participate more on an individual basis. That means that the scope of this chapter is broader than was originally intended for this collection; it is not restricted to community involvement but covers participation by individuals in the legal system as well. This widening of the scope is necessary because the Netherlands does not allow for a great deal of participation by civilians in its legal system, let alone for *community* involvement. For making a relevant contribution to the volume, inclusion of participation by civilians *in general* is therefore required.

Forms of participation by the public and by individual civilians in the criminal justice system are relevant for confidence in the system and its legitimacy. The chapter therefore starts with exploring the concepts of confidence, satisfaction with the system and legitimacy.

## Confidence, satisfaction with the criminal justice system and legitimacy

The media suggest that there is public dissatisfaction with the legal system. A recent compilation of Dutch survey findings concerning confidence in the judiciary, however, shows that trust in judges is relatively high in the Netherlands, both compared with other institutions in our country and compared with other countries (van der Meer 2004). A number of surveys have investigated public trust in the criminal justice system in the Netherlands. In general, confidence in public institutions, including the criminal justice system, has decreased since the 1980s. However, this has not only occurred in the Netherlands, but also in other Western European countries. Confidence in the judiciary appears to be related to confidence in the police (van der Meer 2004). Confidence can be regarded as a central component of the concept of 'legitimacy'.

'Legitimacy' is not a clear concept. Citizens' perceptions of the performance of the legal system are highly relevant for legitimacy. Legitimacy is something in the minds of citizens which makes them accept authority, comply with legal norms and cooperate when the system asks them to do so. In this sense, judges and their decisions would, when considered acceptable by the general public, be 'legitimate'. 'Legitimacy', in this primary meaning, can be defined as the *a priori* preparedness of citizens to comply with judicial decisions, as well as to legal and other relevant norms. It is not totally clear which characteristics of a legal system lead to perceptions of legitimacy. Psychological theories, as well as theories in the fields of law, sociology and public administration, give a number of indications, however, about the characteristics that are relevant in this respect. So the secondary meaning of 'legitimacy', namely the characteristics of the legal system, of judges and their decisions that actually determine 'legitimacy' in its primary sense, is not clear-cut and should be more thoroughly investigated.

Related to legitimacy are the *expectations* that are entertained in society about the effectiveness of the criminal justice system. Both the general public and legislators and politicians have high expectations of the Dutch criminal justice system and about punishing offenders. These expectations appear from the fact that, in the Netherlands, the maximum penalties for a number of crimes have recently been raised and drafts exist for further extensions of penalties. New laws have increased the number of situations in which a person may be prosecuted. Certain actions performed in preparation for committing a crime have themselves been made punishable, whereas previously only the actual *execution* of a criminal act itself could be prosecuted. Membership of an organisation that commits crimes has been criminalised as well. New laws have been drafted to raise the maximum punishments for criminal acts committed with the intent to commit terrorist acts, and to increase the powers of law enforcement officials in case there are indications that certain terrorist activities might either be executed or are in a stage of preparation.

All these – new and old – developments show that both politicians and the general public entertain high expectations of the powers of the criminal justice system to solve certain societal, as well as political, problems. In addition, greater possibilities for victims to claim compensation and to deliver a statement about the consequences of the crime on them at trial may contribute to these expectations. Deception, leading to a reduced confidence in the criminal justice system, may ensue. When a criminal justice system, in spite of all expectations, appears not to be able to reduce crime, to increase safety or to really satisfy victims, it risks, in the long run, losing its legitimacy.

Developments within society may contribute to such loss of confidence and legitimacy. General attitudes to authorities have changed since the 1960s and 1970s. Authorities have become subject to general criticism like any other civilian group. Civilians themselves have become more emancipated. Professionals, such as doctors, lawyers and professors, are no more in a position to merely rely on their own authority and university degrees for making the public accept their decisions and opinions, but have to explain and substantiate them. Patients, students, clients and civilians in general are now more prepared to question these professionals about the knowledge they offer and the suggestions they make. Communication between authorities and civilians, as a consequence, plays a substantially larger role now than a century ago, and has, to a certain degree, replaced a top-down decision-making model. As a consequence, nowadays, the legitimacy of authorities has continually to be sought, to be gained and to be maintained (Malsch 2003).

Research has suggested that legitimacy bears a strong and positive relation with compliance to both judicial decisions and legal norms (Tyler 1990; Tyler and Lind 1992; Sherman 1993; Paternoster *et al.* 1997). When citizens perceive the legal system as legitimate, they will probably follow legal rules to a greater extent, accept judicial decisions, assist the police in finding a suspect, report crimes to the police, be prepared to cooperate as witnesses in criminal trials when summoned so to do and, last but not least, not take the law into their own hands (Malsch 2004). Particular characteristics of the *procedures* that are followed in the administration of justice are highly relevant in this respect. Courts need to be independent and impartial; defendants should be able to make use of the services of counsel and have opportunities to defend themselves; and trials should conform in other respects to the basic principles laid down in Article 6 of the European Convention on Human Rights. But a number of more psychological aspects of procedures are relevant for legitimacy as well. The theory of *procedural justice* (Lind and Tyler 1988; Tyler and Lind 1992) and *defiance theory* (Sherman 1993; 2002) both pay attention to non-legal aspects of procedures that are relevant for their acceptance by those involved in the procedures, satisfaction with the decision made and with the judge, and willingness to cooperate with authorities. Procedures in which process participants are treated with respect, and in which they can have a certain degree of input, lead to greater satisfaction with the system.

These theories, as well as the case law of the European Court of Human Rights, are not discussed further here. In this chapter, the position is taken that a minimum degree of participation and opportunities to have input in a legal system by the public and/ or individual civilians is needed for guaranteeing confidence in the system and maintaining its legitimacy. We discuss below the characteristics of the Dutch criminal justice system which determine its openness for participation by civilians and their opportunities to have input into it.

## The professional nature of the Dutch criminal justice system

In the Dutch legal system, lay elements have almost totally

disappeared. The system does not make use of juries, and lay judges, as far as they are involved, are all experts in a certain field. *Juries* operated in the Netherlands only during the occupation by the French from 1811 to 1813. The jury system was abolished immediately after the Netherlands had again become independent from France. The principle of open justice was taken away at the same time, but was restored in 1838 (Bossers 1987). Juries have never been popular in the Dutch legal system.

Lay persons operate as judges in a limited number of areas of the Dutch legal system. These *lay judges* try tenancy cases and military criminal cases, and can become part of a court that tries cases concerning the imposition of detention (penitentiary court). All these lay judges are experts in specified non-legal fields, and many of them share a similar academic and cultural background, values and norms with professional judges. The Dutch criminal justice system also makes use of *part-time judges*, who participate in 'regular' cases in all legal areas. These part-time judges all have a university degree in law, and they must have had professional experience as a lawyer for at least six years in order to be able to acquire a position as a part-time judge. 'Real' lay people, in the sense of people who have not enjoyed higher academic education and who are not expert in a specific domain, are not involved in the trial of cases in the Netherlands. This is in contrast to most countries surrounding the Netherlands, which either have juries or lay judges without an academic background, or both.

## The principle of open justice

Related to the subject of legitimacy and the professional nature of the Dutch criminal justice system is the question to what degree the system is 'open' to the public. The so-called 'principle of open justice' is considered to be a pillar or bulwark of the Dutch criminal law system, as it is in most countries in the Western world (Hoekstra and Malsch 2003; Malsch and Nijboer 2005). Courts should be open to anyone who wishes to attend, so that the public and the media can see how cases are tried. In legal systems without a substantial lay involvement, such as the Dutch legal system, ensuring the openness of trials is even more important than for systems that make use of lay participation to a greater extent.

Research has demonstrated that Dutch criminal trials, however, are not as open as is suggested by this generally accepted principle of open justice (Malsch and Nijboer 2005). From the public gallery, the trial of cases is not always totally comprehensible, largely caused by insufficient audibility of what is being said. In addition, the language that is used by the professional participants in the process is not always comprehensible to lay people. Because of the absence of lay involvement, the professionals in the system do not have a strong incentive to use more colloquial language. The justification of court decisions in a criminal trial is poor in the Netherlands (Malsch *et al.* 2005).

The media have access to criminal trials, but cameras are admitted only to a small degree in the Netherlands. Audio-visual coverage of criminal trials is in most cases restricted to the pronouncement of the sentence or the start of the process, with most other parts of the trial not being broadcast. The defendant's name is generally not disclosed, except in cases where a well-known person is accused. The same applies to victims. In general, the Dutch media are reserved and honest when reporting criminal trials. Some changes are, however, beginning to emerge in this area.

Of special relevance for the principle of open justice is the fact that in Dutch criminal cases, most investigation is done by the police and the investigating judge in the pre-trial stage. Findings are reported in the case file, and at the actual trial there are, most of the time, no witnesses and experts present to be interrogated. Judges base their decisions primarily on the written reports in the case files rather than on oral evidence from witnesses at the trial. There is, thus, a lot of paperwork in Dutch criminal cases (Malsch and Nijboer 1999). A continually increasing proportion of cases is dealt with by the police and the public prosecutor in the stage before the trial, with criminal proceedings then being dismissed (Blank *et al.* 2004). Because there is then no trial in open court, such procedures reduce the visibility of the criminal justice process to a high degree (Malsch and Nijboer 2005).

A conclusion from this brief description of the Dutch criminal justice system might be that lay participation in the criminal justice system is mostly absent. The principle of open justice is, for the various reasons depicted, not fully able to compensate for the absence of lay participation. This leads to the question whether, aside from a 'full' criminal trial involving oral witnesses, there are procedures or programmes where lay people have more influence on the procedure adopted and/or on the disposal of criminal cases. It appears that there are such procedures.

## Justice in the Neighbourhood (*Justitie in de Buurt* – JiB)

In the late 1990s, a number of small-scale offices were opened in neighbourhoods all over the country, in which police officers and public prosecutors were to work. These offices, called *Justitie in de Buurt (JiB)* offices, have as their primary aim to establish an immediate link with social programmes in the neighbourhood and to cooperate with youth care, schools and community services (Boutellier 2001). Collaboration has also been established with the police, the Child Care and Protection Board, the probation service and victim support organisations. The region that is covered by the work of each JiB ranges from a neighbourhood or an urban district to an entire town or city. Handling safety problems is one of the functions that JiBs seek to fulfill (Boutellier 2001).

A few years ago, about 25 JiBs were started in a variety of neighbourhoods in the Netherlands, and their operation and functioning has been evaluated. It appears that each JiB employs a different set of methods in handling cases and problems. An evaluation report (IPIT 2002) makes a distinction between JiBs that focus primarily on the treatment of cases, JiBs that direct their attention to a broader problem definition involving solutions outside the criminal justice system and pay special attention to victims, and, finally, JiBs that orient themselves towards local governance and community safety in general.

The official aims of JiB are as follows:

- The first aim is to establish an immediate link with social programmes in the neighbourhood and to cooperate with youth care services, schools and community services. The evaluation of individual cases in joint team meetings with representatives of all organisations with which JiB collaborates is an important activity in this respect. The police play an important role in providing cases to the JiB. Problems that occur at the level of the neighbourhood that is covered by the JiB may be tackled by interaction between the organisations involved rather than leaving action to one partner.

- A second aim of JiB is to increase the visibility of justice and law enforcement in the community. Justice must be seen to be done, and should not only take place in large buildings far away from the general public. The small-scale JiB offices aim to serve as an easily accessible place where members of the community can enter and discuss their problems caused by crime and lack of safety. These functions proved, however, difficult to fulfill (IPIT 2002): citizens were not eager to actually contact the JiBs. The visibility of JiB to the other professional organisations involved was, however, substantial.

- Thirdly, JiBs have focused on extra-legal treatment of problems caused by crime, troubles and nuisance taking place in the community. A preventive approach has been chosen such that potential offenders receive a warning if it seems that they may be taking the wrong path. The treatment of 'cases' is tailored to the circumstances of suspects and those who notify JiB that crimes or problems are taking place. As far as possible, cases are diverted from the criminal justice system. Mediation and compensation for damage therefore play a central role in the work of the JiBs. The criminal justice system remains in the background as an option in case the alternatives do not work or the defendant refuses to pay the agreed compensation.

As a consequence of this cooperation between organisations, cases are resolved within a shorter period of time than when 'regular' criminal proceedings are followed. For example, when a suspect does not perform his or her community service in time, he or she can be called to account much more easily than in cases dealt with by the Public Prosecutor's Office. JiBs are evaluated positively by members of the public living in the neighbourhoods where they operate.

JiB presents the most obvious example of community involvement in legal decision-making of all the programmes discussed in this paper. Residents or others living or working in a neighbourhood are offered the opportunity to express their wishes and concerns, and to cooperate in solving problems. Mediation and compensation for damage are among the solutions, which also imply input from members of the community. How far and to what extent JiB has realised actual input by the community in the criminal justice system remains unclear, however, especially in view of the finding that members of the community do not often enter the JiB offices on their own initiative.[1] The Ministry of Justice is of the opinion that JiBs are relatively expensive and inflexible.[2] As a result, it is thought JiBs will disappear in the years to come, or will be modified and be incorporated into other initiatives located in neighbourhoods that focus on community safety and security problems.

## Restorative practices in the Netherlands

The treatment of criminal cases by the criminal justice system is often not satisfying to either the defendant or the victim or their family members and other relations. Offenders are isolated from their homes, family and work as a consequence of the criminal trial and the penalties imposed. Victims often remain with unanswered questions and do not receive apologies or adequate compensation for their injuries, losses and psychological suffering (Malsch and Carrière 1999). By participating in a so-called *Eigen Kracht* or *Echt Recht* (restorative justice) conference,[3] defendants, victims and their relatives have an opportunity to discuss their feelings about what happened and the reasons why it happened. While talking about the crime and its consequences, possibilities are created to solve problems and to restore relations that were destroyed by the crime. A condition for such a conference occurring is that the offender admits having acted as he allegedly did and is prepared to take responsibility for the criminal acts. Each person participates voluntarily in these conferences. The result of each conference is an agreement to restore losses and suffering, signed by each participant.

Each conference needs substantial preparation, during which the supervisor (facilitator) discusses the ins and outs of the conference with each participant. During the conference itself, the supervisor asks the defendant what he has done and what his thoughts were during this act. Next, the victim and the relatives are asked to talk about what happened and what their feelings were. Then, the defendant's family and relatives are asked to do the same, and the defendant may react. The next step is that the victim explains his or her wishes as to what might happen after the conference. A provisional agreement is made. After definitive consensus is reached, the supervisor ends the 'formal' part of the conference and starts putting the agreement in writing. All participants sign the agreement. Then the informal part of the conference starts, with the participants talking to each other informally and person to person. This part of the conference is the most important with respect to the reintegration of the defendant.

A number of distinct features of the *Echt Recht* and *Eigen Kracht* conferences are relevant in comparison to regular criminal proceedings, as shown by the evaluation. One of these features is the opportunity that victims and their families have to confront the offender with their feelings and thoughts about what happened, and to ask the offender questions. Most offenders appear to make apologies during the conferences, and these seem more often genuine than in formal criminal proceedings. Many offenders are prepared to pay compensation and actually *do* pay. Victims and their families appear to be conspicuously generous when it comes to the actual assessment of the damages the victim suffered. Images that offenders and victims have of each other appear to change during the conferences, with offenders often becoming more 'human' in the eyes of the victim and his or her relatives. As a consequence, it becomes possible to discuss damages and to reach consensus as to possible compensation. Many conferences lead to insights on the side of offenders into what they have done and what that meant to the victims. The process of conferencing itself seems much less stigmatising than regular criminal proceedings, and leads more often to rehabilitation. It appears that most participants to these conferences are satisfied with the procedures and the outcomes.[4]

*Echt Recht* and *Eigen Kracht* have been inspired by the New Zealand model of 'family group conferencing'. A number of Dutch organisations are active in the introduction and execution of the practice of *Echt Recht* and *Eigen Kracht*. All over the country, supervisors, while still being employed by organisations such as victim support, the police, the prosecution and other organisations, are involved in supporting the ideas and methodologies of *Echt Recht* and *Eigen Kracht*. Each year, some hundreds of conferences are organised.

The Dutch government has supported a number of other experiments with restorative justice. In the cities of The Hague and Rotterdam, as well as in districts of The Hague and Den Bosch, small-scale experiments have been conducted with restorative justice meetings between offenders and victims both before and after a sentence has been pronounced in these cases. In some cases, conferences have been organised in prisons. However, these latter experiments, although positively evaluated, have been discontinued (Pauwelsen and Blad 2004; Homburg *et al*. 2003). Over the last few years, about 300 restorative justice meetings have been organised (Homburg *et al*. 2003).

In conclusion, restorative justice, which allows for participation by members of the community as well as by individual citizens, is not applied on a large scale in the Netherlands. Initiatives to mount programmes involving restorative justice have been taken both by the Ministry of Justice and through private initiatives. Because of recent EU regulations,[5] the Dutch government is envisaging the introduction of the possibility for victims and offenders to meet and communicate about the crime and its consequences. The outcome of such contact, however, is not intended to influence criminal proceedings against the defendant.

## Halt

Some restorative elements of the Netherlands criminal justice system are of special relevance for young people. One of them is *Halt*, which means 'the alternative' in Dutch. *Halt* aims to provide alternative resolutions for criminal acts committed by young offenders, outside the criminal justice system. This initiative has existed since 1981. Most 'clients' of *Halt* are youngsters accused of vandalism, including such acts as scribbling or painting graffiti, the destruction of bus stops and windows, aggressive acts and threats, thefts from shops, etc. Young offenders are referred by the police to a local *Halt* office that organises work by the young person to be done as an alternative to a criminal sanction. This work is intended to have a relation to the crime that was allegedly committed, such as the cleaning and repair of damaged property or property on which graffiti have been drawn, or working for a parks and public gardens department, etc. In 60 per cent of cases, a relationship between the vandalism and the prescribed work has been achieved (Kruissink and Verwers 1989). Certain educational goals for the young offender are also expected to be served by the *Halt* process, and at the same time the victim is compensated.

Youths that have been involved in *Halt* appear, from evaluations, to commit fewer new criminal acts than they did previously (Kruissink and Verwers 1989). One of the reasons for this success may be that the period between committing the vandalism and the start of the work to be done is quite short: in general two months. Participants in *Halt*, however, do not usually belong to the most problematic groups of youngsters, which makes a reliable determination of success difficult.

Damage suffered by victims and others are compensated in most *Halt* cases. The result of a mediation by *Halt* may be that the youth pays financial compensation, but it may also be that the youngster performs some work with a restorative character. In any case, the relation between the criminal act and the work done is stressed. The offender learns about the consequences of his acts, and the victim is compensated, thereby serving the goals of restorative justice.

In 2005, about 22,000 cases were concluded by *Halt* (Halt 2005). The community element is present in *Halt*, in the sense that young offenders are often ordered to restore public property and that many of the buildings which are cleansed of graffiti are public buildings.

### Alternative sanctions

Alternative sanctions[6] can also contain a number of restorative aspects. In 1983, the application of alternative sanctions for juveniles was started on an experimental basis. Later, these sanctions were also introduced in statutory form for adults. The number of these sanctions imposed each year has increased substantially and continues to increase up to the present day. It has become the sanction most widely used today: in 64 per cent of all cases against youngsters, an alternative sanction was imposed (Blees and Brouwers 1996; Wijn 1997). A court can impose an alternative sanction in place of a principal sanction such as a prison term, and for the past few years this sanction can be imposed independently from any other type of sanction. The type of alternative sanction is determined by the court. The Probation Service supervises the execution of alternative sanctions. Both alternative sanctions in which the perpetrator has to do some work, and other sanctions with an educational character can be imposed. The first are generally served in hospitals, sports clubs, institutions in which animals are nursed, community houses, etc. Some alternatives focus on reintegration into employment. As with *Halt*, the aim is to establish a relation between the criminal act and the alternative sanction. For example, an offender who has damaged the building in which a company was located has to perform work for this company.

Alternative sanctions with an educational goal include courses on the prevention of misuse of alcohol, drugs and gambling, courses on vandalism, certain educational courses, courses aimed at prevention of sexual crimes, and courses about the experiences of victims of crime. Here as well, there are attempts to relate the course to the type of offence committed. Educational alternative sanctions tend to aim at confronting offending behaviour and to be seen as relatively difficult or onerous: the youngsters have to reflect upon what they have done and who they are, and have to discuss their motives and conduct with other participants. Most of them are not accustomed to doing this.

The maximum number of hours for an alternative sanction that may be imposed is 480 hours, of which a maximum of 240 hours may be imposed as community service. In a youth case, the maximum number of hours for an alternative sanction is 240 hours.

Most juveniles (87 per cent) are able to complete the sanction (work or course). Juveniles who have served an alternative sanction that includes work have a slightly lower recidivism rate than juveniles who have served a traditional sanction (69 per cent versus 74 per cent; Wijn 1997).

Acceptability of alternative sanctions by the general public is high. Bottlenecks exist where insufficient places for serving the alternative sanction can be found. The two unifying elements in terms of (restorative) elements of practice for the alternatives described in this chapter are, essentially, confrontation with the consequences of a crime and the preference for attempting to integrate offenders back into a conformist/law-abiding lifestyle rather than excluding them from society/their community. In some of the alternative sanctions that are imposed, a clear community element is present. As with *Halt*, offenders are sometimes ordered to clean streets or to perform some work which will benefit society, though normally the relation between local community benefit and the sanction is less obvious for these alternative sanctions than with *Halt*.

## Victim compensation for damages caused by the offence

In the Netherlands, individuals who suffer damages through an offence can try to obtain compensation using a civil law procedure. Victims of crime have a few additional options, namely the joining procedure, the compensation order, mediation and out-of-court settlements. Each procedure is briefly outlined below (Malsch and Carrière 1999).

### The civil procedure

Both material and immaterial losses can be claimed in a 'normal' civil procedure. These procedures, however, generally take a long time and are expensive. There is a risk that the plaintiff has to pay all the legal costs of the procedure if he or she loses. Defendants may have too limited or no assets, making financial compensation difficult or impossible to achieve. With a crime, these problems may have even more impact on the victim than in a 'normal' civil law suit. On top of the victimisation resulting from the crime, the victim also risks thwarted expectations in terms of not receiving restitution. Regular civil procedures, therefore, do not seem to be an optimal solution for victims of crime in the Netherlands, as in other countries.

## Joining procedure

A victim of a crime can submit a civil claim for compensation against the accused during the criminal court process (joining procedure – *voeging als benadeelde partij*). If the accused is found guilty of the crime, and if it is proved that the damage to the victim has been caused by the crime, the court can order the offender to pay for the losses. A condition that has to be met is that the case and the assessment of damages are relatively simple. Compensation for non-material damage ('pain and suffering') can be claimed (and awarded) in this procedure, and this does happen on a regular basis. Non-monetary compensation can also be claimed using this procedure.

## Compensation orders

A compensation order (*schadevergoedingsmaatregel*) is requested by the public prosecutor and is imposed by the judge at the time of sentence. The court must first decide whether the accused is guilty of the crime. Furthermore, the compensation order can be imposed only if the offender is liable for the damage according to civil law. The size of the compensation is determined by the amount of damage that was caused. The offender has to pay the compensation to the state, which refunds the sum of money to the victim. This is the most obvious difference with the joining procedure that was discussed above: it is the task of the state to enforce the claim, and not that of the victim. The compensation order also provides the opportunity to obtain compensation for non-material damage. Compensation orders only allow for monetary compensation; other modes of restitution (e.g. work for the victim) are excluded.

## Mediation

There are guidelines for the treatment of victims by the police and the prosecution. These guidelines stipulate that the police and prosecution should try to reach a pre-court arrangement between the accused and the victim on the compensation of damage by the accused. If the effect of this 'mediation' (*bemiddeling*) is that compensation results, then either the case against the offender is dismissed or the prosecutor requests a lower penalty at court. Police officers and specially trained employees perform the actual mediation. In most cases, in practice, only material losses that are easy to assess are taken into account. The mediation procedure largely takes place through the exchange of letters and by telephone, and the so-called mediator is a kind of intermediate. It is a very fast procedure. A direct meeting between the accused and the victims hardly ever takes place. Mediators generally do not consider organising face-to-face meetings as one of their tasks (Malsch and Carrière 1999). An experiment with *out-of-court settlement*, which involved more aspects of a restorative nature than do the mediation procedures, has been stopped by the Ministry of Justice because of its lack of cost-effectiveness. Other types of mediation have been developed as well (for an overview, see Spapens 2000).

Most procedures for claining compensation depicted here are used regularly. Compliance with agreements reached in mediation and out-of-court settlement procedures appears to be much higher than for 'regular' civil procedures: most experiments result in a 70 to 80 per cent compliance rate. Evaluations of both mediation and out-of-court settlement have shown that the satisfaction of both defendants and victims with these procedures was actually quite high (for overviews and discussion of these programmes: see Malsch and Carrière 1996, 1999).

The programmes for claiming compensation for damages described above allow for more input by defendants and victims in the process of decision-making than do formal criminal proceedings. That may be the reason why they lead to a higher degree of satisfaction, and maybe also to more confidence in the system and more legitimacy in the first sense described at the beginning of the paper: the preparedness of citizens to comply with judicial decisions. Community involvement, however, is, strictly speaking, absent in these procedures: only individuals are involved. The same is true of the statutory ability for victims to deliver a statement at trial about the consequences of the crime they have suffered ('victim impact statement'). This relatively new phenomenon in Dutch criminal trials also offers opportunities for a group of civilians to have actual input in a criminal trial, but this is again on an individual basis.


## Conclusions

Although not overwhelming, there has been a decrease in the perceived legitimacy of the Dutch criminal justice system: there is reduced confidence in the system and citizens are less prepared to comply with legal norms and judicial decisions. There is supposedly a gap between judges and the general public, caused by scant lay participation in procedures and in the decision-making of the court.

The operation of the system is not transparent, and the visibility of justice has decreased because of legal actors' powers to decide cases outside the forum of the open court, which have grown substantially over the years. Such tendencies can be discerned in many countries; however, the specific circumstances of the Dutch criminal justice system, with its lack of substantial opportunities for lay participation, makes our country even more vulnerable to these effects.

Other, more general tendencies have also contributed to reduced legitimacy of the criminal justice systems of many Western countries. The attitudes of citizens to authorities have changed, leading to a reduced *a priori* preparedness to obey authorities and comply with legal decisions and norms. The growing number of members of minority groups in many countries gives rise to special problems with regard to law enforcement; there are indications that acceptance of the national criminal justice system is less obvious among these groups than it is among the native Dutch population.[7] Victims have acquired a more important formal role and function in the criminal process, but this leads in itself to greater expectations of the criminal justice system that may appear to be unjustified. If the legal system and process do not appear to be able to fulfil such expectations, dissatisfaction and a loss of confidence may ensue.

While highly professional by nature, the Dutch criminal justice system seeks methods to bridge the gap with the 'community', or more generally the gap to civilians who become involved in criminal procedures or who suffer from attacks on their safety as a consequence of crime. A number of these initiatives have been depicted in this chapter. The question remains whether these initiatives have actually succeeded in bridging the perceived gap between the criminal justice system and the community; evaluations of the programmes do not, as yet, shed sufficient light on this issue. New programmes, initiated by the government, are not intended to form an alternative to a criminal prosecution. In principle, the trial of the defendant and the execution of a penalty are not influenced by the outcome of a meeting between the defendant and the victim. This implies that the development of new initiatives with community involvement and initiatives of a restorative nature remain largely left to private organisations.

## Notes

1 The website of the Ministry of Justice www.justitie.nl does not provide recent data on JiB; the numbers of JiB offices currently in operation,

as well as the number of cases dealt with, could not be found by the author.

2 See www.om.nl, press release of 15 January 2004.

3 The *Eigen Kracht* model focuses on aid for juveniles, the *Echt Recht* model is applied in schools and in legal settings. See www.eigen-kracht.nl.

4 www.eigen-kracht.nl.

5 'Framework Decision on the Standing of Victims in Criminal Proceedings' (2001/220/JHA), 15 March 2001.

6 Alternative sanctions (*taakstraffen* in Dutch) consist of *werkstraffen* which include the performance of work and *leerstraffen* which consist of attending courses that serve certain educational goals.

7 For a compilation of research findings on this subject, see Bijleveld *et al.* (forthcoming).

# References

Bijleveld, C., Malsch, M. and Goudriaan, H. (forthcoming) *On Ethnic Minorities and Confidence in the Dutch Criminal Justice System: Facts and Anecdotal Evidence.*

Blank, J., Ende, M. van der, Hulst B. van and Jagtenberg, R. (2004) *Bench Marking in an International Perspective. An International Comparison of the Mechanisms and Performance of the Judiciary System*, Rapport geschreven in opdracht van de Raad voor de rechtspraak. Rotterdam: Ecorys-NEI.

Blees, L. W. and Brouwers, M. (1996) *Taakstraffen voor Minderjarigen: Toepassing en Uitvoering opnieuw Belicht.* Arnhem: Gouda Quint.

Bossers, G. F. M. (1987) *Welk een Natie, die de Jury Gehad Heeft, en ze weder Afschaft.* Dissertation, University of Amsterdam.

Boutellier, H. (2001) 'The convergence of social policy and criminal justice', *European Journal on Criminal Policy and Research*, 9 (1): 361–80.

Halt (2005) *Jaarbericht 05.* Leiden: Halt.

Hoekstra, R. and Malsch, M. (2003) 'The principle of open justice in the Netherlands', in P. J. van Koppen and S. D. Penrod (eds), *Adversarial versus Inquisitorial Justice.* New York: Kluwer Academic/Plenum Press, 333–46.

Homburg, G., Jonker, I. and Soethout, J. (2003) *Eindrapport Regioplan over Herstelbemiddeling.* Den Haag: Ministerie van Justitie.

IPIT (2002) *De Gebiedsgebonden Politiezorg als Uitdaging.* Den Haag: BZK.

Kruissink, M. and Verwers, C. (1989) *Halt: een Alternatieve Aanpak van Vandalisme.* Arnhem: Gouda Quint.

Lind, E.A. and Tyler, T.S. (1988) *The Social Psychology of Procedural Justice.* New York: Plenum Press.

Malsch, M. (ed.) (2003) *De Burger in de Rechtspraak. Ervaringen en Percepties van Niet-professionele Procesdeelnemers. (Special van Recht der Werkelijkheid.)* Den Haag: Elsevier.

Malsch, M. (2004) 'De Aanvaarding en Naleving van Rechtsnormen door Burgers: participatie, informatieverschaffmg en bejegening', in P. de Beer and C. J. M. Schuyt (eds), *Bijdragen aan Waarden en Normen (WRR-Verkenning 2)*. Amsterdam: Amsterdam University Press, 77–106.

Malsch, M. and Carrière, R. M. (1996) 'Dading en Bemiddeling: geschikt voor het strafrecht?', *Recht der Werkelijkheid*, 1: 25–38.

Malsch, M. and Carrière, R. (1999) 'Victims' wishes for compensation: the immaterial aspect', *Journal of Criminal Justice*, 3: 239–49.

Malsch, M. and Nijboer, J. F. (eds) (1999) *Complex Cases: Perspectives on the Netherlands Criminal Justice System*. Amsterdam: Thela Thesis.

Malsch, M. and Nijboer, J. F. (2005) *De Zichtbaarheid van het Recht. Openbaarheid van de Strafrechtspleging*. Deventer: Kluwer.

Malsch, M., Efstratiades, C. and Nijboer, H. (2005) *Justification of Court Decisions in Criminal Cases: Continental Western European Countries Compared*, Rapport NSCR-2005-5. Leiden: NSCR.

Paternoster, R., Bachman, R., Brame, R. and Sherman, L. W. (1997) 'Do fair procedures matter? The effect of procedural justice on spouse assault', *Law and Society Review*, 31: 163–204.

Pauwelsen, J. and Blad, J. (2004) 'Eindevaluatie Herstelbemiddeling', *Tijdschrift voor Herstlerecht*, 1: 57–62.

Sherman, L.W. (1993) Defiance, deterrence, and irrelevance: a theory of the criminal sanction', *Journal of Research in Crime and Delinquency*, 30: 445–73.

Sherman, L. W. (2002) 'Trust and confidence in criminal justice', *NIJ Journal*, 248: 23–31.

Spapens, A. C. (2000) *Bemiddeling Tussen dader en Slachtoffer. Bemiddelingsvonnen voor, Tijdens en na het Strafproces*. Tilburg: IVA.

Tyler, T.S. (1990) *Why People Obey the Law*. New Haven, CT: Yale University Press.

Tyler, T.R. and Lind, E.A. (1992) 'A relational model of authority in groups', *Advances in Experimental Psychology*, 25: 115–91.

van der Meer, T. (2004) 'Vertrouwen in de Rechtspraak: empirische bevindingen', *Rechtstreeks*, 1 (1): 1–56.

Wijn, M. (1997) *Taakstraffen. Stand van Zaken, Praktijk en Resultaten*. Den Haag: Ministerie van Justitie.

## Chapter 7

# Refiguring the community and professional in policing and criminal justice: some questions of legitimacy

*Adam Crawford*

The last two decades in England and Wales, as in other industrialised societies, have seen various initiatives in 'community safety', 'community policing' and 'community justice'. They all evoke a quest for, and an attempt to cement, greater attachment between local publics and the institutions of policing and criminal justice. Not only do they stem from a perceived crisis of legal authority that expresses itself through a lack of confidence and declining trust in the apparatus of criminal justice, but also from an increasing acknowledgement of the state's limitations in its capacity to guarantee and maintain public order through its own efforts alone. This chapter explores one of the subterranean, and often unspoken, themes that permeate much of the debate concerning the linkage between 'community', 'civil society' and 'justice', namely questions of legitimacy. Behind diverse governmental attempts to develop a geographically closer or more socially proximate relationship between 'community' and 'justice' are concerns that the state-sponsored systems of policing and criminal justice have become detached from the publics upon which they rely for support in a manner that signifies authentic deficits in legitimacy. Debate, however, is rarely phrased in this explicit terminology. More often, reference is made to unwillingness on the part of the citizenry to cooperate with institutions of policing and justice on the basis of declining public confidence, a loss of trust or a lack of deference to authority. What connects these sentiments and concerns, I argue, are questions of legitimacy regarding the exercise of power and authority.

The quest to realign 'community' and 'justice' over the past two decades has been an awkward and problematic one for at least two reasons. First, it has been forced to coexist alongside a very different emphasis within public policy on what is variously described as 'modernisation' or 'managerialism'. This has often served to marginalise community involvement and erode the basis of trust in legal authorities. Second, there remain a number of important questions about the nature, source and role of legitimacy in relation to policing and criminal justice which policy has largely failed to address. This has exacerbated declining public confidence and eroded citizens' connections with, and attachments to, formal institutions of legal authority. In this chapter, I will seek to illustrate some of the problematic implications for legitimacy of contemporary policy initiatives and attempts to reinvigorate public participation in policing and criminal justice. I shall draw upon two (analogous but distinct) examples of the involvement of community panel members in responses to youth offending and the creation of a new breed of police patrol employee without the full powers or training of police constables.

## A historical excursion

The construction of the modern penal-welfare state has seen an emphasis upon state-centred approaches to managing crime. In Weber's (1978) terms, the state alone was perceived to exert a monopoly over the legitimate use of physical violence. The modern police represent the public face of Hobbes' Leviathan, wielding legitimate force on behalf of the state. Developing this line of thinking, Bittner identified the 'special competence' of the police institution in the *capacity* of constables *for decisive action* and their authority to intervene where force may have to be used: 'The role of the police', Bittner suggests, 'is best understood as a mechanism for the distribution of nonnegotiable coercive force employed in accordance with the dictates of an intuitive grasp of situational exigencies' (1970: 46). This generic coercive authority, although relatively rarely used, differentiates the police from other public servants. It also structures the relationship between police and publics in ways that the police may be called upon to use coercive force against some citizens in the name of good order or public protection. The concept of 'policing by consent' relies on the recurrent reaffirmation of the rightfulness and legitimacy of the police function. Hence public perceptions of the legitimate authority of the police determine their capacity to act in every exigency in which force may have to be used. The special mandate implied in 'policing by consent', rather than through brute force, derives from the public trust that coercion will only be used where necessary in extreme situations. The fragile competence upon which policing rests, therefore, consists of 'retaining recourse to force while seeking to avoid its use, and using it only in minimal amounts' (Bittner 1974: 40).

The modern police, as the symbolic street-level face of legal authority, sought public acceptance largely in relation to processes of professionalisation, legality, bureaucratisation and specialisation. These pillars of legitimacy and public confidence conform broadly to Weber's 'rational bureaucratic authority'. From their inception in 1829, the historically constructed 'mythical image' of the British Bobby was founded on a differentiation from continental policing which was perceived as centralised, oppressive and intrusive. Police reformers, such as Peel, were well aware of the great hostility that the early police encountered. In the face of opposition, the 'new' police were fashioned emphasising minimal force, the rule of law, local accountability, a service function and a connection to the citizenry. In the event, as Reiner (2000: 58) notes, police legitimacy was not easily secured but had to be won through locally negotiated policing settlements and wider social changes from the mid-nineteenth to mid-twentieth centuries, most notably the incorporation of the working class 'gradually, unevenly and incompletely' into political and social institutions.

The notion of the police as 'citizens in uniform' has held an emblematic place in the engineering and construction of *policing by consent*.[1] The police historian, Reith, captured this notion in the phrase: 'the police are the public and the public are the police' (1956: 56). This ideal drew figuratively upon the tradition that all citizens have a civic duty to assist in the arrest and prosecution of offenders, and posited the notion of the constable performing 'on a paid basis what all citizens had the power and social duty to do' (Reiner 2000: 55). 'In this sense', as Banton remarked, 'the constable is a professional citizen: he is paid to discharge obligations which fall upon all citizens, and his obligations are to the community as a whole' (1964: 7). The authority that the 'new' police exercised was that of citizen constable. While this image of the police has always been contested as a reflection of empirical fact, as a normative principle it has an enduring legacy. The history of policing, however, has seen the veracity and sway of this principle eroded as police officers have been given greater powers, equipment and technology that have increasingly distanced them socially, organisationally and culturally from the citizenry they serve.

To some degree, the idea of social distance between the police and the policed was entrenched in the genesis of the modern police. As early police managers noted, to break the prior association with the arbitrariness and corrupt practices of feudal authority, the 'new' police necessitated an arm's length relationship between legal authorities and those over whom they exercised power. The kind of legitimacy that arises from 'formal rationality', as Weber (1978) suggested, eschews the vagaries of personal characteristics or social position. Forms of social and organisational distance between the police and the community were required. New recruits were often brought in from outside the geographical communities they were to police. Furthermore, the qualifications for entry into the police were raised by Rowan and Mayne, the first Metropolitan Police Commissioners, and disciplinary codes strictly applied. This served to underline a new professionalism and a departure from the earlier reliance on 'amateur volunteers'. As the police became more professional and bureaucratic, they also refigured their relations with the public. Despite the ideal of the police as 'citizen in uniform', increasingly real citizens were expected to support and assist the police (and criminal justice agencies) but not to be, or act, like them.

From an institutional perspective, legitimacy often appeared to be grounded upon an instrumental reading of effectiveness and efficient performance by the police and criminal justice system in controlling crime. Public support and organisational credibility were associated with increasing professionalism in fighting crime. This focus on instrumental performance served to downgrade proactive crime prevention and emphasised the reactive elements of policing within the organisation. Yet the capacity of the police to impact upon crime has always been limited. Hence, the quest for legitimacy through professionalised performance necessitated what Manning (1977) described as the 'manipulation of appearances' in the face of the police's inability to accomplish their self-proclaimed 'impossible mandate' of controlling crime and maintaining order. Part of this 'manipulation' entailed the propagation of the dual 'myths' that the police emblematically reflect the monopoly of coercive power in the state and the police can make a significant impact upon the level of crime.

These myths regarding state monopoly and effectiveness also permeated the elaborate institutional division of labour in the tasks of crime control and processing of offenders that was constructed since the nineteenth century. Emphasis was placed upon expert judgement. This bureaucratic state-centred approach to crime control also saw declining 'publicness' in two allied senses. First, there was less public involvement in the processes of criminal justice and punishing. Second, there was reduced space for the expression of popular sentiments within the act of punishing (Garland 1990). In this context, victims' involvement was marginalised within formal responses to crime. In Christie's account (1977) victims and communities had their disputes 'stolen' by state-sponsored professionals and experts. The formal institutions of criminal justice assumed a monopolistic and paternalistic approach to the public with regard to crime control. The underlying message was 'leave it to the professionals'. This resulted in an 'outsourcing approach to crime' (Leadbeater 1996: 1), whereby the public were encouraged and came to expect specialist institutions to solve most problems of security and safety. The dominant assumption was that justice was best served not by too close an involvement of the community, civil society or individual citizens.

Technology too played its part in this separation of the public from those charged with regulating their behaviour and social order. Most notable was the introduction to the police of radios and response vehicles. As communication between one officer and another improved, as did the ability of patrol officers to speed from one incident to the next, there was less opportunity for face-to-face contact between police and policed. Technological advances prioritised a reactive 'fire-brigade' style of policing which served to reduce informal community interactions. The combined effect was noted by early promoters of 'community policing' (Alderson 1979), who argued that by the late 1970s policing left little space for proactive, non-conflictual contact between the police and public. Hence there was limited foundation for the construction of public consent.

The 1970s heralded what Garland (2001) has called a 'crisis of penal modernism', which exposed many of the assumptions upon which the criminal justice complex had been shaped. As recorded crime rates increased dramatically from the 1960s onwards, the limited capacity of criminal justice institutions to meet their self-proclaimed aims of effectively controlling crime and reforming offenders became increasingly evident. Victimisation surveys prompted the growing realisation that most crimes do not come to the attention of formal institutions, raising fundamental questions about the effectiveness of public policing and the uncertain deterrent effects of state administered punishments. Moreover, the importance of institutions of civil society and informal control in sustaining order and conformity were increasingly acknowledged. Perversely, this appeared to occur precisely at the historic moment of their demise, as social and cultural trends loosened and undermined traditional bonds of family, kinship and community.

As faith in traditional criminal justice and policing began to wane, practitioners and policy-makers looked elsewhere. Previously, crime control had been shielded from the gaze of political criticism by a broad consensus that it was best served by 'expert' judgement rather than public opinion. This insulation was increasingly breached as law and order became the subject of debate, notably with the growth of social movements that championed the previously ignored victims of crime. With declining clear-up rates, congested courts and overcrowded prisons, the realisation grew that government promises ran ahead of performance. Politics came to embrace views about the limited capacity of government to effect significant social change. At the same time, issues of law and order became politically salient, saturated with wider concerns about contemporary insecurities.

Consequently, we have seen a *volte-face* as policy-makers have come to realise the fundamental role that the public play in policing and crime control, as witnesses or victims, through informal social control – as parents, peers, families and communities – and in giving support to legal authorities and institutions of criminal justice. The somewhat awkward new message reconfigures citizens as 'partners against crime' (Crawford 1997). Across diverse fields of public policy, governments have sought to mitigate and reverse the acknowledged decline of social capital within civil society by encouraging public participation and lay involvement in public services.

## The limits of coercion

The arguments explored here take as their starting point an acknowledgement that order and crime control are largely sustained not by the activities of formal institutions but through informal control mechanisms. Most conflicts are resolved far from the reach of state institutions or the law. Police and legal authorities are usually only called upon when these voluntary modes of control and conflict resolution have broken down or are deemed inappropriate. A related premise is the belief that effective policing and criminal justice demand and operate through public assistance. This cooperation takes two different but interrelated forms. First, regulation, authority and control work best where the norms and values are internalised and self-realised. Raw coercion is costly in time and effort and somewhat inefficient. Voluntary compliance and self-regulation are not only preferable, but also vital. They are preferable because they are easier to enlist and more effective. If people comply with rules only because they fear coercion, then as soon as the threat of coercion is not immediately apparent motivations to comply will dissipate. Legal authorities – the police and courts notably – depend upon their ability to activate internal motivations for obeying the law for their effectiveness. Self-regulation, where social norms, obligations and responsibilities are internalised, will operate whether or not formal institutions of control are present and able to exercise powers or resources. Over the long term, voluntary deference is more reliable than instrumentally motivated compliance as the latter may be contingent upon circumstances or situations which may change.

A further sense in which public cooperation is vital to effective policing and crime control relates to the crucial role that the public play in assisting the police and justice system, primarily through the provision of information but also through participation in crime prevention activities. Even in their reactive tasks of solving crimes, police and criminal justice are reliant upon the public to report crimes, provide information and serve as witnesses. Without this vital information justice would grind to a halt. In sum, the actions of the police and other legal authorities can only succeed if most people comply most of the time and some people some of the time provide earnest support and information. Hence they can only be effective to the extent that people believe they are exercising their authority legitimately. An effective strategy for encouraging cooperation demands supplementary reasoning above and beyond instrumental assessments of performance: 'Trust me because I'm good at catching criminals and clearing up crime' is less persuasive as a basis for citizen cooperation than 'Trust me because I am a legitimate authority'.

## Public confidence

Most indicators suggest that the public have declining confidence and trust in legal authorities. According to British Crime Survey (BCS) findings, overall public confidence in the criminal justice system is low and diminishing (Mirrlees-Black 2001). National and local surveys indicate a significant decline in public confidence in the police since the 1980s. Figure 7.1 shows recent BCS data with regard to the police and magistracy. While confidence in the police is higher than in all other criminal justice agencies, it has declined most sharply over recent years.

Generally, the public have limited contact with the police and criminal justice system. Successive sweeps of the BCS demonstrate that people's opinions about criminal justice are generally founded on poor knowledge of crime and sentencing practice (Hough and Roberts 1998). There is a clear correlation between how much people know about the different constituent agencies of the criminal justice system and their perceived effectiveness. The police are, by far, the most well known agency and are rated as having the greatest impact on crime in the local area. However, the experience of contact with the police does not itself bring a higher level of confidence. On the contrary, those who report higher levels of contact with the police also tend to report lower levels of confidence in them, as well as lower levels of satisfaction with their work. This is evidenced both in local surveys (Smith 1983; Fitzgerald *et al.* 2002) and national surveys (Allen *et al.* 2006). Unsurprisingly, those who had adversarial contact with the police hold particularly critical views of them. More surprisingly, those who experienced non-adversarial contact with the police also tend to have lower levels of confidence than those who had no contact with the police. This is particularly evident among minority groups.

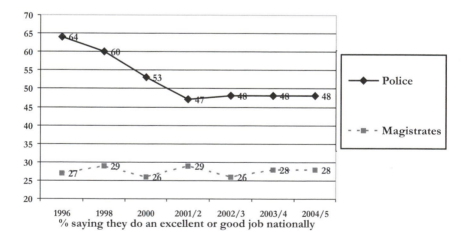

**Figure 7.1** Public confidence in the police and magistracy 1996–2004/5. *Source*: Allen *et al.* (2006: 9).

Worryingly, victims of crime express lower levels of confidence than do non-victims. As with adversarial contacts, the effect is additive; the more experiences, the more critical people tend to be. The number of experiences of victimisation is consistently and strongly related to critical views, even where there was no obvious connection between the substance of the views and the experience (Smith 1983: 274–301). According to BCS data, victim satisfaction with police response has declined steadily over time from 68 per cent in 1994 to 58 per cent in 2004/5 (Allen *et al.* 2006: 19). Generally, confidence in the police is the strongest predictor of overall confidence in how well crime is dealt with at a local level (Page *et al.* 2004). When asked directly what would convince them that crime was being dealt with more effectively, 'an increased police presence' was the most frequent answer.

In sum, a significant section of the population has no contact with the police and tends to hold an idealised, 'mythical' image of them. It would seem that contact with the police is liable to erode that image. Another section of the population, the subjects of police-initiated endeavours, has unwanted adversarial contact with the police, the experience of which generates critical views. Assessing the data, Smith (2007: 297) concludes:

> [T]he suggestion is that police officers are taboo objects: sacred and set apart. One section of the population avoids contact with them and regards them as perfect. Those who come close to them find the experience disturbing, and as the taboo is broken, their image of the police becomes more realistic, and therefore more critical.

This fits well with the historically constructed 'myths' of policing outlined earlier. Problematically, recent US research demonstrates a significant asymmetry in the impact of encounters with the police, such that unfavourable and favourable experiences do not have comparable consequences for people's assessment of the police service. Survey data from the US found that while having a positive experience 'helps little', having a bad experience 'hurts a great deal' (Skogan 2006: 112). This holds true for both citizen-initiated and police-initiated contact, despite their different characters and contexts. The research shows the impact of having a bad experience in contact with the police is 4 to 14 times as great as that of having a positive experience. This 'negativity bias' has significant implications for policy and practice, suggesting that favourable experiences of police treatment are easily trumped by negative encounters.

Much of the research focus is on public perceptions of effectiveness, reflecting the preoccupation of recent policy on improving public sector performance. However, as already implied, instrumental judgements of effectiveness are not particularly illuminating with regard to legitimacy. A stark illustration is the lack of correlation between public confidence in institutions of criminal justice, public perceptions of their effectiveness and actual crime rates. In the last decade, aggregate crime rates have consistently fallen, reversing a sustained rise in crime which had preoccupied both criminological attention and policy debate.[2] Decreasing crime rates have not produced any significant benefits in terms of a reversal in the long-term decline in levels of confidence. If legitimacy is based upon instrumental judgements regarding the capacity of institutions to reduce crime, one might have expected some kind of dividend from the significant reductions in crime rates. Yet this has not been forthcoming.

There has been a belated realisation that public confidence is not necessarily tied to performance and may need to be addressed as a fundamental issue in its own right. Launching the reassurance policing programme in 2004, the then Home Secretary, David Blunkett, declared: 'If you don't feel it, you don't believe it – only when people begin to feel safer will we know that we are beginning to make a real difference.'[3] More recently, the then Prime Minister Tony Blair articulated a similar paradox: 'The real point is not about statistics, *it is about how people feel* ... because the fear of crime is as important in some respects as crime itself.'[4] In this light, feeling safer is as much a priority as objective reductions in risks of victimisation (Crawford 2007). This recognises the expressive, normative and symbolic dimensions to institutions of control over and above instrumental assessments (or measurements) of their performance.

Hence, the formal aim of 'improving public confidence in justice' has become central to Home Office plans, one that is now shared across various departments with an interest in criminal justice. The National Policing Plan 2005–8 states that a key priority is to 'provide a citizen-focused police service which responds to the needs of communities and individuals, especially victims and witnesses, and *inspires public confidence in the police*, particularly among minority ethnic communities' (Home Office 2004: 1, emphasis added). While legitimacy is related, albeit not reducible, to public confidence, this new-found emphasis is an acknowledgement that public perceptions matter.

## Managerialism and (dis)trust

A contention of this chapter is that the new public management reforms introduced since the mid-1980s have both limited the scope for community involvement and further eroded the basis of legitimacy and public trust. However, it would be wrong to suggest that this has been a unidirectional development. Managerialist reforms have also served to promote the voluntarisation and civilianisation of public services (including the police and other criminal justice agencies) through the contracting out of service provision, via quests for cost-efficiencies and by challenging professional cultures and practices through new forms of accountability (Hood 1991; Power 1997). On one hand, managerialist reforms have encouraged a 'deprofessionalisation' by challenging paternalistic notions of professional expertise, opening up markets for services to greater competition and championing the sovereignty of the consumer. On the other hand, managerial reforms have ushered in 'reprofessionalisation' and 'delocalisation' on the basis of centralised standards, performance measurements and cost efficiencies. Ambiguously, managerial reforms have opened up new circuits of power between the demands of communities and citizens and those of providers of public services.

By focusing institutional efforts on securing economies and efficiencies, managerialist reforms have left little room for non-core activities such as community involvement. They have prioritised organisationally measurable outputs at the expense of less easily quantifiable social outcomes. In relation to policing and community safety, the preoccupation with performance indicators has been associated with a narrow focus on crime fighting at the expense of order maintenance. In a managerialist culture in which 'what gets measured gets done', public engagement and reassurance through locally tied visible patrols has largely lost out. This has served to reduce the public's investment in formal professional policing (Crawford and Lister 2006).

The idea of justice as entailing participation and deliberation by citizens and non-professional judgement has deep normative and historic roots. In England and Wales, the central practices of participatory democracy within criminal justice have been the institutions of the jury system and the lay magistracy, both of which share the notion of 'judgement by one's peers'. However, both have become subject to critical governmental attention. The right to trial by jury has been eroded by successive legislation; so too, there has been an increased reliance upon professional stipendiary magistrates,[5] partly at the expense of the lay magistracy. To an extent, this is due to a perception in government circles that the lay magistracy 'as a symbol of the unmodernised court' is 'under pressure as never before' (Raine 2000: 19). Largely due to concerns over cost and efficiency, the managerial agenda has promoted declining lay participation in court processes and increased reliance on paid and legally qualified professionals.

There are two further ways in which legitimacy has been challenged by new public management reforms. First, by introducing various 'rituals of verification' (Power 1997), they have tended to problematise trust and institutionalise distrust, notably in professional expertise. They represent a challenge to the 'cosy cultures of professional self-regulation' and feed off critiques of 'self-serving professional élites' (Power 1997: 44), replacing traditional forms of trust in professional authority with new forms of accountability. These developments express a loss of faith in deference to professional authority. They do not merely empty out trust, but provoke an active suspicion of public institutions and those who wield authority. Paradoxically, these technologies of managerial control are contrived, in part, in the hope of restoring trust in organisational competence. Rather than resolving trust deficits these are dispersed into the fabric of the organisational environment. Simultaneously, new 'guardians of trust' are introduced in the form of inspectors, quality controllers and auditors. In the medical field, for example, the old adage 'trust me, I'm a doctor' is now replaced by 'trust me, my performance scores and inspection results are comparatively better than other doctors'. In the name of managerial accountability, professional discretion has been significantly encircled and curtailed. One unintended consequence of the proliferation of information on professional performance may actually be a greater public scepticism regarding the quality of performance measurement itself (O'Neil 2002).

A second challenge comes in the growing involvement of the private sector in delivering policing and criminal justice, fostered by new public management reforms. The privatisation of criminal justice has opened up novel questions about the legitimacy of public enterprises previously shielded from critical scrutiny (Sparks 1994). The fragmentation of policing agencies and the growth of private security as a commodity has also weakened the symbolic link between policing and the state and questioned the unique status of the police

(Crawford *et al.* 2005). Increasingly, corporate bodies not only provide policing but are also sources of its authorisation and direction, such that 'the state is no longer a stable locus of government' in the governance of security (Johnston and Shearing 2003: 148). This pluralisation presents new challenges as state monopoly has become increasingly exposed.

## Legitimacy

Legitimacy lies at the heart of all forms of government. This is particularly so for criminal justice and policing. According to Beetham (1991: 16), power can be said to be legitimate to the extent that it meets three criteria:

i   it conforms to established rules;
ii  the rules can be justified by reference to beliefs shared by both dominant and subordinate; and
iii there is evidence of consent by the subordinate to the particular power relations.

While all systems of power and authority seek legitimation, such criteria are rarely met entirely. Furthermore, each dimension of legitimacy has an analogous form of non-legitimate power. Where power fails to conform to its own established legal rules of validity it may be said to be 'illegitimate'. By contrast, 'legitimacy deficits' arise where there is either 'the absence of shared beliefs' or a 'discrepancy between rules and supporting beliefs' (Beetham 1991: 20). Finally, a crisis of 'delegitimation' exists where power fails to find legitimation through expressed consent or where consent has been withdrawn.

From Beetham, we can identify two distinct levels at which legitimacy operates. First, it is to be found in broad normative principles to which a system seeks to adhere and which are believed to inform the exercise of power. These may be explicit constitutional principles of legality or implicit normative assumptions that systems of social power generate. We might call these *legitimating ideologies*. However, Tyler notes they may be better described as 'legitimising myths' (2005: 212). Secondly, legitimacy circulates at the level of conferred consent by those individuals who are subjected to systems of power. This may be analysed in terms of public levels of trust or confidence in systems of power (and those that operate them) and in the extent of compliance by those governed by such systems of power. It may be argued that legitimate social arrangements will generate commitments to compliance not only on the basis of utilitarian or pragmatic grounds but also on normative or moral grounds. Specific minority populations, less incorporated into the dominant belief systems of a given society, may serve as a particular barometer of levels of trust and confidence.

While policing and criminal justice are ultimately bound up with coercive power, they rely upon a degree of 'quasi-voluntary compliance' on the part of citizens, as evoked in the notion of 'policing by consent'. Such consent is not purely self-interested or instrumental but also has a normative base, strongly linked to perceptions of legitimacy. It is important because, as noted earlier, the coercive powers of criminal justice officials and police are themselves limited and only used as options of last resort. The police and courts invariably rely upon citizens' cooperation. It is only if compliance breaks down that there is recourse to coercive legal powers. Given the limits of coercive power, authorities must depend upon 'consensual' deference to their decisions by most of the people they interact with most of the time. Much of the literature on compliance has focused on the instrumental dynamics of policing and law enforcement, namely the risks associated with non-compliance – the threat of sanction. This has largely revolved around issues regarding the certainty and alacrity of detection and the severity of the punishment. This deterrence model of behavioural motivation ignores the normative dimensions as to why people conform and defer to authority. People are not only self-interested but also moral agents. Legitimacy, as Weber noted, constitutes important moral glue that informs people's internal motivational systems and guides behaviour.

Judgements about the legitimacy of legal authorities are crucial to why people obey the law and comply with decisions taken. Tyler (1990) identifies two forms of legitimacy in this context. First, personal legitimacy resides in the competency and honesty of legal authorities. Second, institutional legitimacy exists where the role of legal authorities entitles them to make decisions which ought to be deferred to, complied with and obeyed. According to Tyler and Huo (2002), the relationship between the legitimacy of legal authorities and personal experiences resides in judgements that the agents of the legal authority have treated them with respect and in a procedurally just manner.

## Procedural justice

Procedural justice entails being treated fairly and with dignity. It relates to both the quality of decision-making and inter-personal treatment. It includes qualities of participation (procedures that allow citizens voice and the opportunity to explain their situation and express their views), neutrality, respectful treatment and trusting decision-makers' motives (Tyler 2004). Where authorities are seen to care about the needs of individuals and to be acting out of 'a sincere and benevolent concern' (Tyler 2004: 95) experiences of procedural justice are likely to be enhanced. This highlights the importance of both *processes* – where decisions are made through procedures that members of the public view as fair – and *people* – where decisions are made by people perceived as legitimate in that their character and motives are trusted. Conversely, experiences of disrespect reduce compliance (McCluskey *et al.* 1999).

Importantly, perceptions of procedural justice are different from judgements about institutional effectiveness or even the favourability of outcomes. This does not mean that outcomes are irrelevant. However, both willingness to accept outcomes and feelings about the decision-maker have been shown to be influenced by reactions to the process (Sunshine and Tyler 2003). At a policy level, this has considerable significance. The police and legal authorities have greater control over their interactions with people than they do over crime rates and perceptions of safety, with implications for their own legitimacy.

Much of the research into the linkages between procedural justice and legitimacy has tended to focus on narrow experiences of process-based treatment at particular times and places by given legal authorities. This we might refer to as the *internal* attributes of legitimacy. There is less focus on the fairness of how or why an individual came to the attention of legal authorities or the legitimacy of the laws or rules that those authorities are seeking to enforce. While an authority may be deemed legitimate, the rules required to be enforced may be perceived to be illegitimate. This we might call the *external* attributes of procedural justice. Individuals may differentiate between procedurally just treatments by a legal authority in a particular setting and harbour an acute sense of injustice regarding the context in which they find themselves. Research suggests that procedural justice may be more important in shaping compliance when people do not view the laws and rules being enforced as legitimate (Murphy and Tyler 2005). Procedural justice may be more important precisely because individuals who do not support the underlying goals of the law place more salience on their experience to compensate for the fact that they may be complying with a rule they disagree with.

In complex chains of interactions with legal authorities, such as those involved in criminal justice, individual experiences – as victim, witness or offender – may be 'contaminated' by contacts with other legal authorities in relation to the same or connected matters. Experiences of procedural justice further down the criminal justice chain may be affected by earlier experiences with the police or prosecution authorities. This compounding effect also works in other ways. Citizens seem to generalise from their experience with one or a few legal agents to the entire legal system (Tyler 2004). This highlights the importance of policing for the legitimacy of criminal justice generally.

## Beyond professionalism?

Let us consider some of the possible implications for legitimacy raised by recent attempts to align relations between 'community' and 'justice' through lay involvement and deprofessionalisation in the context of policing and responses to crime. Why might greater lay or civilian involvement enhance legitimacy? First, it accords with long-standing normative principles of justice, most particularly notions of 'trial by one's peers' and the historic allusion to the police as 'citizens in uniform'.

Second, it affords ways of introducing significant numbers of under-represented groups into policing and criminal justice personnel, allowing legal authorities better to reflect and fully represent the communities they serve. One of the considerable contemporary challenges to the legitimacy of organisations wielding public power has been their inability to reflect the increased diversity of the British population, notably in terms of ethnicity and cultural or religious values. Making public institutions truly representative has been a long-standing problem, notably with regard to perceptions on the part of sections of the minority ethnic communities that they are differentially treated by the police and courts.

Third, it allows greater synergy between formal and informal systems of control and a more effective flow of information and understanding between the two. It may foster greater community engagement. This is especially relevant given the weakening of traditional cultural bonds, the apparent decline of social capital and the collapse of diverse intermediary institutions of social control.

Fourth, it may render legal institutions more responsive and directly accountable to the communities that they serve. It can facilitate the 'opening up' of otherwise introspective professional cultures and afford a broader skills mix among personnel. It may ensure more open, deliberative processes of decision-making that may otherwise be dominated by technical, bureaucratic or managerial demands. In so doing, it can accord greater space to the emotional and expressive needs of policing and responses to crime.

Fifth, the direct experience of involvement by lay people may give them a greater appreciation of the workings and limitations of legal authorities, and an engagement with the operations of justice. Recent research in England suggests that jurors had a more positive view of the jury system after completing jury service than they did before (Matthews *et al.* 2004). Not only did the experience enhance their confidence in the system, notably in terms of the fairness of the process, but it also increased their understanding of the criminal trial.

Finally, it may offer savings in terms of efficiency, cost or freeing up the time of professionals to dedicate to more specialist or technical activities.

## Lay participation in youth justice

The Youth Justice and Criminal Evidence Act 1999 established the referral order as a new primary sentencing disposal for 10–17 year olds pleading guilty and convicted for the first time. Under it, the courts are required to refer young offenders not given an absolute discharge or custody to a youth offender panel for a specified period of three to 12 months depending on the seriousness of the crime. Referral to a panel has become *the* mandatory criminal justice disposition for most young offenders appearing in court for the first time and pleading guilty to at least one offence for which they are charged. Like family group conferences and restorative justice inspired interventions (Daly 2001), the intention is that panels provide a forum away from the formality of the court where the young offender, his or her family and, where appropriate, the victim can consider the circumstances surrounding the offence and the effect on the victim. The panel agrees a 'contract' with the young offender, which lasts for the duration of the referral order. It is intended that the work of panels be governed by the principles underlying the concept of restorative justice: defined as 'restoration, reintegration and responsibility' (Home Office 1997). Importantly for our purposes, panels consist of a mix of at least two community volunteers, recruited and trained by the Youth Offending Team (YOT), and a professional YOT member. One of the two community volunteers has responsibility for chairing and leading the panel deliberations. Panels should be held in locations as close as possible to where the young person lives and from which the volunteers are drawn. After initial pilots, panels were implemented throughout the 156 YOTs across England and Wales from April 2002. Referral orders now account for over a quarter of all youth court orders.

Research evidence suggests that youth offender panels provide a constructive new forum in which to address young people's offending behaviour in novel and different ways (Newburn *et al.* 2002). Panels received high levels of satisfaction from young people, parents and victims on measures of procedural justice, including being treated fairly and with respect (Crawford and Newburn 2003). The involvement of community panel members has been at the heart of the changes. Though not unproblematic, their involvement may be one of the most important safeguards against the excesses of recent managerialist pressures on youth justice. Ensuring diverse volunteer involvement in panels can lead to the inclusion of a broader range of approaches and values than anticipated. It may also generate localised practices which, because they are influenced and owned by volunteers rather than professionals, are relatively resistant to the demands of bureaucratic managerialism. Consequently, panels potentially open a space for a different type of dialogue to occur in response to incidences of crime.

The participation of ordinary citizens in the deliberative processes of justice can also help to ensure that proceedings which may otherwise be dominated by bureaucratic or managerial demands also accord to the emotional and expressive needs of responses to crime. It can help break down inward-looking cultures and paternalistic attitudes held by professionals and encourage responsiveness to the concerns articulated by citizens. The experience of the youth offender panels is testimony to the seriousness and thoughtfulness that lay people can bring to such forums and to the task of facilitating discussions.

Research findings suggest that volunteers may be seen by young offenders, victims and parents as according legitimacy to the process by the very fact that they are not professionals (Crawford and Newburn

2002). Community involvement can counter scepticism on the part of participants (notably offenders) that decision-makers are removed from their concerns and understandings, precisely because of their professional attachments. Community members at panel meetings often emphasise their sincerity in their concern for the welfare of the offender and the wider community. This is reinforced through reference to their own status as volunteers, implying something unique and important about the voluntary participation of local citizens. As noted earlier, assessments about the motives of decision-makers can be important determinants of perceptions of procedural justice. Non-professionals and volunteers may be more likely to be thought to be acting out of a sincere and benevolent concern. This appears to reinforce findings on community conferencing in Canberra that citizens' personal judgement that the law is moral may depend upon their judgement that the human agents of the legal system have treated them with respect (Sherman *et al.* 2003).

A key element of lay involvement and public participation may lie in the manner in which it enhances perceptions of procedural fairness. Yet the evidence suggests that despite being treated fairly and with due respect during the panel meeting, young people may nevertheless feel that the referral order itself was not a proportionate or fair response to what had occurred or disagree with the legitimacy of the laws themselves (Crawford and Burden 2005: 71). The *internal* legitimacy of the process may be circumscribed by the lack of *external* legitimacy of the criminal justice response or normative rules. No matter how fair or procedurally just the panel meeting may be, it may always be tainted by wider perceptions of legitimacy and justice which precede it.

Furthermore, lay involvement may help strengthen interactions between local formal and informal systems of control. It may permit processes of restorative justice to operate through relations of interdependencies and mutual understanding. In so doing, it can promote the importance of local capacity and knowledge (Shearing 2001). Lay participation may herald an attachment to 'the affective and effective world of local affairs' (Shapiro, cited in Doran and Glen 2000: 10). The experience of youth offender panels has much to contribute to, and learn from, debates about 'community justice' and the recent experiment to establish a Community Justice Centre in north Liverpool (Fagan and Malkin 2003). Furthermore, working with volunteers as equal partners in an inclusive process presents real challenges to the way in which professional YOT staff work. In the pilot sites, though making significant progress, panels only uncovered a small part of the potential contribution of volunteers. There is clearly still much more that could be done in relation to their involvement as a broader resource in delivering a form of justice that links panels to wider communities in which they are located and the latent forms of social control that reside therein. Panels potentially suffer the same dichotomy identified by Karp and Drakulich (2004: 682), in relation to analogous Reparative Boards in Vermont, USA: 'competency building is one of the most theoretically exciting but practically disappointing' elements. This highlights the need for significant institutional support for lay volunteers to maximise their potential.

Research highlights the practical difficulties of ensuring a representative composition of lay volunteers (Crawford and Newburn 2002). Nevertheless, panels have also allowed a wider diversity of people to be drawn into the process of responding to youth crime in a decision-making capacity. A national survey found that by the end of 2002 there were 5,130 volunteers across England and Wales who had completed training and were sitting on panels, with a further 2,009 awaiting training (Biermann and Moulton 2003). Despite an over-representation of women (65 per cent), panel members broadly reflected the general population, as against recent census data (see Table 7.1). Certainly, panel volunteers are more representative of the population than lay magistrates, particularly with regard to age and ethnicity.

If the role of community panel members is to reflect the composition of the wider community, then YOTs appear to have done well in attracting a representative group of volunteers. Naturally, there are

**Table 7.1** The diversity of panel volunteers, as against lay magistrates

|  | Census 2001 | Panel volunteers 2002 | Lay magistrates 2001 |
|---|---|---|---|
| Female | 52% | 65% | 49% |
| Under 40 | 35% | 37% | 4% |
| 60–75 | 19% | 12% | 32% |
| Black | 2% | 7% | 2% |
| Asian | 4% | 3% | 3% |
| Other non-white | 2% | 1% | 2% |
| Unemployed | 3% | 3% | N/A |

*Source*: Adapted from Biermann and Moulton (2003).

important local variations.[6] Nevertheless, YOT managers continue to seek to attract greater numbers of people from ethnic minority backgrounds, notably young men. There are good reasons to suggest that the over-representation of volunteers from these groups is consistent with the idea that volunteers should reflect those young people (and victims) referred to panels who are themselves more likely to be drawn from such populations.

The implementation of youth offender panels presents a number of core challenges to the culture and organisational practice of youth justice. Working with victims presents deep-rooted difficulties for YOTs and panel members. Presenting victims with real choices over attendance and input requires adaptations of cultural assumptions and working practices. One worry is that in practice there may be a tension between community involvement and victim participation. In the pilot sites, victims attended panels in 13 per cent of relevant cases (Crawford and Newburn 2003: 186). In a recent study of Leeds YOT, with one of the largest caseloads in England, victims attended in only 9 per cent of relevant cases (Crawford and Burden 2005). This reinforces the findings of research into Reparative Boards where 'substantial community involvement' coexisted alongside 'limited victim involvement' (Karp and Drakulich 2004: 678). The concern is that involvement of community representatives can serve to sideline direct victim input. Community representatives may feel themselves capable of bringing a victim perspective through their own role as an indirect victim of crime. This expanded notion of victim feeds into restorative justice models of harm, but may limit the involvement of actual victims. This does not imply that community involvement will always function in this way, rather, in a system that is reluctant to accord to victims a central stake, community participation can be used as an excuse for victim non-attendance.

Organising panels presents considerable administrative hurdles that can disrupt community involvement. Holding panels in the evening and at weekends requires different working patterns; facilitating the attendance of the diverse stakeholders and finding appropriate venues all present difficulties of organisation and timing. Experience shows that administering panels creatively and flexibly often sits awkwardly within a risk-averse professional culture. Rotas of community volunteers, for example, are not ideal ways of constituting panels but present a rational means of managing them. So too does the strategy of scheduling numerous back-to-back panels. Nevertheless, these all limit the restorative potential of panels and circumscribe the nature of community involvement. In practice, balancing the demands of rational management and accommodating the expressive and human dimensions of community justice constitute fundamental but precarious dynamics. Under such pressures, there are dangers that panel meetings increasingly become routinised and formalised, losing their creative and flexible party-centred approach. Standardised hours of community reparation, pre-packaged activities drawn from a list (like coats off a peg) and standard-term contracts, while understandable, all leave less scope for the deliberative qualities of community participation.

Fundamentally, lay involvement may affront cherished notions of 'non-partisanship', key criteria in the legitimate exercise of power. Ambiguously, the more attached to the community lay panel members are, the less likely they are to hold the required 'detached stance' which constitutes a central value in facilitator neutrality. As noted, neutrality, even-handedness and lack of bias are key elements in perceptions of procedural justice. The more facilitators or panel members represent (or are perceived to represent) particular interests or value systems, the greater the danger that the interests of one of the principal parties may become sidelined. Ironically, it is this pressure to provide neutral and detached facilitators that increases the likelihood of professionalisation of panel members and the formalisation of otherwise fluid restorative processes. Experience suggests that over time many community justice schemes come to rely upon a group of 'core' volunteers who increasingly are seen as semi-professionals by virtue of their workload, training and experience. Evidence suggests that often a group of core panel members is increasingly relied upon for much work. Consequently, panel members may begin to represent and behave more like 'quasi-professionals' than ordinary lay people.

These challenges are as relevant for professional legal authorities as they are for non-professionals. They are merely brought to light in the analysis of the contribution of lay people and paraprofessionals where issues of representation and local attachment are defining validations. One explicit justification that differentiates lay people from professionals relates to questions of cost. Governments looking for savings have viewed lay people and civilians as cheaper alternatives to established and costly professionals. This is evident in diverse areas of justice and policing. However, as the experience of community panel members testifies, lay involvement may not amount to a cheaper overall service. Volunteers often introduce new costs and perceived 'inefficiencies' into practices. They frequently generate new workloads. There are costs associated with training, advice and information provision for volunteers, as well as other supporting infrastructures that are required because volunteers are involved. Volunteers also tend to work at a slower pace than do professionals. This was one reason for the expansion of the professional magistracy over their lay counterparts. This may be a positive outcome if, as with community panel members, their involvement allows greater time and space for the human and deliberative aspects of justice. For governments keen to speed up justice and remove inefficiencies, such consequences of lay involvement may jar with wider managerialist goals.

The chair of the Youth Justice Board may be correct in his recent assessment that youth offender panels constitute the 'jewel in the youth justice crown' (Morgan 2005). Nevertheless, there is a fine balance to be struck between providing volunteers with the training and support which they want and need, without professionalising their role such that it either displaces the important involvement of actual victims or erodes the innovative and human approach to reparation which their non-professional voices are intended to introduce into proceedings.

## Police and policing

In response to widespread criticism over the professional police's incapacity to provide adequate levels of community-based patrols, the Police Reform Act 2002 introduced a new type of employee, a 'community support officer' (CSO). The Metropolitan Police Commissioner, Sir Ian Blair (2002), suggested that their arrival constitutes a major 'revolution' in British policing, by providing an important 'second-tier force' with significant implications for community engagement and the collection of local intelligence. Operating under the formal direction of the chief officer, CSOs are intended to address public concerns over fear of crime, anti-social behaviour and the perceived lack of police visibility in local neighbourhoods. CSOs have limited powers but may detain a person for up to 30 minutes pending the arrival of a constable. Since their introduction in London in late 2002, the number of CSOs has expanded incrementally through successive waves of central government funding. By 2006, the number had risen to over 6,500 CSOs in England and Wales. In 2004, the government announced its intention to expand the ranks of CSOs exponentially to 24,000 by March 2008 and has put in place funding to support this. If realised, this will dramatically transform the face of front-line policing.

The separation of the patrol function from reactive demands means that CSOs are not subject to the same reactive burdens on police constables. Hence, they are able to spend more time on the streets in public contact. Implicitly, through their proactive and judicious interactions with the public they can enhance the legitimacy of the police more generally. CSOs also represent a means of responding to growing competition from the private sector, which has begun to encroach upon the police dominance of visible patrols (Crawford and Lister 2006). CSOs are freed from most of the pressures that serve to abstract constables from dedicated contractual arrangements that often stymie the commercial marketing of police officers (Crawford et al. 2003). The arrival of CSOs has coincided with a rise in the cost of private security patrols generated by the introduction of national licensing and regulation under the Private Security Industry Act 2001. While recent research commissioned by the Home Office reveals considerable disparities in pay and conditions of CSOs across force areas (Accenture 2006), these are largely explained by local market conditions.

Evaluations of CSOs have highlighted their capacity to provide high-visibility patrols that are well received by members of the public (Crawford et al. 2004, 2005; Johnston 2005, 2006; Cooper et al. 2006). Evidence suggests CSOs are playing an important role in working with partner agencies to deliver safer environments, providing effective crime prevention advice and engaging with different groups in ways that police officers find difficult given the pressures upon them. CSOs have demonstrated that they can deliver effective patrols without the need for the full range of powers vested in police constables. Where introduced as part of neighbourhood policing teams, CSOs have impacted significantly on 'perceptions of crime and antisocial behaviour, feelings of safety and public confidence in the police' (Tuffin et al. 2006: ix.).

Importantly, CSOs also contribute to the goal of diversifying the police workforce. Historically, the under-representation of minority groups among police recruits has been a cause of concern, reflecting tense relations with negative implications for legitimacy. With this in mind, government now expects police forces across England and Wales by 2009 to have an ethnic composition proportionate to that of the local population they serve (Home Office 1999). Table 7.2 shows the number of CSOs from black and minority ethnic populations by March 2005 exceeded their relative representation within the population.

**Table 7.2** Percentage of black and minority ethnic police (31 March 2005)

|  | Census 2001 | Police officers | CSOs |
| --- | --- | --- | --- |
| All England & Wales | 8.7% | 3.5% | 14.3% |
| London | 28.9% | 6% | 35% |

*Source*: Home Office (2006a)

The CSO role has attracted significant numbers of women. Recruits tend to be older than their police constable colleagues, with past work experience and skills to draw upon. This presents a challenge to police in avoiding the creation of a bifurcated service with predominantly white policemen supported by a body of largely female and black or minority ethnic colleagues in less well paid civilian roles. However, the fact that a significant number of recruits from under-represented groups have subsequently joined the constabulary suggests that the CSO role is potentially a useful recruitment resource for the wider police organisation. According to the national evaluation, over 42 per cent of CSOs said they joined 'as a stepping stone to becoming a fully sworn police officer' (Cooper *et al.* 2006: 47), which holds for ethnic minority CSOs (Johnston 2006: 393). Nevertheless, this recruitment benefit also presents challenges as the high level of staff turnover can impact adversely on the organisational status of the CSO role and the ability to retain officers dedicated to specific neighbourhoods.

Undoubtedly, the challenge of delivering a more demographically diverse and genuinely representative police organisation extends beyond simply a head count from minority backgrounds. It must include the capacity of the police to adapt to the cultural and organisational challenges presented by a diverse workforce and become more sensitive to the needs of the various communities it polices. Given the pace of recruitment and deployment of CSOs, there is some evidence that police forces have not provided the necessary support and infrastructure to integrate CSOs fully within the police organisation as a whole (Crawford *et al.* 2004; Johnston 2005). It is likely that this will impact more upon ethnic minority recruits, precisely because they may have greater need for support given their historic under-representation within the police.

Research highlights a significant degree of public confusion over the role of CSOs and the powers available to them (Crawford *et al.* 2005). Legally, the chief officer of a police force has the discretion to confer on CSOs any powers from a list prescribed in the Act.[7] The patchwork of powers across forces is likely to continue to engender public confusion. Furthermore, the limited powers available question the extent to which CSOs conform to Bittner's 'special competence', whereby the use of 'non-negotiable coercive force' is available. CSOs are unlikely to qualify for this 'special competence' and the public are likely to be uncertain as to the extent of their competency. In the absence of clarity over CSOs' responsibilities and limitations the public are often left to assume that they can act like police officers. This may furnish CSOs with a greater reassurance premium but, conversely, suggests false expectations may arise among the public over precisely what CSOs can legitimately do. Research highlights that some members of the public differentiate between the immediate reassurance value of a CSO derived from their visible presence, and the capacity of CSOs to deal with specific incidents, notably in difficult situations, which was seen to have implications for their longer-term reassurance (Crawford *et al.* 2004). Public uncertainty may lead to experiences where people's expectations are disappointed with negative consequences for legitimacy. Government's response to concerns over the variable powers available to CSOs has been to propose a standardisation of powers, while also allowing for a host of discretionary powers (Home Office 2006b).[8] This response is unlikely to clear the muddied waters.

Similar, but less dramatic, questions may be raised with regard to the granting of powers to 'suitably skilled and trained' accredited officers. The Police Reform Act 2002 makes provision for community safety accreditation schemes and, in certain circumstances, the granting of limited (fixed penalty notice) powers to those accorded accreditation status by the chief officer of the local police. Accredited officers may be local authority, housing association or private security employees. While these officers are not employed by the police or under police control, their accreditation by the local police force lends them a certain degree of 'received' legitimacy. Conversely, the police may be held vicariously responsible, in a legal and non-legal sense, for the inactions or misdemeanours perpetrated by such policing agents.

More broadly, the commodification of policing raises fundamental questions about future legitimacy. Not only have police forces been given greater commercial freedoms to 'sell' their services to private interests, but also the private sector has been given a greater role in policing public places. In the context of this complex division of labour in which public values jostle with private and parochial interests, it is less easy to differentiate the 'special competence' of the public police. As specialisation and differentiation has gained momentum within the police, through workforce modernisation (HMIC 2004), the idea of the omni-competent constable has given way to a plethora of different skills-related tasks, with different entry-points, training requirements and career trajectories. This raises questions about the potential dilution of the state police 'brand' and, hence, the enduring significance of the mythical 'police image'. The employment of CSOs and the accreditation of third-party policing may have adverse implications for the future legitimacy claims, cultural authority and symbolic power of the British police. Their distinctiveness, as they increasingly enter the commercial world while working alongside other 'plural policing' providers, is likely to become less rather than more evident.

Given the historic linkage between questions of legitimacy and state power, contemporary quests to revive legitimacy in public authorities can also be read as defensive attempts to reassert state control over the governance of public security. In large part, the introduction of CSOs provides the police with a commodity with which to secure scarce resources and compete within the unfolding market. In this context, questions of legitimacy are likely to become muddled, as the police operate simultaneously as regulator, accreditor and provider of policing. The pluralisation of policing should allow us to ask fundamental questions about who should govern policing and in whose interests? It should provoke scrutiny of the manner in which legitimacy is secured and contested in the authorisation of private and parochial power, notably where conferred legitimacy via the state is absent. At the same time, questions about the basis of authority are likely to become more salient as private providers valorise the conditions upon which legitimacy is constructed by offering more instrumental identifiers of brand reputation and quality assurance than that historically presented by the British Bobby.

## Conclusion

Community-based initiatives that seek to foster lay-connectedness raise fundamental issues regarding the appropriate basis of detached reasoning that has informed principles of justice. What should be the relationship between those who exert legal authority and the citizenry? While the intention of recent developments may be to narrow the social distance between legal authorities and communities, it is undesirable for justice to be compromised by partisan relations or potential conflicts of interest. The experiences of youth offender panel volunteers and police CSOs suggest that they prefer not to work in areas where they live or know people too well. As well as concerns for personal safety and reprisals, this is often explained in terms of the inappropriateness of exerting power and authority over those with whom they are closely associated. To do so might conflict with fundamental perceptions of justice and procedural fairness which adhere to neutrality and even-handedness.

This chapter has explored recent quests to realign communities and state professionals in the fields of policing and responses to crime through the lens of legitimacy. It has sought to show that recent initiatives have had ambiguous effects, often serving to undermine the historically insecure foundations of legitimacy and intensify legitimacy deficits. Yet the involvement of lay people and a new breed of paraprofessional have simultaneously reinvigorated the capacity of legal authorities to reflect, and be responsive to, the needs of a diverse society. Through their non-professional voices and experiences, they have (re-)introduced creative and inter-personal approaches to policing and justice deliberations, serving as a bulwark against some of the excesses of managerialist reforms. Yet the ambivalent policy initiatives that are refiguring community and professional relations convey an incoherent conception of statecraft, vacillating between extensive governmental ambitions and limited capacities for action. In an era when the myth of state monopoly in securing public safety has been unmasked and public and private power have become confused, there is a need to renegotiate legitimate public expectations over the competency and authority of state professionalism.

## Notes

1 To be found explicitly articulated in the 1962 Royal Commission Report that informed the 1964 Police Act.
2 According to the BCS, since peaking in 1995 the overall crime rate fell by 44 per cent (Walker *et al.* 2006).
3 www.reassurancepolicing.co.uk/Latest_Details.asp?id=28
4 www.number-10.gov.uk/output/Page9040.asp
5 Now referred to as district judges.
6 For example, black people sitting as panel members ranged from 0 to 62 per cent.
7 Extended by the Anti-Social Behaviour Act 2003, Serious Organised Crime Act 2005 and Clean Neighbourhoods and Environment Act 2005.

The national evaluation found variable implementation: 'Most forces had delegated between 14 and 28 powers from over 40 that were available. A quarter of forces had designated 30 or more powers, a quarter 28 to 19, a quarter between 18 and 15 and a quarter between 14 and nine. One force had not granted any powers to their CSOs' (Cooper *et al.* 2006: 19).

8  The Police and Justice Act 2006.


# References

Accenture (2006) *Police Community Support Officer Terms and Conditions Study.* London: Home Office, at: www.crimereduction.gov.uk/cso03.htm.

Alderson, J. (1979) *Policing Freedom.* Plymouth: McDonald & Evans.

Allen, J., Edmonds, S., Patterson, A. and Smith, D. (2006) *Policing and the Criminal Justice System – Public Confidence and Perceptions.* London: Home Office.

Banton, M. (1964) *The Policeman in the Community.* London: Tavistock.

Beetham, D. (1991) *The Legitimation of Power.* London: Macmillan.

Biermann, F. and Moulton, A. (2003) *Youth Offender Panel Volunteers in England and Wales, December 2003.* London: Home Office.

Bittner, E. (1970) *The Functions of Police in Modern Society.* Chevy Chase, MD: National Institute of Mental Health.

Bittner, E. (1974) 'Florence Nightingale in pursuit of Willie Sutton', in H. Jacob (ed.), *The Potential for Reform of Criminal Justice.* Beverly Hills, CA: Sage, 17–44.

Blair, I. (2002) 'The policing revolution: back to the beat', *New Statesman*, 23 September, 21–3.

Christie, N. (1977) 'Conflicts as property', *British Journal of Criminology*, 17 (1): 1–15.

Cooper, C., Anscombe, J., Avenell, J., McLean, F. and Morris, J. (2006) *A National Evaluation of Community Support Officers.* London: Home Office.

Crawford, A. (1997) *The Local Governance of Crime.* Oxford: Clarendon Press.

Crawford, A. (2007) 'Reassurance policing: feeling is believing', in A. Henry and D. J. Smith (eds), *Transformations of Policing.* Aldershot: Ashgate, 143–68.

Crawford, A. and Burden, T. (2005) *Integrating Victims in Restorative Youth Justice.* Bristol: Policy Press.

Crawford, A. and Lister, S. (2006) 'Additional security patrols in residential areas: notes from the marketplace', *Policing and Society*, 16 (2): 164–88.

Crawford, A. and Newburn, T. (2002) 'Recent developments in restorative justice for young people in England and Wales', *British Journal of Criminology*, 42 (3): 476–95.

Crawford, A. and Newburn, T. (2003) *Youth Offending and Restorative Justice.* Cullompton: Willan.

Crawford, A., Lister, S. and Wall, D. (2003) *Great Expectations: Contracted Community Policing in New Earswick*. York: JRF.

Crawford, A., Blackburn, S., Lister, S. and Shepherd, P. (2004) *Patrolling with a Purpose*. Leeds: CCJS Press.

Crawford, A., Lister, S., Blackburn, S. and Burnett, J. (2005) *Plural Policing: The Mixed Economy of Visible Patrols in England and Wales*. Bristol: Policy Press.

Daly, K. (2001) 'Conferencing in Australia and New Zealand', in A. Morris and G. Maxwell (eds), *Restorative Justice for Juveniles*. Oxford: Hart, 59–83.

Doran, S. and Glenn, R. (2000) *Lay Involvement in Adjudication*. Belfast: Stationery Office.

Fagan, J. and Malkin, V. (2003) 'Theorising community justice through community courts', *Fordham Urban Law Journal*, 30: 897–953.

Fitzgerald, M., Hough, M., Joseph, I. and Qureshi, T. (2002) *Policing for London*. Cullompton: Willan.

Garland, D. (1990) *Punishment and Modern Society*. Oxford: Clarendon.

Garland, D. (2001) *The Culture of Control*. Oxford: Oxford University Press.

Her Majesty's Inspectorate of Constabulary (2004) *Modernising the Police Service*. London: HMIC.

Home Office (1997) *No More Excuses*. London: Home Office.

Home Office (1999) *Dismantling Barriers to Reflect the Community We Serve: The Recruitment, Progression and Retention of Ethnic Minority Officers*. London: Home Office.

Home Office (2004) *National Policing Plan 2005–08*. London: Home Office.

Home Office (2006a) *Statistics on Race and the Criminal Justice System 2005*. London: Home Office.

Home Office (2006b) *Regulatory Impact Assessment: Powers of Community Support Officers*. London: Home Office.

Hood, C. (1991) 'A public management for all seasons?', *Public Administration*, 69: 3–19.

Hough, M. and Roberts, J. (1998) *Attitudes to Punishment: Findings from the 1996 British Crime Survey*. London: Home Office.

Johnston, L. (2005) 'From "community" to "neighbourhood" policing', *Journal of Community and Applied Social Psychology*, 15: 241–54.

Johnston, L. (2006) 'Diversifying police recruitment?', *Howard Journal*, 45 (4): 388–402.

Johnston, L. and Shearing, C. (2003) *Governing Security*. London: Routledge.

Karp, D. and Drakulich, K. (2004) 'Minor crimes in quaint settings: practices, outcomes and limits of Vermont Reparative Probation Boards', *Criminology and Public Policy*, 3 (4): 655–86.

Leadbeater, C. (1996) *The Self-Policing Society*. London: Demos.

McCluskey, J.D., Mastrofski, S.D. and Parks, R.B. (1999) 'To acquiesce or rebel: predicting citizens' compliance with police requests', *Police Quarterly*, 2: 389–416.

Manning, P.K. (1977) *Police Work*. Cambridge, MA: MIT Press.

Matthews, R., Hancock, L. and Briggs, D. (2004) *Jurors' Perceptions, Understanding, Confidence and Satisfaction in the Jury System*. London: Home Office.

Mirrlees-Black, C. (2001) *Confidence in the Criminal Justice System*. London: Home Office.

Morgan, R. (2005) Speech to conference on 'Building on Success: The West Yorkshire YOTs, Five Years On', West Yorkshire Playhouse, Leeds, 20 May.

Murphy, K. and Tyler, T. (2005) *Rethinking Legitimacy*. Paper given at RegNet Conference, Australian National University, 7/8 December.

Newburn, T., Crawford, A., Earle, R., Goldie, S., Hale, C., Masters, G., Netten, A., Saunders, R., Sharpe, K. and Uglow, S. (2002) *The Introduction of Referral Orders into the Youth Justice System*. London: Home Office.

O'Neil, O. (2002) *A Question of Trust*. Cambridge: Cambridge University Press.

Page, B., Wake, R. and Ames, A. (2004) *Public Confidence in the Criminal Justice System*. London: Home Office.

Power, M. (1997) *The Audit Society*. Oxford: Oxford University Press.

Raine, J.W. (2000) 'Whither local justice?', *Criminal Justice Matters*, 40: 19–20.

Reiner, R. (2000) *The Politics of the Police*. Oxford: Oxford University Press.

Reith, C. (1956) *A New Study of Police History*. London: Oliver & Boyd.

Shearing, C. (2001) 'Transforming security: a South African experiment', in H. Strang and J. Braithwaite (eds), *Restorative Justice and Civil Society*. Cambridge: Cambridge University Press, 14–34.

Sherman, L. and Strang, H. with Woods, D. (2003) 'Captains of restorative justice', in E. Weitekamp and H.-J. Kerner (eds), *Restorative Justice in Context*. Cullompton: Willan, 229–56.

Skogan, W. (2006) 'Asymmetry in the impact of encounters with the police', *Policing and Society*, 16 (2): 99–126.

Smith, D.J. (1983) *Police and People in London: Vol. I – A Survey of Londoners*. London: Policy Studies Institute.

Smith, D.J. (2007) 'New challenges to police legitimacy', in A. Henry and D.J. Smith (eds), *Transformations in Policing*. Aldershot: Ashgate, 279–305.

Sparks, J. R. (1994) 'Can prisons be legitimate?', *British Journal of Criminology*, 34: 14–28.

Sunshine, J. and Tyler, T. (2003) 'The role of procedural justice and legitimacy in shaping public support for policing', *Law and Society Review*, 37: 513–48.

Tuffin, R., Morris, J. and Poole, A. (2006) *An Evaluation of the Impact of the National Reassurance Policing Programme*. London: Home Office.

Tyler, T.R. (1990) *Why People Obey the Law*. New Haven, CT: Yale University Press.

Tyler, T.R. (2004) 'Enhancing police legitimacy', *The Annals*, 359: 84–99.

Tyler, T.R. (2005) 'Legitimating ideologies', *Social Justice Research*, 18 (3): 211–15.

Tyler, T.R. and Huo, Y.J. (2002) *Trust in the Law: Encouraging Public Cooperation with the Police and Courts*. New York: Russell Sage Foundation.

Walker, A., Kershaw, C. and Nicholas, S. (2006) *Crime in England and Wales 2005/6*. London: Home Office.

Weber, M. (1978) *Economy and Society: An Outline of Interpretive Sociology*, eds G. Roth and C. Wittich. Berkeley, CA: University of California Press.

## Chapter 8

# Who owns justice? Community, state and the Northern Ireland transition

*Kieran McEvoy and Anna Eriksson*

In Northern Ireland, throughout the decades of conflict and in its immediate aftermath, crime rates remained stubbornly low in comparison with other industrialised nations (O'Mahony *et al.* 2000). 'Justice' functions such as policing were complicated by the involvement of not only the state justice system but also Republican and Loyalist paramilitaries who were engaged in 'policing' activities including shootings, beatings and exiling of alleged offenders (Feenan 2002). The actions of each of these actors were in turn shaped by complex (and distinct) sets of relationships with local communities affected by crime (McEvoy and Mika 2001, 2002). As paramilitary activities have gradually waned over the years since the Good Friday Agreement of 1998, a number of state agencies have appeared determined to reassert the dominance and monopoly of the state in justice provision. Some communities, particularly in working-class Republican and (to an extent) working-class Loyalist areas, have retained considerable misgivings about the motives and capacity of such state justice agencies. This keenly fought contest over justice ownership during the conflict has continued to mark the development of a relationship between state and communities during the period of transition.

A number of particular challenges emerge from the Northern Ireland transition. On the one hand, elements of the state appear to retain an ingrained suspicion of strong, cohesive communities. Such communities, particularly in Republican areas, were traditionally viewed as the waters in which the paramilitary 'fish' thrived (Sluka 1989). Paradoxically, that suspicion remains in a context where, as with the rest of the United Kingdom, there is considerable emphasis on the need for closer state–community cooperation, community responsibility and 'empowerment' in crime prevention, community safety and related activities (Crawford 1999; Criminal Justice Review 2000; Hughes 2006). For key state agencies, the notion of 'partnership' being promoted is arguably one which is firmly on the terms outlined by the agencies themselves (McEvoy *et al.* 2002). On the other hand, the working-class communities most affected by crime and anti-social behaviour are manifestly in need of a more effective formal justice system which commands local respect and legitimacy. The Irish Republican Army (IRA) is no longer involved in 'policing' or indeed any other activities of note in Republican areas (IMC 2007). As of May 2007, one of the principal Loyalist organisations (the Ulster Volunteer Force – UVF) committed itself to a similar trajectory of dissolving its 'military' structures.[1] In 2007 Sinn Fein, the political wing of the now defunct IRA, held a special party conference to permit its ruling executive to support policing and justice structures.[2] For the first time since the creation of the state, senior Republicans have called for community support of the police in tackling a number of high-profile crimes.[3] Following the elections to a local power-sharing Assembly in March 2007 and the ground-breaking decision by the Democratic Unionist Party (DUP) and Sinn Fein to share power in a devolved assembly, Sinn Fein has nominated three members to take up their seats on the Policing Board for Northern Ireland.[4] However, while there is significant movement at the macro-political level, 30 years of antipathy, violence from and towards the agents of the state, and indeed simple lack of familiarity with the police in particular, will not be magically resolved by the formalising of 'the policing deal' (Mulcahy 2006).[5] Bridge-building between the state and strong but historically estranged communities requires a concurrent emphasis on organic and bottom-up styles of partnership, a willingness from the state in particular to cede some ownership and control, and a commitment on all sides to the development of real relationships based upon trust and mutual respect.

In exploring these themes in the Northern Ireland context we have chosen to focus in particular on the development of community-based restorative justice programmes as a potentially key vehicle in the development of such relationships. The programmes have received significant national and international attention (Mika and McEvoy 2001; Braithwaite 2002; McEvoy 2003; Sullivan and Tifft 2006).[6] They were established with the theory of restorative justice as an explicit guiding focus for practice and aim to find non-violent and lawful alternatives to paramilitary punishment attacks (McEvoy and Mika 2002). Since their establishment in 1998, the projects have become a permanent presence in the local and indeed national broadcast and print media and have dominated public and professional discourses in the jurisdiction on criminal justice policy and practice. As is discussed below, they have been the subject of a specific paper in the Northern Ireland peace negotiations, of a substantial discussion in the review of the Northern Ireland criminal justice system and of a number of high-profile investigations by bodies such as the International Monitoring Commission and the Northern Ireland Select Committee. Moreover, several attempts have been made at draft protocols (designed to regulate relations between these projects and the formal system) by senior executives of the main criminal justice agencies in Northern Ireland. This is quite an unusual amount of attention to be paid to approximately a dozen very localised community-based restorative justice projects. As one exasperated local voluntary sector chief executive told one of the authors: 'I have not been at one single conference or public discussion on criminal justice in the past few years where community restorative justice has not been at the very top of the agenda. There are other things happening you know.'[7]

One of the oft-cited reasons why the projects have received such arguably disproportionate attention is that they were established in direct dialogue with armed groups and involve former Loyalist and Republican combatants among the staff and volunteers (McEvoy and Mika 2001). Certainly the political prominence of the debate on policing in Northern Ireland also contributed significantly to any suggestion that local community structures might be involved in localised 'problem-solving' (Feenan 2002). In addition, however, we would argue that it is precisely because the work of these projects speaks directly to the question of who 'owns' justice in a transition that they have preoccupied so many politicians, policy-makers and opinion-formers in the jurisdiction. That context is precisely why they are such a useful site to develop some of the broader theoretical and practical issues which such a struggle entails.

For the purpose of this paper we have grouped the evolving relationship between the state and the community-based projects into three broad phases. Although these phases undoubtedly overlap, it may be useful to offer them as distinct heuristic models for seeing state/community justice relations in this particular transition. We have termed these phases defensive formalism, party politicking, and regulation and standard setting. Before examining these phases in more detail, however, it would be useful at this juncture to provide some background to the notion of both 'community' and state in the context of the Northern Ireland transition.

## The contested community and the Northern Ireland transition

Across a range of social science disciplines, the notion of community has been described as having a multitude of meanings (Butcher *et al.* 1993). It has been described as 'interlocking social networks of neighborhood, kinship and friendship' (Crow and Allan 1994: 178–9), and as something shared in common between people whether in terms of territoriality, ethnicity, religious background or occupational or leisure pursuits (Willmott 1987). Communities may in effect be socially constructed (Cohen 1985). A community may be viewed in some contexts as a 'feel-good' concept (Hughes 1998), an idealised or utopian notion towards which we all strive (Bauman 2001) and a focal point around which individual, communal and indeed national life is collectively 'imagined' (Anderson 1991). In other more exclusionary notions of community, it may be viewed as a way of defining not only those who are part of the community, but also those who are *not*, those who are *outside* or *beyond* this imagined collective (Cohen 1987: 14; Dignan and Lowey 2000).

Within the relevant literature on informal and restorative justice (Abel 1982; Crawford 1999; Pavlich 2005), the concept is also highly contested. For example, Matthews (1988) has argued that the concept of community is one of the most ambiguous, overused and under-defined within the social sciences. Similarly within restorative justice writings, where community is frequently portrayed as a key to the entire justice equation, there is comparatively little literature which analyses the role of community within restorative justice practices beyond the superficial.[8] In some contexts, such as state-led 'community prevention' initiatives, community is almost exclusively defined as a geographical space (Crawford 1999). In such instances, its usage is often deployed strategically by state agencies, occasionally morphing into 'a convenient political and rhetorical device used like an aerosol can, to be sprayed on to any social programme, giving it a more progressive and sympathetic cachet' (Cochrane 1986: 51, cited in Foster 2002: 173). Community actors for their part are often equally cognisant of the power of community as a basis for claims-making (Pavlich 2005).

Such a construction of community boundaries between 'us' and 'them' is occasionally starkly evident in the Northern Ireland context. The conflict was too often portrayed in an overly simplistic fashion as a binary one between two warring communities refereed by a 'neutral' and ultimately benevolent British state (see, for example, O'Leary and McGarry 1995; Ruane and Todd 1996). That said, it is indisputable that the notion of community can have strongly negative connotations in the jurisdiction. In Northern Ireland, words such as the Catholic/Protestant, Nationalist/Unionist or Republican/Loyalist community are terms which can be deployed in an exclusionary and sectarian fashion. The lived reality for many working-class urban communities in particular is highly segregated (Shirlow and Murtagh 2006).

In contrast, it is also true that despite high levels of socio-economic deprivation, significant numbers of such communities are characterised by strong civil society and communal structures. Although it is occasionally over eulogised, for those of us who live and work here there is a self-evident energy and vitality to a broad range of grass-roots work in local communities. In some Republican areas such as West Belfast and parts of Derry in particular, the *resistant* character of such community structures grew in part from a deep suspicion of the state and a culture of self-reliance and self-help developed. In addition, as we have discussed elsewhere, it is arguably the best amongst the ex-combatant community, including those who work on the restorative justice projects discussed below, who have shown real leadership in challenging sectarian and exclusionary attitudes both within and beyond such working-class communities (McEvoy 2004, 2005; McEvoy and Eriksson 2006).

To recapitulate, community is a contested notion both in the relevant social sciences literatures and within scholarly writings on justice in particular. In Northern Ireland the particularities of community as a basis for exclusionary claims-making are well rehearsed. However, we would contend that the restorative justice schemes discussed herein are examples of projects which, while located in the lived reality of sectarian division, have demonstrated a willingness and capacity to transcend that context. They have shown increased abilities to develop working relationships with historically estranged 'others', including not just the (arguably easier) restorative justice programmes which work on the 'other' side of the sectarian divide but also the agencies of the formal justice system. Of course, for such relationships to flourish, concurrent willingness and capacity is required from such state agencies as well.

## The contested state and the Northern Ireland transition

There is an enormous criminological literature on the role of the state and its practical and symbolic functions with regard to the delivery of justice.[9] The importance of the state's monopoly over 'the legitimate use of physical force' has long been regarded as central to the very core of the state as a 'human community' (Weber 1948: 78). However, increasingly in 'settled' (i.e. non-transitional) societies, there has been a tendency to delegate justice functions upwards (towards supra-state structures), sideways to private sector entities and downwards to voluntary and community sector structures (Johnston and Shearing 2003). This 'hollowing out' of state justice functions, wherein the state has increasingly 'rowed rather than steered' (Osborne and Gaebler 1992), has not, however, been accompanied by a loosening of state control functions. Rather as Braithwaite (2000), Levi-Faur (2005) and others have argued, the emergence of this 'neo-liberal' state has arguably seen a growth in regulation by or on behalf of the state. States have not relinquished sovereignty over justice or security in such contexts; rather they have reshaped the ways in which it is controlled, governed or delivered (Wood and Shearing 2007).

In transitional and post-conflict contexts other than Northern Ireland, huge energies have been invested in 'rule of law' programmes designed to secure a fairer and more efficient delivery of justice through improvement of state criminal justice systems (Brookman 2003). The description of the 'failed state' in places like Somalia or Liberia is often viewed as synonymous with the absence of a proper justice and policing system which is capable of guaranteeing the security of its citizens. Indeed lawlessness, usually interpreted as the absence of state justice, is often used as a catch-all phrase to describe a Hobbesian version of violence and anarchy (Rotberg 2004). The reassertion of the authority of the state is seen in such contexts as central to the move away from conflict and respect for 'the rule of law'. It is frequently the yardstick by which such progress is measured (Cherif Bassiouni 2002). Judicial and legal reform, the reform of the police, courts, prisons and related efforts to improve the capacity and standing of state justice have become typical elements of the 'transitional justice template' (McEvoy 2007).

At a theoretical level, the development of such institutions speak to the tendency towards what Scott (1999) has referred to as 'seeing like a state'. This is an anthropological perspective which suggests that often governments which are attempting to realise politically or socially complex ends – in this case the construction of Brasilia or major collectivisation projects – oversimplify their vision and delivery mechanisms into state-like institutions simply to better 'see' the project through to its completion. Whatever their myriad failings, state-like institutions are familiar, indeed comforting, ways of envisioning complex concepts through to practice (Bartelson 2001; Steinberger 2004). Such institutions, as Mary Douglas (1986) and others have argued, have a particular tendency to develop and reproduce their own rationality, their own reason for being.

However, one of the reasons Scott suggests why 'state-centric' grand schemes often fail spectacularly is that they oversimplify. They fail to take account of local customs, expertise and practical knowledge and to properly engage with community and civil society structures. Such a lack of engagement – often done in the name of efficiency, lack of trust in the capacity or intent of community, professional expertise or simply 'getting the job done' – may in turn lead to incompetence, maladministration or even encourage grass-roots resistance to state-led initiatives (Scott 1999). Such unease at ceding power or authority to non-state structures may in turn obscure the need on the part of the state to invest in thicker forms of accountability or legitimacy from the communities which it claims to serve (Beetham 1991; Roche 2002, 2003).

In post-conflict contexts, where the power and legitimacy of the state have been directly and violently challenged, the impetus towards a firm reassertion of the state's monopoly over justice is arguably all the more powerful. In particular, when actors within such institutions develop a self-image of serving higher goals such as 're-establishing the rule of law' or re-imposing the authority of the state, the temptation to see violence-affected communities as 'othered' constituencies which are treated with suspicion and distrust, rather than citizens to whom the state must be accountable, becomes all too real (Schärf 2001). Since those who make criminal justice policy tend to think of justice as *belonging to* the institutions of the state justice system, state ownership over justice is inevitably conceived as the norm and the ceding of such ownership is viewed with considerable suspicion.

It is apparent that despite the contemporary prominence of 'neo-liberal' theorising about the role of the state in general, many states are in reality highly reticent about divesting regulatory authority (at least) over justice functions. States which are in transition from conflict in particular often display a marked unwillingness to cede authority over such areas of policy and practice.

The state's reluctance to give up any such authority over justice functions in the Northern Ireland transition can be explained in part by the particular exigencies of the conflict. Although there were discernable shifts in government policy, and indeed periods where a coherent overall strategy appeared absent (O'Leary 1997), the dominance of security policy remained a conspicuous constant through the 'troubles' (Cunningham 1991).[10] Throughout the conflict, control over justice and security was viewed as absolutely central to the state's effort to tackle political violence (e.g. Heath 1998). Indeed it was a dispute between the Conservative government and the Unionist administration at Stormont over which had ultimate sovereignty over security policy which ultimately led to the dissolution of the latter in 1972 and the imposition of direct rule from London (Kelly 1972). Throughout the conflict, there was little effort to engender any genuine sense of community ownership or sovereignty over justice functions. Operational independence in the police and army, judicial independence and a tendency to appoint largely uncritical elements of 'the great and the good' to any body with (usually very limited) oversight powers arguably inculcated a culture in the Northern Ireland justice system which was immune to community control or critique.[11] Allied to such a culture were a range of distinct security strategies including brutal army tactics, paramilitary-style policing by the Royal Ulster Constabulary (RUC), internment without trial, torture, emergency legislation and non-jury Diplock courts. Such measures clearly impacted directly (and largely negatively) on the relationship between the criminal justice system and the communities most affected by them (Amnesty International 1994; Criminal Justice Review 2000). In addition, concurrent 'policing' efforts by paramilitary groups emerged which filled the policing vacuum in such communities with brutal forms of punishment violence (McEvoy and Mika 2001). In the case of Republicans, such actions directly questioned the political legitimacy of the state. In the case of Loyalists, they spoke at the very least to the limitations of the state's claim to a monopoly on the use of coercion (Feenan 2002).

In brief, the Northern Ireland conflict produced a state system which privileged control over justice and security, which eschewed any meaningful community control or accountability over such functions and which was directly challenged by the violent activities of paramilitaries. It is perhaps little wonder that the emergence of community-based restorative justice programmes in the transition from conflict was treated with suspicion by many of the key institutions of the state and influential others whose views were formed during that conflict.

## Background to community-based restorative justice in Northern Ireland

The detailed origins of the community-based restorative justice projects in Northern Ireland have been extensively detailed elsewhere (McEvoy and Mika 2001, 2002; Mika and McEvoy 2002). For current purposes it is only necessary to provide sufficient details to inform the arguments below.

On the Republican side, the origins of the projects lay in dialogue between Republicans and elements of civil society in Northern Ireland. In 1996, one of the authors (McEvoy) and a number of colleagues who had been active in the human rights and voluntary sectors were approached by Republican activists to begin discussion and training on finding alternatives to punishment violence. Following two months of dialogue, intensive training and a residential meeting in the Irish Republic, a discussion document was drawn up which was circulated widely within the Republican Movement and the British and Irish governments. In December 1997, following considerable consultation with a range of statutory organisations, community representatives, political parties and others, the authors published a report ('The Blue Book') which documented the process and proposed a model for a non-violent community-based justice project based upon the principles of restorative justice (Auld *et al.* 1997). That document was subsequently endorsed by Sinn Fein and the IRA.

From the outset the authors, and indeed Sinn Fein themselves, made clear that these projects were not viewed as supplanting the formal justice system, but rather the informal system of paramilitary punishment violence. Indeed the Blue Book formally recommended the development of partnerships with a range of statutory organisations in the management and delivery of the projects (including the Probation Service, Youth Service and Social Services) but recognised that it was politically untenable for the projects to cooperate with an unreformed police service. After the report was published, independent funding for four pilot projects was secured and the projects became known as Community Restorative Justice Ireland. The work of these four initial projects (and the others which subsequently came on line) has focused on the familiar normal restorative justice activities of preparation of victims and offenders, mediation, family group conferencing and the monitoring of agreements. As noted above, while the initial focus of the projects was upon finding alternatives to punishment violence, in practice their remit expanded considerably to a much more generalised service focused upon community mediation, dispute resolution and other work which might be broadly termed community safety.[12]

On the Loyalist side, the projects which emerged were on a smaller scale but no less impactive in the areas in which they operate. In 1996 a former life-sentenced UVF prisoner, under the auspices of the Northern Ireland Association for the Care and Resettlement of Offenders (NIACRO) carried out research in the Shankill area of West Belfast on the viability of non-violent interventions on punishment attacks (Winston 1997). The subsequent report, based upon interviews with paramilitary, statutory and other community actors, suggested that such interventions were possible with one faction – the Ulster Volunteer Force. While the UVF stipulated that they would not countenance restorative justice style interventions concerning internal paramilitary discipline, disputes between paramilitary organisations, offences related to sexual offences or disputes regarding the sale of drugs, interventions regarding punishments on other matters were possible. That research was followed by two intense residentials and the project 'The Greater Shankill Alternatives' was created.

Operating within the parameters laid down by the paramilitaries, Alternatives initially limited itself to a narrow focus within its local area, namely to provide an alternative to punishment violence for young offenders in that community. Participants on the programme are normally between 13 and 22 years of age. If a member of the client base is viewed as being under threat, programme staff contact representatives of the Ulster Volunteer Force (UVF) to verify that the threat exists and then negotiate so that the punishment threat may be lifted on condition the individual successfully participates in the Alternatives programme. Staff liaise with the individual young person and their family to explain the programme and invite participation. Young people who refuse to become involved, or who fail to complete the programme, are referred to Base 2 for possible relocation outside of Northern Ireland.[13] Participants are assigned a caseworker and a contract is drafted which specifies actions on offending behaviour, victim restitution and community reparation. The young person also makes a presentation to a community panel who judge the adequacy of the contract and regular contact between the panel, the caseworker and the young person is maintained. After what is usually several months, the young person again appears before the panel to certify the contract is completed and (if satisfactory) the young person is discharged, normally with some provision of monitoring or aftercare services. Alternatives has subsequently expanded, establishing similar projects in North Belfast, East Belfast and Bangor. While in the early days the majority of referrals came from the UVF themselves, their referral base has broadened considerably to include community referrals, statutory agencies (including the police) and self-referrals. Like the projects in Republican areas, Alternatives broadened their case-load to include activities which would not meet a criminal threshold and have also attempted to mediate between disputing Loyalist factions.

Between 2003 and 2007 the staff at Alternatives (18 in total) worked with a total of 1,964 young people, 1,719 victims and had a total of 268 volunteers (Northern Ireland Affairs Committee 2007: para. 12). Community Restorative Justice Ireland (CRJI) currently has a staff of 15 and approximately 160 volunteers (although they have previously had as many as 360 volunteers). Our review of their case files suggests that they processed a total of 1,005 cases in 2006, involving work with 4,412 people, and approximately 700 cases each from 2003 to 2005. Mika (2006) reports that in the eight sites which he evaluated between 1999 and 2005 (his focus did not include all of the projects ultimately established), the projects were involved in almost 500 documented cases which, without their intervention, would almost certainly have led to a punishment attack by paramilitaries.[14] For example, Mika (2006: 23) argues that Community Restorative Justice Ireland was successfully intervening in 94 per cent of potential paramilitary assaults in their operational areas and Northern Ireland Alternatives in 90 per cent by the end of 2005.[15] By comparing levels of punishment violence generally and in comparable neighbourhoods in Belfast and Derry where no restorative justice projects were established, Mika (2006: 26) again concludes that 'it would therefore appear that NIA and CRJI interventions have caused a noticeable drop in the number of beatings and shootings compared to baseline over time'. While levels of punishment violence are of course also related to other local and broader political developments concerning the peace process, these figures are nonetheless impressive. As is discussed below, the quality of the work conducted in both sets of projects has garnered considerable praise from even the most unlikely sources.

Despite the myriad difficulties in conducting such difficult and occasionally dangerous work,[16] few community restorative justice workers or volunteers would dispute that by far the most difficult element of their work has been the relationship with the agencies of the state. It is to those relationships that we now turn our attention.

## Defensive formalism and justice ownership in transition

The various reactions of the state are discussed under the themes of *defensive formalism, party politicking* and *standards and regulation.* In the wake of the political negotiations which culminated in the Good Friday Agreement, the criminal justice system was, like other aspects of civic and political life, required to change as a result of the peace process. However, unlike the Independent Commission on Policing under the chairmanship of Chris Patten which was also established under the terms of the Agreement, the Criminal Justice Review was 'to be carried out by the British Government through a mechanism with an independent element' (Good Friday Agreement 1998: 27). Ultimately the Review was conducted by civil servants with a number of prominent independent criminal justice specialists.

The Review was far reaching and well beyond the parameters of this chapter. In broader terms, however, its origins as a government-led process are evident. The tone of the Review was set by the former Secretary of State, or at least her civil servants, in the introduction to the Criminal Justice Review's original consultation document: 'The criminal justice system has served Northern Ireland well over the past thirty years, often in the face of considerable difficulties' (NIO 1998: i). Unlike in the Patten Report,[17] the Review contains little by way of honest acknowledgement of the unhappy past of the criminal justice system in Northern Ireland (which for many Republicans at least was largely a symbol of repression) and the ways in which that past has impacted on relations with different communities.[18] While many of the changes recommended by the Review undoubtedly offered the framework for a more modern and professional criminal justice system, a central fault-line which runs through its various provisions is its failure to properly internalise that those failings of the past *required* greater community involvement and ownership in justice.

For example, as has been argued elsewhere (McEvoy *et al.* 2001), the Review could have gone considerably further to outline practical means to achieve a more balanced workforce in the criminal justice sector (large swathes of the system have a significant Catholic under-representation), or 'outcomes' by community background – issues which remain mired in bureaucratic wrangling seven years after it reported. Similar progressive measures, such as the introduction of youth conferencing for the youth justice system, have struggled to achieve meaningful community involvement in their daily working practices (Campbell *et al.* 2005). Most instructive for current purposes, however, are the elements which concern community restorative justice. These sections illustrate neatly an institutional mindset which was determined not to cede sovereignty over justice functions to any local community structures. Such a mindset may be characterised by what Maureen Cain (1985) has famously characterised as defensive formalism.

As noted above, given their small size and precarious financial position,[19] the projects appear to have been afforded a disproportionate amount of time and energy in official circles. In 1998 the government position was outlined in a paper which was viewed as sufficiently important to be included as an appendix to the consultation document which established the Criminal Justice Review (NIO 1998: appendix D).

The Review mirrors more or less exactly the government position as outlined in that paper. The Review oscillates between derision and a desire for domination: 'Community-based schemes which have no or only tenuous links with the formal criminal justice system will by definition not lie at the heart of mainstream approaches ... We do not therefore see these as central ... but, in view of the interest in them and their existence in parts of Northern Ireland, we address the issues that they raise at the end of this chapter' (Criminal Justice Review 2000: para. 9.57). This patronising comment obfuscated the reality of the public and private battles which had followed the publication of the 'Blue Book' and the fact that, at that time, apart from a very small number of cases being processed through a couple of police-led pilot projects (O'Mahony *et al.* 2002), these projects were to all intents the ones actually *doing* the bulk of restorative justice work in Northern Ireland. The Review was supported in its views by a commissioned research report, conducted by Dignan and Lowey (2000), which placed considerable emphasis on the dangers of authoritarian and exclusionary variants of communitarianism.[20] The Review concluded that while community-based schemes may have a role to play in dealing with low-level crimes, they should only receive referrals from a statutory criminal justice agency rather than from within the community (with the police being informed of all such referrals), be accredited by and subject to standards laid down by the government, be subject to regular inspection by the independent Criminal Justice Inspectorate and have no role in determining the guilt or innocence of alleged offenders (Criminal Justice Review 2000: para. 9.98). While the projects appeared to have little difficulty with the latter two criteria, the prohibition on receiving referrals from the community which they served and the compulsory involvement of the statutory agencies (in particular the police for Republicans) presented considerable obstacles for several years.

In short, as evidenced by the Criminal Justice Review, the initial reaction of the key policy-makers in the criminal justice system in Northern Ireland was one of defensive formalism towards these projects. The notion that the presence of the formal justice system was required in order to 'guarantee' the rights of those involved was treated as a source of mirth by some of the ex-prisoners involved in the community projects.[21] The origins of the projects, of unapologetic dialogue with paramilitaries, the fact that they were located in communities in which the state had historically struggled to 'do' justice, and the high level of take-up even in the early days of the projects (particularly when compared with the low numbers in the sole statutory scheme at the time), all contributed to an approach which sought to impose state control over referrals to the programmes and compel a relationship with the police, regardless of local political and social circumstances. The recommendations of the Criminal Justice Review and the Justice Act which implemented it were reflective of a mindset which *feared* genuine community involvement and ownership in the process of justice, particularly when those communities might be ones traditionally alienated from state structures. Drafted primarily by civil servants with long histories within the criminal justice system of the 'conflict era', it failed to deliver a new vision of state/community partnership more appropriate to a society in post-conflict transformation.

## Party politicking and justice ownership in transition

A second key dynamic which has influenced the debate on community restorative justice in Northern Ireland has been the significant prominence of the projects in both local and indeed national (UK) politics. Of course the notion that criminal justice policy is core business in contemporary politics is now a given in contemporary criminology (see, for example, Newburn and Sparks 2004). However, as is argued above, the significance of the criminal justice system in general and of policing in particular is given a particular edge in a transition from political conflict. It is arguable that the seemingly inextricable linking of the work of the projects (both Loyalist and Republican) to the debate within Republicanism on policing has been the factor which has done most to maintain the high profile of the projects in party politics.

Following the publication of the Patten Report, the British government (under the stewardship of the then Secretary of State Peter Mandelson) introduced the Police Bill (Northern Ireland) which was designed to give effect to the report's recommendations. Mandelson, who has since indicated his intuitive sympathy to Unionist perspectives on the conflict and transition[22] was accused by some key commentators of having substantially diluted the Report[23] and by one prominent member of the Patten Commission of having 'gutted' it.[24] The envisaged powers of the Police Board were dramatically curtailed, the centrality of human rights downplayed, the Police Ombudspersons' powers were reduced and much of the detail on training, ethos, restructuring, decentralisation, etc. were to be left to an 'Implementation Plan' which was to be left in the hands of the Northern Ireland Office and the RUC Chief Constable. Despite Mandelson's protests to the contrary that he had remained faithful to Patten, Mulcahy's assertion that the Bill was a 'pale shadow' (2006: 169) of the original report is hard to contest. There was some movement over the course of the passage of the legislation. The Social Democratic and Labour Party (SDLP), Sinn Fein's principal rival in nationalist politics in Northern Ireland, tabled 150 amendments, 100 of which were ultimately accepted (Ryder 2004: 308). Even these, however, were insufficient and in the end neither of the main nationalist parties endorsed the legislation. This represented a significant feat of political mismanagement given that much of the impetus behind Patten had been designed to secure nationalist support for policing for the first time since the formation of the state. Finally, after a further round of political negotiations at Weston Park in 2001, an updated implementation plan was issued by the government (NIO 2001) and additional legislation was agreed which eventually resulted in the Police (Northern Ireland) Act 2003. The changes agreed at Weston Park were enough to satisfy the demands of the SDLP and they took up their seats on the Policing Board when it was established in November 2001 and on the local district policing partnership boards when these came on line in 2003.

Sinn Fein refused to endorse these changes. They accused the British government of 'not having done enough' to implement Patten in full. They also charged the SDLP of having 'jumped too early' and having 'accepted half a loaf' on policing, thereby breaking the nationalist consensus on maximising change to the policing establishment.[25] For their part the SDLP accused Sinn Fein of 'yelping on the sidelines' and of not having 'the political courage and capacity to make policing work'.[26] This wrangle within Irish nationalism in Northern Ireland has continued to flavour the political debate on the development of community-based restorative justice until the present day.

At one level, the political sparring between Sinn Fein and the SDLP is hardly surprising. The transition from conflict has seen significant shifts of political allegiance within the two dominant political blocks. In a similar fashion to the struggle between the two main unionist parties (the Democratic Unionist Party and Ulster Unionists), transitional politics in the jurisdiction have been fiercely contested. While the IRA were involved in armed struggle, support for their political wing Sinn Fein appeared stuck at an apparent ceiling of around one-third of the nationalist vote, with the SDLP taking the other two-thirds (Feeney 2003). Since the IRA ceasefires, however, Sinn Fein has largely eclipsed the SDLP as the largest political party in the nationalist community. In the most recent Assembly elections, Sinn Fein took 28 seats compared with the SDLP's 16.[27] Since Sinn Fein were involved in the discussions which led to the creation of Community Restorative Justice Ireland and have continuously given vocal support to the projects, and since the projects include many former IRA prisoners among their staff and volunteers, SDLP opposition is hardly surprising. There were, however, deeper political and ideological issues at stake.

Although the SDLP has consistently declared itself in favour of restorative justice per se, they have long held suspicions that the projects which emerged from the Blue Book were part of a broader plot to maintain paramilitary hegemony in working-class Republican areas. As one SDLP dossier explained: 'What is bad is when this concept [restorative justice] is abused by a political party, allied to a private army, in order to keep control of nationalist areas. What we are faced with then is not, in fact, restorative justice, it's vigilantism (2006:1)'. This long-standing concern, the merits of which are discussed below, appears to have been crystallised by a number of factors.

Following the SDLP's decision to join the policing structures, they (together with the British and Irish governments and other influential actors) invested considerable energies in seeking to pressurise Republicans of all hues to begin to do business with the police. To the extent that CRJI (like many other community-based projects in Republican areas) was unwilling to formally cooperate with the police until recently, this made them an obvious target for similar pressure. This came to a head when, as is detailed below, the government eventually produced draft protocols designed to regulate the relationship between the projects and the state. The SDLP became convinced that not only were these too 'lax' but that they removed the pressure from Sinn Fein to sign up to the policing deal. As one SDLP advisor candidly told one of the authors:

> Our fear is, that they [the projects] will try to take the money, without cooperation, working with the police. Meanwhile, Sinn Fein may not get onboard for policing for years yet ... Meanwhile you have this culture embedding itself. And, also, an alternative method has been given to the Sinn Fein, or what they call an alternative method, for dealing with the problem, which allows them to postpone their decision on policing instead of to confront it. And we want to keep pressure, this is about human rights and protection of individuals, it is also about we want to keep pressure on Sinn Fein to ensure that they do the real solution on policing, as opposed to putting into place something that is very unsatisfactory.[28]

In addition, however, many SDLP members and others were particularly horrified by the events concerning the murder of Robert McCartney.[29] Although we are unaware of any accusation being made that CRJI personnel were involved in the McCartney murder or cover up, the SDLP consistently used the case to illustrate the dangers of the Republican community failing to cooperate with the police.[30] Since CRJI was the embodiment of Republican reluctance to full engagement with the Police Service of Northern Ireland, their non-involvement in the McCartney killing appeared to become blurred in the frenzy of media activity surrounding the case. A well-meaning but ill-judged effort to mediate subsequent community tensions between supporters of the McCartney family and some of those accused in the media of having been involved made matters worse.[31] As one senior Republican summed up to one of the authors:

> It was a mess from start to finish. The murder and the cover-up was wrong and disgraceful, immoral and a complete failure of local leadership. The IRA's response was cack-handed. Sinn Fein appeared to twist themselves in knots saying everything but 'of course witnesses should go to the police'. Meanwhile I think the family got used in the media feeding frenzy and the Stoops [derogatory term for the SDLP] made hay about it, using the McCartney case as justification for them having jumped first on policing. An absolute fucking mess.[32]

The party politicking concerning restorative justice in Northern Ireland was not confined solely to the nationalist political bloc. While the main unionist parties have been predictably hostile to 'former terrorists' being involved in justice work, they have not expended anything like the political capital of the SDLP in opposing these projects.[33] The Conservatives in Britain have on the other hand given the issue increased prominence in recent years. In particular, in the wake of the government's publication of the draft protocols discussed below, elements of the Conservative party appeared to regard the issue as one with the potential to tarnish Labour's otherwise strong record on the Irish peace process. For example, the government was accused by the Conservatives of 'licensing a paramilitary mafia'.[34] Explicitly taking their briefings from the SDLP on the topic, the Tories too saw restorative justice as a pressure point for Republicans on policing.[35]

This local and national party politicking concerning the policing debate in Northern Ireland arguably obscured more meaningful analysis on what the projects actually do. As one British Minister acknowledged in a meeting attended by both authors, the heat generated by the SDLP and the Conservatives ensured that discussion on the quality of the actual work on the ground was largely lost in the ensuing political melee.[36] The political linkage of progress on restorative justice to Republican acceptance of formal policing structures was a source of frustration for restorative justice practitioners in both communities. For those working in Republican areas, CRJI repeatedly reiterated that they were pro-policing, willing to provide leadership for Republican communities in building relationships with the police and indeed were involved in 'quiet' cross referrals in a small number of cases (CRJI 2005). This bottom-up style of transition was consistently stymied by the larger debate on policing and the assumption (repeatedly and persuasively reiterated to the authors as erroneous) that CRJI was highly influential to the overall Republican decision-making process on the topic.[37] The frustrations for Alternatives operating in the Loyalist community were all the more acute. Alternatives have since their establishment sought to develop relationships with all of the statutory organisations and retained a place on their board for the police which was ultimately accepted. However, they have been unable to access mainstream statutory funding because of what they perceived, with some justification, as government reluctance to be seen to favour the funding of Loyalist projects over Republican ones.[38] Obviously their influence over Republican moves on policing was even less. What *has* arguably shifted the debate in both communities, apart from Sinn Fein's recent endorsement of policing, has been the consistently high quality of the work and the willingness of both sets of projects to commit themselves to external evaluation and regulation.

## Standards, regulation and justice ownership in transition

Northern Ireland actually has a more mature debate on standards and principles of restorative justice than any society I know. It is certainly a more sophisticated debate than in my home country of Australia. I suspect this is because Northern Ireland has a more politicised contest between state and civil society models of restorative justice than can be found in other places. Such fraught contexts are where there is the greatest risk of justice system catastrophes. But they also turn out to be the contexts with the richest prospects for rising to the political challenges with a transformative vision of restorative justice. (Braithwaite 2002: 572)

John Braithwaite's comments concerning the debate on standards in restorative justice in Northern Ireland followed his attendance at a conference in the jurisdiction and a week of interaction with both the community projects themselves and the various statutory agencies involved. His argument, that it is precisely the highly politicised context which makes the debate on restorative justice standards so acute, is well made. It is also true that Northern Ireland has a particularly lively 'human rights culture' so the level of sophistication generally concerning rights discourses in the jurisdiction is arguably much higher than in most non-transitional settings (see Harvey 2001). Given the background of the projects and the presence of ex-combatants among their staff and volunteers, these programmes have been aware since their formation that they would have to 'go the extra mile' in seeking to demonstrate their bona fides to those who were suspicious of their work and motivations.[39] This they have sought to do through two overall strategies. First, they have been (broadly) amenable to a diverse range of visits, inspections and commentary from a wide range of actors 'from above' who have taken an interest in their work. Second, they have successfully developed a range of practical working relationships with statutory agencies 'on the ground' in the communities in which they work. Cumulatively these strategies have developed reserves of goodwill which have, ultimately, served the projects well in retaining a degree of focus upon the standard of their practice among all of the political machinations.

Both Northern Ireland Alternatives and Community Restorative Justice Ireland have worked hard at outreaching to a range of important policy-makers, evaluators, visiting scholars and others interested in their work. Quite apart from the long-running independent evaluation by Mika (2006) discussed above, they have also been the subject of a range of both formal and informal reviews and related interventions. Indeed, they have received supportive commentary from sources which one might have assumed were not intuitively sympathetic to community justice initiatives.

For example, Lord Clyde, head of the Justice Oversight Commission, a body established to oversee implementation of the recommendations of the Criminal Justice Review, made a number of important commentaries on the operation of the schemes. Clearly impressed with the quality of the work, his assessments are laced with an appreciative, pragmatic and 'problem-solving' approach. He suggested (JOC 2004: 101) that CRJI and NIA are 'engaged in valuable and effective work', that their growth 'gives evidence to the value they have', and that 'they share a common intention and motivation to make a positive and peaceful contribution to the welfare of the communities in which they serve'. Lord Clyde acknowledged the need to find ways for the projects to engage with the statutory system but suggests that 'to require all cases to be processed through any elaborate state monitoring before they could be dealt with by the local scheme might well take the edge off the efficiency and effectiveness of the local scheme' (JOC 2004: 102). He criticised the Northern Ireland Office for their failure to produce guidelines for the projects (as obligated under the Criminal Justice Review Implementation Plan) and concluded that 'the development of these community restorative justice schemes which was recommended by the Review and has been accepted by the Government is a matter of considerable importance and should be pursued in an active, forward-looking, cooperative, sensitive and open-minded spirit' (p. 102). In his third report in January 2005 he once more referred to the unacceptable delay in the production of the government guidelines and again reiterated his view that 'the schemes provide an opportunity for engagement with the community and should not be seen as a threat but a possible advantage for the whole system' (JOC 2005: 105).

Similar, and perhaps even more surprising, has been some of the commentary from the International Monitoring Commission (IMC).[40]

The IMC is regularly lambasted for its uncritical reliance upon and publicising of security force briefings, unsourced intelligence information and 'rumours' by nationalist, loyalist and other seasoned commentators on Northern Ireland.[41] In its third report, while stressing the need for human rights protections and safeguards in the schemes and mechanisms to ensure that they were not 'paramilitary front' organisations, the IMC concluded 'we have received evidence which we find convincing that community restorative justice can under the right conditions help offer alternatives to paramilitary violence and intimidation ... with the right standards and safeguards, we believe community restorative justice has its part to play in helping transition from paramilitarism' (2004: 36). In their fifth report they reiterated these views, also going on to suggest that restorative justice could help 'repatriate the administration of justice' back to the communities through getting local people involved and responsible, and again stressed the role of community restorative justice in helping communities 'break free from paramilitarism' (2005: 42). Although their eighth report in 2006 was less positive, repeating verbatim some of the allegations contained in the SDLP 'dossier' outlined above, it too reconfirmed the earlier comments about the positive role and potential of the projects. In the round, for the projects to have been given such broadly positive reportage by the International Monitoring Commission during the transition was quite remarkable. As one CRJI activist joked to one of the authors, 'for us to have got such positive coverage from the three spooks and the Lord [IMC] is ruining my credibility amongst Republicans'.

A central thread running through the commentary of the Justice Oversight Commissioner and the IMC has been the need for appropriate statutory guidelines which might not only guide the work of the projects but also offer a template around which to structure their relationship with statutory organisations. As was noted above, 'informal' working arrangements had been developed with a range of statutory organisations including probation, the social services, the police, youth agencies, the housing executive and others, but none of these had been sufficiently 'formalised' at a more senior management level to enable the projects to access mainstream statutory funding. Eventually in December 2005 a version of these protocols was published. After consulting widely on these guidelines, the government announced in July 2006 that it intended to publish a new draft Protocol to address the concerns raised during the initial consultation, concerns raised mainly by the SDLP. The final draft Protocol was published on 20 September 2006 and was subject to another 12 weeks' consultation. As part of the consultation, the NIO Minister for Criminal Justice visited both projects and an inquiry was conducted by the Northern Ireland Affairs Committee, where staff from both projects and a range of statutory and political representatives gave evidence (Northern Ireland Affairs Committee 2007).

The key areas for concern during the consultation process, and the reasons behind the redrafting of the Protocols, were around the issues of the scheme's relationship with the police; the suitability of those working in the schemes (particularly in relation to politically motivated ex-prisoners); the distinction between criminal and non-criminal matters; the handling of complaints by participants in the schemes and the need for an independent mechanism to deal with such complaints; and the nature and extent of an inspections regime in relation to everyday practice by the schemes. Several different solutions were proposed during the consultation to deal with the above controversies but the final Protocol published on 5 February 2007 decided on adding or adapting the following features in response to concerns expressed in regard to previous drafts.

Summarising some of the key issues for the sake of brevity, the new protocols include the following provisions:

1 that the previous suggestion that schemes could report an offence to the PSNI through a third party (i.e. the Public Prosecution Service) be removed;
2 that the previous suggestion that the schemes could only receive referrals from a statutory criminal justice agency rather than from within the community be removed;
3 that a 'panel' should be established which would determine the suitability of staff and volunteers. The issue of past politically motivated convictions of staff and volunteers has been a major issue for political parties and statutory agencies. However, the relevant Minister for Criminal Justice has consistently stated that individuals with criminal convictions dating back to before the Good Friday Agreement, i.e. 1998, should be allowed to work in community restorative justice schemes, but that individuals with convictions after this cut-off date will be excluded from practice;[42]
4 that the Probation Board of Northern Ireland will establish an independent complaints mechanism for victims and offenders who may have cause to raise concerns about how a scheme has handled their case;

5  that the schemes be subject to 'rigorous, regular, and unannounced inspections' by the Criminal Justice Inspectorate.

Following an indication that Northern Ireland Alternatives were willing to 'sign up' to the revised government protocols, in May 2007 the Criminal Justice Inspectorate published a report which recommended that the scheme be accredited by the government. The Chief Inspector Kit Chivers, indicated that he was impressed by the 'high standard of professionalism and dedication' of the staff, and that record keeping, training and child protection policies were good and in place. He also explored fears that community-based restorative justice schemes were a front for paramilitary organisations or that people were forced into taking part in restorative justice by paramilitaries and 'found no evidence that there was any such problem in relation to Northern Ireland Alternatives or its schemes. There was no evidence of the schemes being driven by paramilitaries and every indication to the contrary' (Criminal Justice Inspectorate 2007: 4). In April 2007, Community Restorative Justice also indicated a willingness to sign up to the government protocols. In the same month, they held their first preliminary meeting with senior police officers to see how the protocols might be operationalised in practice. At the time of writing (May 2007), a similar preliminary inspection is slated to happen within weeks, and providing the Inspectorate deems the organisation capable of accreditation, live cases should begin (between the schemes and the formal system including the police) by the end of the summer of 2007. A full ten years after the Blue Book was published, these developments herald the potential for a real organic relationship developing on the ground between Republican communities, the police and other elements of the formal justice system. Although the word historic is over-used in the Northern Ireland context, the term is appropriate in this instance.

## Conclusion

Defensive formalism, party politics and tortuous negotiations concerning regulation and standard setting concerning the work of projects are doubtless dynamics that would be present in any interaction between community-based and state structures engaged in a contest over justice ownership. As was argued above, however, the particular edge to these tussles in Northern Ireland has been as a direct result of their peculiar prominence as ex-combatant led projects engaged in real 'on the ground' reconciliation at the end of a violent 30-year conflict. The success of the projects in not only surviving in an initially hostile political climate but actually developing highly professional and impactive services to violence-affected communities and ultimately persuading sufficient numbers of wary criminal justice professionals and more open-minded politicians of their bona fides is quite remarkable.

In a context where peace has apparently broken out between the formal justice system and the community-based programmes, they will now face a new challenge, albeit one which is familiar to many other community-based justice projects with strong ties to the state. As Cain (1985), Matthews (1988), Fitzpatrick (1992) and others writing on the informal tradition have argued, such is the hegemonic power and will to dominate of the justice system that it can 'swallow up' community-based programmes, professionalise them and reconfigure them into the image of the state to such an extent that they ultimately lose their specific community focus and indeed legitimacy. Such a debate is well rehearsed in the restorative justice literature as well (e.g. Boyes-Watson 1999; Olson and Dzur 2004; Aertsen *et al.* 2006). It is of course too early to say with any certainty if such will be the fate of these programmes in five or ten years. Certainly the projects themselves appear acutely aware of the need to hold onto their distinct community identity in the new dispensation.

The protocols designed to regulate relations between the state and community projects do not mean that disputes over justice ownership are magically resolved in Northern Ireland. Rather, they provide an agreed framework within which such disputes can be addressed. As we have argued elsewhere (McEvoy and Eriksson 2006), the tenacity and durability of the projects to date are due in no small part to the leadership skills of those same ex-combatants whose presence in them has proved so controversial for so long. Their commitment to the respective communities has remained undented throughout the long years of conflict and transition. Based upon our cumulative personal knowledge of the individuals involved over the last 14 years or so, we are hopeful. If any community justice projects can receive statutory funding, be subject to independent oversight, develop strong partnership arrangements with the formal justice system and *still* retain their unique community ethos, it is these.

## Notes

1 'UVF "deactivates" and agrees to put weapons "beyond reach" ', *The Independent*, 4 May 2007.

2 The motion before the Sinn Fein: Ard Fheis empowered the party's executive to: 'Support the Police Service of Northern Ireland (PSNI) and the criminal justice system; Hold the police and criminal justice systems north and south fully to account, both democratically and legally, on the basis of fairness and impartiality and objectivity; Authorise our elected representatives to participate in local policing structures in the interests of justice, the quality of life for the community and to secure policing with the community as the core function of the PSNI and actively encouraging everyone in the community to co-operate fully with the police services in tackling crime in all areas and actively supporting all the criminal justice institutions.' See Ard Fheis Motion passed by the Sinn Fein Ard Fheis – 28 January 2007, at: www.sinnfeinonline.com/policies (last visited 7 March 2007).

3 'PSNI praise Sinn Fein for murder probe help', *Belfast Telegraph*, 17 February 2007.

4 Amongst Sinn Fein's nominees were Alex Maskey, a former internee and Lord Mayor of Belfast, and Martina Anderson, a former Republican prisoner convicted of the bombings in England and released under the provisions of the Good Friday Agreement.

5 For example, O'Mahony *et al.* (2000: 80) found that in working-class Republican areas in Northern Ireland just over 1 per cent of respondents knew a police officer to speak to and 9 per cent knew an officer by sight.

6 For a fuller discussion of the significance of the programmes to broader international debates concerning 'transitional justice from below', see McEvoy *et al.* (forthcoming).

7 Interview with voluntary sector chief executive, 17 January 2007.

8 For a useful critique see Roche (2003).

9 See Loader and Walker (2007) for an excellent overview.

10 For an overview of distinct phases in government criminal justice policy see McEvoy (2001), especially Chapters 8–10.

11 For a useful critique of the effectiveness of the widely discredited Police Authority of Northern Ireland (replaced by the Policing Board under the Patten reforms) see Mulcahy (2006: ch. 2).

12 See Hughes (2006) for a discussion on the meaning of this term.

13 Base 2 is a NIACRO-run project which has been involved in relocating and supporting those under paramilitary threat for the past 15 years (see Base 2, 1992–2006).

14 Documented cases were those where a paramilitary group confirmed that a person was under threat.

15 It is important to note also that other paramilitary groups (other than the mainstream IRA and the UVF) also carry out punishment violence in these communities. Such 'dissident' groupings, some of whom remain opposed to the peace process, are much less susceptible to interventions from the projects.

16 One prominent community restorative justice worker was shot and wounded while trying to mediate a dispute and several have been threatened at different junctures during the peace process.

17 For example, para. 1.3 of the Patten Report (1999) notes: 'In contested space, the role of those charged with keeping the peace has itself been contested. The roots of the problem go back to the very foundation of the state ... Both in the past, when the police were subject to political control by the Unionist government at Stormont, and more recently in the period of direct rule from Westminster, they have been identified by one section of the population not primarily as upholders of the law but as defenders of the state, and the nature of the state itself has remained the central issue of political argument. This identification of police and state is contrary to policing practice in the rest of the United Kingdom. It has left the police in an unenviable position, lamented by many police officers. In one political language they are the custodians of nationhood. In its rhetorical opposite they are the symbols of oppression. Policing therefore goes right to the heart of the sense of security and identity of both communities and, because of the differences between them, this seriously hampers the effectiveness of the police service in Northern Ireland.'

18 'We were asked to "bring forward proposals for future criminal justice arrangements". And in that sense we looked forward to the future, not backwards to the past. But we did listen carefully to genuinely and strongly held views, from differing perspectives, about past events. It was important for us to understand these points of view if we were to develop recommendations for arrangements most likely to inspire the confidence of all parts of the community in the future. We do not express any opinion about the validity of views about past events and wish to stress that where we suggest change, this should not in itself be taken as implying criticism of what has gone before' (Criminal Justice Review 2000: para. 1.20).

19 From their establishment to the time of writing, the projects have received virtually no statutory funding and instead have been reliant on private charitable funding from the US-based philanthropic organisation, Atlantic Philanthropies.

20 For a critique of that research, see McEvoy and Mika (2002).

21 'They tell us that we need the RUC [Royal Ulster Constabulary] and the NIO [Northern Ireland Office] involved in CRJI in order to protect people's rights, that's a joke. I have been interned by the NIO, I have been beaten and tortured by the RUC in Castlereagh and by the screws

in Long Kesh. I have had friends killed in shoot to kill operations and in collusion with the Loyalists … What is really annoying them is that we are processing hundreds of cases because the community has confidence in us and what we are doing.' Interview, CRJI activist, 23 January 2003.

22 'Blair guilty of capitulating to Sinn Fein – Mandelson', *The Guardian*, 13 March 2007.

23 Prominent political scientist and author of a key text on the RUC Brendan O'Leary argued that 'The Bill is a fundamental breach of faith, perfidious Britannia in caricature. It represents old Britain; it was drafted by the forces of conservatism, for the forces of conservatism. It keeps or preserves the powers of the Secretary of State, the Northern Ireland Office and the Chief Constable' (Brendan O'Leary, 'Perfidious Britannia', *The Guardian*, 15 June 2000).

24 'The core elements of the Patten Commission's Report have been undermined everywhere. The district policing partnership boards that are so vital to the Patten Commission's vision have been diluted … So have its recommendations in the key areas outlined in its terms of reference – composition, recruitment, culture, ethos and symbols. The Patten Report has not been cherry picked, it has been gutted … It will not serve the people of Northern Ireland, nor will it serve the many, many dedicated persons within the RUC who have been looking for a new vision for policing that will move and inspire them to police in partnership with the community they serve' (Clifford Shearing, 'Patten has been gutted', *The Guardian*, 14 November 2000).

25 See, for example, 'Sinn Fein renews attacks on SDLP over Policing Board', 7 August 2002, at www.4ni.co.uk/northern_ireland_news.

26 See for example, 'SDLP man hits out at Sinn Fein over policing', *Belfast Telegraph*, 21 September 2002.

27 Northern Ireland Election Overview, 13 March 2007, at news.bbc.co.uk/1/shared/vote2007/nielection/html/main.stm.

28 Interview, 17 February 2006.

29 Mr McCartney was stabbed to death and a colleague was injured outside a Belfast bar after a dispute inside with a number of local Republicans in January 2005. After the killing, Republicans entered the pub, removed CCTV footage and 'cleaned up' other forensic evidence. Police described the subsequent investigation as being met with a 'wall of silence' by those who were inside the packed pub at the time. The IRA expelled three members some weeks later and subsequently offered to shoot those responsible, an offer which was declined by the McCartney family. SDLP leader Mark Durkan accused the IRA of orchestrating a cover-up, claiming that the 'full force of the IRA has been used to intimidate witnesses and prevent the killers from being brought to justice'. Gerry Adams, President of Sinn Fein, expelled a number of members from the party and urged witnesses to come forward to 'the family, a solicitor, or any other authoritative or reputable person or body', also saying, 'I want

to make it absolutely clear that no one involved acted as a republican or on behalf of republicans'. However, until recently when Sinn Fein's position on policing changed, he stopped short of urging witnesses to go directly to the police. The high-profile campaign for justice by the McCartney family, which included visits to the White House and European Parliament, was highly embarrassing to Sinn Fein and the Republican Movement. See: 'Brutal killing turns republicans against IRA', *The Guardian*, 14 February 2005. In June 2005, two men were charged with the McCartney murder; the charges against one were subsequently dropped. See: *The Guardian*, 9 February 2005; 'Grieving sisters square up to IRA', *The Observer*, 13 February 2005; 'We can't let it go, not what happened to Robert', *Irish News*, 29 January 2006; 'Sinn Fein should back police inquiry', *Irish News*, 17 July 2006.

30  'McCartney killing has changed the North', *Irish News*, 1 March 2005.

31  'SDLP call for suspension of CRJ Funding', *Irish News*, 10 July 2006.

32  Interview, 12 January 2006.

33  Interview with DUP policing and justice spokesperson, 20 January 2006.

34  HC Debates, *Hansard*, 23 November, 2005, col. 1499.

35  'Let us hear Sinn Fein members urge those of their supporters who witnessed the murder of Robert McCartney to go to the police with their evidence. Let us see republicans working with the police and the other agencies of law and order to make restorative justice a reality of the kind that we have seen elsewhere in the United Kingdom, rather than trying to operate community restorative justice organisations as a private judicial system and an instrument of intimidation and social control.' Liddington, *Hansard HC debates*, 13 May 2006, col. 1182.

36  Meeting with NIO Minister and CRJI board, 23 October 2006.

37  As one CRJI board member told the authors: 'My real frustration is that while the Shinners [Sinn Fein] have been dragging their feet on policing, the good work of CRJI is getting lost in all of the mud-slinging. There is an assumption that squeezing CRJI will make the Shinner jump, nothing could be further from the truth. Such a view completely overestimates the influence of CRJI on the broader Republican movement. In fact, I am pissed off that CRJI hasn't been a key negotiating demand from Sinn Fein to the Brits. It hasn't, their eyes are on the big prize and we aren't even on the list of priorities or confidence building measures.' Interview, CRJI board member, 16 December 2006.

38  Speech by Northern Ireland Alternatives Director Tom Winston to Belfast Community Safety Partnership Conference, 23 November 2006.

39  Interview, CRJI activist, 23 January 2003.

40  The IMC is a highly controversial organisation in Northern Ireland. Under pressure from Unionists in particular, it was established by the British and Irish governments in 2004 to monitor the activities of paramilitary organisations, security normalisation and 'the activities of Assembly Parties'. Its members are a former leader of the moderate Unionist Alliance Party of Northern Ireland, a former Deputy Director of

the Central Intelligence Agency, a former Deputy Assistant Commissioner of the Metropolitan Police Service and a former Director General of the Department of Justice in Dublin. Sinn Fein lodged an unsuccessful legal challenge to the legality of the commission wherein they claimed, *inter alia*, that it was biased and failed to offer any evidence to support its conclusions.

41 See 8 February 2006, D. Morrison 'IMC land', *Andersontown News*; 5 May 2004, 'Progressive Unionist Party rebuttal of the first IMC report', *The Blanket*; April 2004, 'IMC needs to make amends', editorial, *Irish News*; 27 April 2004, B. Feeney, 'IMC suits the last ditchers in the DUP', *Irish News*.

42 In addition a recent set of government guidelines on dealing with 'conflict-related' convictions suggests that there should be a presumption that such convictions are not relevant for most employment, that the seriousness of an offence is not per se relevant in making assessments of relevance and that offences should only be considered as a bar to employment (or volunteering) when they are 'manifestly incompatible' with the post in question (OFM/DFM 2007).

# References

Abel, R. (ed.) (1982) *The Politics of Informal Justice: Vol. 1 The American Experience; Vol. 2 Comparative Studies*. New York: Academic Press.

Aertsen, I., Daems, T., and Robert, L. (eds) (2006) *Institutionalizing Restorative Justice.* Cullompton: Willan.

Amnesty International (1994) *Political Killings in Northern Ireland*. London: Amnesty International.

Anderson, B. (1991) *Imagined Communities: Reflections on the Origin and Spread of Nationalism*, revised edn. London: Verso.

Auld, J., Gormally, B., McEvoy, K. and Ritchie, M. (1997) *Designing a System of Restorative Justice in Northern Ireland*. Belfast: The authors.

Bartelson, J. (2001) *The Critique of the State*. Cambridge: Cambridge University Press.

Base 2 (1992–2006) *Annual Report of the Base 2 Projects*. Belfast: Northern Ireland Association for the Care and Resettlement of Offenders.

Bauman, Z. (2001) *Community: Seeking Safety in an Insecure World*. Oxford: Blackwell.

Beetham, D. (1991) *The Legitimation of Power*. London: Macmillan.

Belfast Agreement (1998) *The Agreement Reached in Multi-Party Negotiations*. Belfast: Northern Ireland Office.

Boyes-Watson, C. (1999) 'In the belly of the beast? Exploring the dilemmas of state-sponsored restorative justice', *Contemporary Justice Review*, 2 (3): 261–81.

Braithwaite, J. (2000) 'Decomposing a holistic vision of restorative justice', *Contemporary Justice Review*, 3 (4): 433–40.

Braithwaite, J. (2002) 'Setting standards for restorative justice', *British Journal of Criminology*, 42 (3): 563–77.

Brookman, F. (2003) 'The new imperialism: violence, norms, and the "rule of law"', *Michigan Law Review*, 101 (7): 2275–340.

Butcher, H., Henderson, P., Smith, J. and Glenn, A. (eds) (1993) *Community and Public Policy*. London: Pluto.

Cain, M. (1985) 'Beyond informal justice', *Contemporary Crisis*, 335–73.

Campbell, C., Devlin, R., O'Mahony, D., Doak, J., Jackson, J., Corrigan, T. and McEvoy, K. (2005) *Evaluation of the Northern Ireland Youth Conference Service*. Belfast: Northern Ireland Office.

Cherif Bassiouni, M. (ed.) (2002) *Post-Conflict Justice*. New York: Transnational Publishers.

Cochrane, A. (1986) *Community Politics and Democracy*. London: Sage.

Cohen, A.P. (1985) *The Symbolic Construction of Community*. London: Routledge.

Cohen, A.P. (1987) *Whalsay: Symbol, Segment and Boundary in a Shetland Island Community*. Manchester: Manchester University Press.

Community Restorative Justice (CRJI) (2005) *Community Restorative Justice Ireland Annual Report*. Belfast: CRJI.

Crawford, A. (1999) *The Local Governance of Crime: Appeals to Community and Partnerships*. Oxford: Oxford University Press.

Criminal Justice Inspectorate (2007) *Northern Ireland Alternatives: Report of an Inspection with a View to Accreditation Under the Government's Protocol for Community Based Restorative Justice*. Belfast: Criminal Justice Inspection Northern Ireland.

Criminal Justice Review (2000) *Review of the Criminal Justice System in Northern Ireland*. Belfast: Stationery Office.

Crow, G. and Allan, G. A. (1994) *Community Life: An Introduction to Local Social Relations*. Hemel Hempstead: Harvester Wheatsheaf.

Cunningham, M. (1991) *British Government Policy in Northern Ireland, 1969–89: Its Nature and Execution*. Manchester: Manchester University Press.

Dignan, J. and Lowey, K. (2000) *Restorative Justice Options for Northern Ireland: A Comparative Review*, Research Report No. 10. Belfast: Stationery Office.

Douglas, M. (1986) *How Institutions Think*. Syracuse, NY: Syracuse University Press.

Feenan, D. (2002) 'Justice in conflict: paramilitary punishment in Ireland (North)', *International Journal of the Sociology of Law*, 30: 151–72.

Feeney, B. (2003) *Sinn Fein: A Hundred Turbulent Years*. Dublin: O'Brien Press.

Fitzpatrick, P. (1992) 'The impossibility of popular justice', *Social and Legal Studies*, 1: 199–215.

Foster, J. (2002) '"People pieces": the neglected but essential elements of community crime prevention', in G. Hughes and A. Edwards (eds), *Crime Control and Community: The New Politics of Public Safety*. Cullompton: Willan, 167–96.

Good Friday Agreement (1998) *The Agreement Reached in the Multi-Party Negotiation*. Belfast: HMSO.

Harvey, C. (ed.) (2001) *Human Rights, Equality and Democratic Renewal in Northern Ireland*. Oxford: Hart.

Heath, E. (1998) *The Course of My Life: My Autobiography*. London: Hodder & Stoughton.

Hughes, G. (1998) *Understanding Crime Prevention: Social Control, Risk and Late Modernity*. Milton Keynes: Open University Press.

Hughes, G. (2006) *The Politics of Crime and Community*. London: Palgrave.

Independent Monitoring Commission (November 2004) *Third Report of the Independent Monitoring Commission*. London: Stationery Office.

Independent Monitoring Commission (May 2005) *Fifth Report of the Independent Monitoring Commission*. London: Stationery Office.

Independent Monitoring Commission (September 2005) *Sixth Report of the Independent Monitoring Commission*. London: Stationery Office.

Independent Monitoring Commission (February 2006) *Eighth Report of the Independent Monitoring Commission*. London: Stationery Office.

Independent Monitoring Commission (April 2007) *Fifteenth Report of the Independent Monitoring Commission*. London: Stationery Office.

Johnston, L. and Shearing, C. (2003) *Governing Security: Explorations in Policing and Justice*. London: Routledge.

Justice Oversight Commissioner (JOC) (2004) *Second Report of the Justice Oversight Commissioner*. Belfast: JOC.

Justice Oversight Commissioner (JOC) (2005) *Third Report of the Justice Oversight Commissioner*. Belfast: JOC.

Kelly, H. (1972) *How Stormont Fell*. Dublin: Gill & Macmillan.

Levi-Faur, D. (2005) 'The global diffusion of regulatory capitalism', *Annals of the American Academy of Political and Social Science*, 598 (1): 12–32.

Loader, I. and Walker, N. (2007) *Civilizing Security*. Cambridge: Cambridge University Press.

McEvoy, K. (2001) *Paramilitary Imprisonment in Northern Ireland: Resistance, Management and Release*. Oxford: Oxford University Press.

McEvoy, K. (2003) 'Beyond the metaphor: political violence, human rights and "new" peacemaking criminology', *Theoretical Criminology*, 7 (3): 319–46.

McEvoy, K. (2004) *Ex-prisoners, Peace Building and the Construction of Leadership*. Paper presented at the Prisoners and the Basque Peace Process, Catalan Parliament, Barcelona, December.

McEvoy, K. (2005) *Restorative Justice, Leadership and Transition from Conflict*. Paper presented at the PSNI Conference on Restorative Justice, 1 March.

McEvoy, K. (2007) 'Beyond legalism: towards a thicker version of transitional justice', *Journal of Law and Society* (34.4 in press).

McEvoy, K. and Eriksson, A. (2006) 'Restorative justice in transition: ownership, leadership and "bottom-up" human rights', in D. Sullivan and L. Tifft (eds), *The Handbook of Restorative Justice: Global Perspectives*. London: Routledge.

McEvoy, K. and Mika, H. (2001) 'Punishment, politics and praxis: restorative justice and non-violent alternatives to paramilitary punishment', *Policing and Society*, 11 (1): 359.

McEvoy, K. and Mika, H. (2002) 'Restorative justice and the critique of informalism in Northern Ireland', *British Journal of Criminology*, 42 (3): 534–62.

McEvoy, K., Mika, H. and Gormally, B. (2002) 'Conflict, crime control and the "re" construction of state/community relations in Northern Ireland', in G. Hughes, E. McLaughlin and J. Muncie (eds), *Crime Prevention and Community*. Buckingham: Open University Press.

McEvoy, K., Mika, H., and McConnachie, K. (2008 forthcoming) *Reconstructing Justice After Conflict: A Bottom Up Perspective*. Cambridge: Cambridge University Press.

Matthews, R. (ed.) (1988) *Informal Justice?* London: Sage.

Mika, H. (2006) *Community Based Restorative Justice in Northern Ireland: An Evaluation*. Belfast: Institute of Criminology and Criminal Justice, Queens University Belfast.

Mika, H. and McEvoy, K. (2001) 'Restorative justice in conflict: paramilitarism, community and the construction of legitimacy in Northern Ireland', *Contemporary Justice Review*, 3 (3): 291–319.

Mulcahy, A. (2006) *Policing Northern Ireland: Conflict, Legitimacy and Reform*. Cullompton: Willan.

Newburn, T. and Sparks, R. (eds) (2004) *Criminal Justice and Political Cultures: National and International Dimensions of Crime Control*. Cullompton: Willan.

Northern Ireland Affairs Committee (2007) *First Special Report: Draft Protocol for Community-based Restorative Justice Schemes: Government Response to the Committee's First Report of Session 2006–07*, at: www.publications. parliament.uk/pa/cm/cmniaf.htmffreports.

Northern Ireland Office (NIO) (1998) *Introduction to the Criminal Justice Review Consultative Process*. Belfast: Northern Ireland Office.

Northern Ireland Office (NIO) (2001) *The Community and the Police Service: Patten Report Updated Implementation Plan*. Belfast: Northern Ireland Office.

O'Leary, B. (1997) The Conservative stewardship of Northern Ireland 1979–1997: sound bottomed contradictions or slow learning?', *Political Studies*, 45: 663–76.

O'Leary, B. and McGarry, J. (1995) *Explaining Northern Ireland: Broken Images*. Oxford: Blackwell Press.

O'Mahony, D., Chapman, T. and Doak, J. (2002) *Restorative Cautioning: A Study of Police based Restorative Cautioning Pilots in Northern Ireland*. Belfast: Northern Ireland Statistics & Research Agency.

O'Mahony, D., Geary, R., McEvoy, K. and Morison, J. (2000) *Crime, Community and Locale: The Northern Ireland Communities Crime Survey*. Aldershot: Ashgate.

OFM/DFM (2007) *Recruiting People with Conflict-Related Convictions: Employers' Guidance*. Belfast: Office of the First Minister and Deputy First Minister.

Olson, S.M. and Dzur, A. (2004) 'Revisiting informal justice: restorative justice and democratic professionalism', *Law and Society Review*, 38 (1): 139–76.

Osborne, D, and Gaebler, T. (1992) *Reinventing Government: How the Entrepreneurial Spirit Is Transforming the Public Sector*. Jackson, TN: Perseus Books.

Patten, C. (1999) *A New Beginning, Policing in Northern Ireland: Report of the Independent Commission on Policing for Northern Ireland*. Belfast: HMSO.

Pavlich, G. (2005) *Governing Paradoxes of Restorative Justice*. London: Glasshouse Press.

Roche, D. (2002) 'Restorative justice and the regulatory state in South African townships', *British Journal of Criminology*, 42 (3): 514–33.

Roche, D. (2003) *Accountability in Restorative Justice*. Oxford: Oxford University Press.

Rotberg, R. (ed.) (2004) *State Failure and State Weakness in Time of Terror*. Washington, DC: Brookings Institute Press.

Ruane, J. and Todd, J. (1996) *The Dynamics of Conflict in Northern Ireland: Power, Conflict and Emancipation*. Cambridge: Cambridge University Press.

Ryder, C. (2004) *The Fateful Split: Catholics and The Royal Ulster Constabulary*. London: Methuen.

Scharf, W. (2001) 'The challenges facing non-state justice systems in Southern Africa: how do, and how should governments respond?', in W. Scharf and D. Nina (eds), *The Other Law: Non-State Ordering in South Africa*. Cape Town: Juta & Co.

Scott, J. C. (1999) *Seeing Like a State: How Certain Schemes to Improve the Human Condition Have Failed*. New Haven, CT: Yale University Press.

Shirlow, P. and Murtagh, B. (2006) *Belfast: Segregation, Violence and the City*. London: Pluto.

Sluka, J. A. (1989) *Hearts and Minds, Water and Fish: Support for the IRA and INLA in a Northern Irish Ghetto*. London: JAI Press.

Social Democratic and Labour Party (SDLP) (2006) *The Issues Explained in a Nutshell*. Belfast: SDLP.

Steinberger, P. (2004) *The Idea of the State*. Cambridge: Cambridge University Press.

Sullivan, D. and Tifft, L. (eds) (2006) *The Handbook of Restorative Justice: Global Perspectives*. London: Routledge.

Weber, M. (1948) *From Max Weber: Essays in Sociology*. Oxford: Oxford University Press.

Willmott, P. (1987) *Policing and the Community*. London: Policy Studies Institute.

Winston, T. (1997) 'Alternatives to punishment beatings and shootings in a Loyalist community in Belfast', *Critical Criminology: An International Journal*, 8 (1).

Wood, J. and Shearing, C. (2007) *Imagining Security*. Cullompton: Willan.

# Chapter 9

# Policing, 'community' and social change in Ireland[1]

*Aogán Mulcahy*

## Introduction

Debate about the proper role of 'community' within the criminal justice system has become increasingly prominent in recent decades (Crawford 1997). Although the policies this has given rise to vary considerably from jurisdiction to jurisdiction, the desirability of maximising community potential as part of a broad-based crime prevention strategy has long been accepted as axiomatic (Hughes *et al.* 2002; Wood and Dupont 2006). Against this international consensus, the Irish context stands in a somewhat anomalous position. When the Garda Síochána Act 2005 established – for the first time in Irish history – legislative provisions for formal consultation between police and public, it represented a considerable break with the tradition of informalism that hitherto dominated the field of Irish policing. In light of this, my chapter poses a straightforward question: why did Ireland prove to be such a late arrival in terms of policy developments in the field of police–community relations?

The answer to this lies, I argue, in the relationship between policing and constructions of community in Ireland. Specifically, I argue that policing functioned as a means through which the canons of Irish cultural nationalism were asserted by privileging specific conceptions of community and identity. Independence had, of course, provided new pathways for social mobility through the various positions to be filled within the state infrastructure, but for the most part Irish nationalism was underpinned by visions of a rural idyll, characterised by asceticism and innocence. The famous 1943 characterisation by

Eamon de Valera (who served as Taoiseach – political premier – and subsequently President of Ireland) of an independent Ireland may from a modern standpoint appear fatally clichéd, but it remains an evocative elaboration of this vision:

> That Ireland which we dreamed of would be the home of a people who valued material wealth only as a basis for right living, of a people who were satisfied with frugal comfort and devoted their leisure to the things of the spirit – a land whose countryside would be bright with cosy homesteads, whose fields and villages would be joyous with sounds of industry, with the romping of sturdy children, the contests of athletic youths and the laughter of comely maidens whose firesides would be forums for the wisdom of serene old age. It would, in a word, be the home of a people living the life that God desires that man should live. (Speech to the Nation, Radio Éireann, 17 March 1943)

Within this framework, social capital was associated with circumscribed notions of community and community life: rural, quiescent, homogeneous, stable. The model of policing that developed in Ireland served to enact, valorise and reproduce these ideals.

This argument is developed as follows. First, I outline the historical development of Irish policing, and the manner in which informal links between police and public were prioritised above formal ones. Second, I consider the factors that challenged the hegemony of this broad vision of policing. Third, I review recent developments in terms of community involvement in the criminal justice system, particularly through the provisions of the Garda Síochána Act 2005. Finally, I consider the implications of these changes for the field of police-community relations in Ireland.

## State, community and the development of policing in Ireland

The origins of An Garda Síochána,[2] the Irish police force, lie in the partition of Ireland in the early 1920s and the subsequent emergence of two states: Northern Ireland, which remained within the United Kingdom, and the Irish Free State, or Ireland, which became a republic in 1949. The political independence of Ireland was reflected in the creation of new state agencies which would reflect Irish interests rather than those of the colonial administration. This transition was managed in several, often contradictory, ways, producing a model of policing that was both fundamentally different from, yet strikingly similar to, that which had preceded it.

First, particularly in light of the social upheaval and political uncertainty that had characterised the years leading up to independence, pragmatism demanded that the policing void which had developed in many parts of Ireland during the war of independence and the civil war be filled as quickly as possible. As such, the organisational structure of An Garda Síochána was closely based on that of its predecessor, the Royal Irish Constabulary (RIC) (Allen 1999; Brady 2000). Although the RIC had been a central part of the British administration in Ireland and had played a military as well as a policing role, its efficiency and effectiveness were widely admired. Moreover, the involvement of several senior RIC officers in designing the new force inevitably ensured that An Garda Síochána enjoyed close similarities with its predecessor. In terms of day-to-day activities, the manner in which gardaí policed was not dissimilar to how the RIC had operated (leaving aside the question of political policing and state security issues). They performed a wide range of duties, a great deal of which had little or no bearing on crime *per se* and was better classified as state administration, such as collecting agricultural statistics and enforcing the Noxious Weeds Act.

Second, the Irish political establishment focused on establishing agencies specifically identified as Irish in symbolic terms. Thus the force was initially named 'the Civic Guard', and soon after renamed 'An Garda Síochána' (Irish for 'guardians of the peace'). This was specifically to distinguish it from the 'constabulary' (i.e. 'foreign' and militaristic) ethos of the RIC. Similarly, the force was routinely unarmed (although detectives are allowed to carry firearms) to reflect its civic – rather than paramilitary – nature, and to emphasise the extent to which its mandate would derive from the explicit consent of the public. As the first Garda Commissioner, Michael Staines, proclaimed, 'The Garda Síochána will succeed not by force of arms or numbers, but on their moral authority as servants of the people' (Walsh 1998: 10).

As a police organisation, An Garda Síochána based its legitimacy firmly on the extent to which it could mobilise itself at two distinct levels. First, it oriented itself to the symbolic task of representing the state – in ways that clearly identified it as an expression of political independence and of the broad community whose interests this independence was argued to represent. Second, it addressed policing at a specifically local level – in ways that demonstrated the organic ties between guards and members of the community, albeit within specific parameters of locality, of being 'from' and 'of' specific communities. This generated a model of policing wherein citizens could affiliate with the police at the abstract level of the state and the more tangible level of organic community and locality links, and the police could accrue the social capital deriving from these macro and micro dimensions of their identity. Constituting the guards as an expression of the national ideal was undertaken in a number of ways that stressed the integration of the guards into Irish cultural life. All told, it involved seeking to establish the guards, in the words of Staines, as 'Irish in thought and action' (McNiffe 1997). This vision of policing was manifested in a number of measures that crafted close links between policing and the cultural nationalism of the day.

One of the immediate concerns An Garda Síochána faced was recruiting individuals sympathetic to this particular ideology. In the early decades of the force, the background of recruits reflected a Western, rural, nationalistic ethos. It was composed entirely of men (women were first appointed in 1959) drawn largely from the west of Ireland. McNiffe's (1997: 48) research demonstrates that in the period 1922–52, the western counties of Cork, Kerry, Clare, Galway and Mayo generated 38 per cent of Garda recruits, and during that same 30-year period, as many recruits joined from county Clare as from county Dublin.[3] The majority of recruits had a background in agriculture or unskilled labour: between 1922 and 1952, 38 per cent came from farming backgrounds, 15 per cent were manual labourers, 5 per cent were clerks and a further 5 per cent were shop assistants. Although this probably corresponded closely with the demographic profile of the RIC, the vast majority of Garda recruits had fought in the war of independence. As McNiffe (1997: 33) notes, 'approximately 96 per cent of the first 1,500 civic guards had been in the IRA'. Although this figure declined in subsequent years, the vast bulk of An Garda Síochána personnel were explicitly identified as loyal to an independent Ireland rather than to the previous political order.

Asserting this allegiance to the 'imagined community' of an independent Ireland was a major component of the Irish policing habitus, as the organisation actively promoted a Gaelic identity that privileged specific notions of Irishness and of the communities most closely associated with this (Allen 1999; McNiffe 1997). This was evident in a number of spheres. For instance, the force gave a particular prominence to the Irish language. At one stage, training was initially provided in English and then repeated in Irish, and recruits were forced to pass an Irish exam as part of their training (instruction in Irish is provided to the present day).

The force also developed close links with the Catholic church. The 1926 Irish census revealed that 93 per cent of the population, but 98.7 per cent of the officers who joined between 1922 and 1952, were Catholic (McNiffe 1997: 135). In 1928, no fewer than 250 officers went on a pilgrimage to Rome, while 340 travelled to Lourdes in 1930 (Allen 1999); up until the 1980s, Garda recruits were marched to a Catholic church for mass every Sunday.

Police involvement in Gaelic sports was another important dimension of An Garda Síochána's identity. In the early years of the force, officers were encouraged to become involved in the development of Gaelic sports (including football, hurling, camogie and handball), organised on an amateur basis under the auspices of the Gaelic Athletic Association (GAA). This was recognised as a strategic means of integration, and cultivating these relationships has become an enduring part of the Irish policing habitus. As Brady put it, 'with their sporting prowess, they were to "play their ways into the hearts of the people"' (2000: 117). Within the force, GAA activity was (and continues to be) a source of pride and status. What is most striking about the involvement of police in the GAA is the framework through which the sports are organised. They are amateur and explicitly local in nature, organised in a spatial hierarchy based primarily on the local parish or club level and subsequently county level. The involvement of Garda officers in amateur and vocally Gaelic sports, organised on a geographic basis in which affiliation with and loyalty to a specific community was pre-eminent, provided a ready means of identifying the police with 'the people' and of signifying police involvement in and affiliation with community life in Ireland.[4] To this day it remains a prominent feature of police culture in Ireland.

### The success of informalism?

This privileging of informal links with the public reflected a wider concern that the establishment of formal links between the police and either the public at large or the political establishment would sully the innate understanding that purportedly existed between police and public, and hark back to a pre-independence era when policing operated along explicitly political lines. However, a number of researchers have suggested that these grand claims had considerable foundation. Successive analyses of Irish policing strongly supported the view that the Garda Síochána had secured the confidence of the wider public and that the force was, as McNiffe (1997: 175) put it, 'one of the striking successes of the new state'. Mac Gréil's (1996) study of prejudice in Irish society found that members of the public were generally more willing to accept police officers as potential neighbours and as part of their kinship network than individuals from other spheres or backgrounds. He characterised members of An Garda Síochána as one of Ireland's 'in-groups' (p. 68), stating that 'the Gardaí are very highly thought of ... It would be difficult to find a police force in any other country with such a high national standing' (p. 271). Allen (1999: 136) concurred, stating that 'their place in the social life of the community could not reasonably have been higher'.

Surveys examining police–community relations have repeatedly found high levels of public confidence in the police. Table 9.1 includes the main survey findings on this issue, and indicates that with the exception of one occasion in 2004, satisfaction ratings ranged from a low of 81 per cent to a high of 89 per cent. The only significant departure from the broad pattern outlined in Table 9.1 is the figure of 57 per cent obtained in a survey in February 2004. This survey was conducted shortly after a programme broadcast on RTE television featured several serious allegations of police misconduct and while several tribunals of inquiry were underway into police actions. Perhaps indicating its exceptional findings, the Garda Research Unit's subsequent 2005 survey found an overall satisfaction level of 83 per cent.

These various factors reflected particular notions of nation and community that privileged the role of the Garda Síochána and limited the scrutiny applied to it. Here it is important to note that

**Table 9.1** Garda public satisfaction ratings 1986–2005

| Year of survey | Overall satisfaction rating (%) |
| --- | --- |
| 1986 | 86 |
| 1994 | 89 |
| 1996 | 86 |
| 1999 | 89 |
| 2002 | 87 |
| 2003 | 81 |
| 2004 | 85 |
| 2004a | 57 |
| 2005 | 83 |

*Sources*: O'Donnell (2004), *Irish Times* (10 February 2004); O'Dwyer *et al.* (2005).

this situation was not limited to policing. Economic stagnation, mass emigration, widespread social conservatism and the dominance of the cultural nationalism which lauded notions of the quiescent rural idyll, all contributed to a wider culture that inhibited overt criticism of and challenge to dominant social institutions (see, for example, Inglis 1998). Nevertheless, the manner in which the police came to embody particular characteristics of the imagined community at the heart of Irish cultural nationalism was especially significant in this regard, for it constituted this institution as self-evidently 'natural' and appropriate to the challenges and demands of policing Irish society. In this context, policing was structured through almost implicit understandings of the proper nature of Irish society, the role of the police and the empathetic manner in which the police would regulate the boundaries of community.

## The changing field of Irish policing

From the 1970s onwards, the hegemony of this informalism was increasingly called into question. A series of changes, in the field of policing specifically as well as in Irish society generally, combined to bring Garda activities and policies under sustained scrutiny.

In terms of factors specific to the policing field, three issues seem particularly significant. First, An Garda Síochána became embroiled in a number of scandals over allegations of police misconduct that undermined the public trust invested in the force. In the 1970s, allegations of misconduct arose in relation to police interrogation of serious criminals and members of paramilitary organisations, resulting in an Amnesty International investigation and an official inquiry. In 1984/5, the force was criticised for its behaviour in the 'Kerry babies case' (Inglis 2003). This centred on allegations that a young woman and her family in rural Kerry had confessed to killing and subsequently disposing of the body of a baby to whom she had given birth, despite forensic evidence indicating that she could not have been the mother of that specific child. A further series of controversies that coincided at the turn of the century raised public concerns about police accountability to new levels. These included the 2000 police shooting of John Carthy after a police siege (Barr Tribunal 2006), police violence towards members of the public at a 'reclaim the streets' march in Dublin in 2002, and several scandals centred around police corruption and misconduct in Donegal which are the subject of an ongoing inquiry (the Morris Tribunal).

Second, from the mid-1960s onwards, the field of crime and crime control increasingly featured on the public agenda (O'Donnell 2005). Crime levels rose dramatically from the mid-1960s onwards, the number of indictable crimes nearly doubling during the second half of the 1960s, and increasing sixfold in the twenty-year period between 1964 and 1983, when for the first time the threshold of 100,000 recorded offences was crossed. Although surveys indicate that the population at large was more concerned with economic and employment issues (Kilcommins *et al.* 2004), increased governmental concern with crime and the police response to it was fully apparent (Association of Garda Sergeants and Inspectors 1982; Vaughan 2004).[5] One key dimension of this was the emergence in the late 1970s of a serious heroin problem concentrated in particular parts of Dublin. Prior to then, problems associated with illegal drugs in Ireland were minuscule by international standards, and attracted little police attention. As such, the rapid upsurge in heroin use found the Gardaí ill-prepared for this development. One survey in a north inner-city area in 1982–83 found that '10 per cent of the fifteen to twenty-four age group had used heroin in the year prior to the survey, with 93 per cent of that group admitting that they had taken heroin at least once a day' (Kilcommins *et al.* 2004: 226). Such drug use had immense ripple effects. Keogh (1997), for instance, estimated that over the course of a single year known drug-users committed two-thirds of all crime in the Dublin metropolitan area. Senior Gardaí interviewed by Brewer *et al.* (1997: 46–7) noted that drugs had been 'the biggest single influence on the crime profile during their time of service', their impact exceeding that of the Northern Ireland conflict, while government officials were 'shaken' by the scale of heroin-related problems in Dublin. The situation was further complicated by the fact that communities in which heroin use was concentrated repeatedly claimed that state indifference had greatly contributed to the escalation of the problem, and that direct community action was necessary against suspected drug dealers. Cumulatively, this volatile mixture of drugs and drug-related crime, marginalisation and vigilantism had an immensely negative impact on police–community relations in many quarters (Bennett 1988; Bissett 1999; Mulcahy and O'Mahony 2005).

Third, the 1990s onwards was a period of unparalleled activism within the broad sphere of 'law and order' politics. While in opposition, the Fianna Fail political party had vocally promoted a package of 'zero-tolerance' measures, and upon entering government (in coalition with the Progressive Democrat party) in 1997 it promptly set about implementing these (O'Donnell and O'Sullivan 2003). The criminal justice system was also subject to the 'Strategic Management Initiative' directed towards modernisation of the public sector generally, which prompted a major review of organisational structures and practices (see, for example, the Garda SMI Implementation Steering Group 2004).

Accompanying these policing changes was a further raft of changes unfolding throughout Irish society as a whole. First, the traditional conception of 'community' that had underpinned cultural nationalism since the 1920s became increasingly anachronistic in the face of widespread and far-reaching changes to the fabric of Irish society. From a position of grinding poverty, Ireland had by the turn of the twenty-first century become one of the wealthiest societies in the world. Images of a rural idyll gave way to the realities of urban sprawl and traffic congestion and, as the agricultural sector contracted dramatically, Ireland's economy became increasingly driven by multinational investment and the rapid expansion of the information technology and pharmaceutical sectors in particular. Moreover, while historically 'Irishness' had been synonymous with 'whiteness', the unparalleled social economic changes associated with the 'celtic tiger' from the 1990s onwards witnessed a significant rise in the ethnic diversification of Irish society, as the demands of the economy attracted an influx of foreign labour. Preliminary figures from the 2006 census indicated that 10 per cent of the population were non-nationals.

Second, by the 1990s discourses of 'partnership' had become a core feature of the Irish political and institutional landscape. Partnership was a key pillar of the multi-agency task force approach developed to address problems associated with the use of illegal drugs (Connolly 2002). It also formed the explicit basis of the economic policy agenda underpinning the 'celtic tiger' through the 'Partnership for Prosperity and Fairness' programmes that specified agreed national wage increases in return for productivity increases and included a range of social inclusion measures. Through its popularity in these spheres, it was inevitable that it would also be considered in any overhaul of policing (National Crime Council 2003).

## Community involvement in the criminal justice system

In charting the various factors that contributed to the emergence of policing onto the public agenda, an important qualification is required: namely, that the informalism that existed did not prevent police–community initiatives from being established. Various types of community policing schemes had, in fact, been in operation for several years and decades.[6] Rather, the significance of informalism was that it helped ensure that any such initiatives that did emerge did so largely in an *ad hoc* fashion, with little direction, coordination or evaluation of their impact (see, for example, Bowden and Higgins 2000). The most pervasive scheme was a nationwide system of neighbourhood watch committees rolled out in the 1980s, but these suffered from the familiar problem of being easiest to establish where they were least needed, and hardest to establish where crime levels were high and police–community relations were poor. Moreover, their impact on crime was never systematically examined, and their role was confined to that of 'talking shops' – they appeared largely devoid of focus or work programme. As one review noted, some 'barely have enough to do to keep them active' (McKeown and Brosnan 2001: 118). Other community policing schemes emerged in parts of Dublin in the late 1990s with the goal of improving police–community relations. These, however, largely reflected the depth of concern over levels of drug use in specific neighbourhoods. One scheme emerged in Rialto in Dublin after a number of anti-drugs activists were implicated in the murder of Josie Dwyer, a heroin addict and AIDS sufferer (Bissett 1999; Mulcahy and O'Mahony 2005). That forum was then merged into a pilot scheme established by the police in various parts of Dublin's inner city. Similarly, the North Inner City Policing Forum was also established in light of problems associated with heroin use in particular (Connolly 2002).

Against this backdrop of long-standing yet diffuse initiatives, the measures contained in the recent Garda Síochána Act 2005 represent the most significant intervention in the field of police–community relations in Irish history. Although changes to the force's structures of accountability and internal management were probably the most prominent features of the Act, it nevertheless broke new ground in police–community relations and the field of community safety more generally. Thus while the Act established an Ombudsman Commission to investigate complaints against the police and an Inspectorate to review organisational effectiveness, the Act's stipulation that the force now has a statutory requirement to obtain the views of the public provided for the first time a legislative footing for police–public consultation in Ireland. Moreover, the Act also provided for the establishment of a Garda Reserve, a voluntary part-time force who would work in support of attested members of the force.

Although some Garda staff associations voiced strong opposition to this measure, characterising it as 'policing on the cheap', the first members of the reserve were appointed in December 2006 and the Minister for Justice envisaged the reserve increasing in due course to a total of more than 4,000 members.[7]

Although less publicly debated than the Act's other provisions, its changes to the role of local authorities are probably of far greater significance. In this respect, the Act significantly extended the mandate of local authorities in relation to the governance of crime and security, specifying that: 'A local authority shall, in performing its functions, have regard to the importance of taking steps to prevent crime, disorder and anti-social behaviour within its area of responsibility' (s. 37.1). The Minister for Justice further noted that responsibility for 'ensuring that our society's policing needs are effectively met' lie with 'the local authorities as much as the Garda Síochána' (Department of Justice 2006: 1). The greater reliance on multi-agency approaches, and on extending the role of local authorities in particular, can be traced back to the influential reports from the Committee of Inquiry into the Penal System (Whitaker Committee 1985) and the Interdepartmental Group on Urban Crime and Disorder (1992). Recognising the limits of the 'fire-brigade' model of policing, these reports highlighted the clear links between crime, deprivation and antagonistic relationships with the police, and emphasised the need for sustained multi-agency partnership approaches to crime prevention issues. This theme of partnership continues to dominate policy debate on these issues (National Crime Council 2003).

Local authorities have taken on a far greater role in this respect and have become one of the key pillars of this putative partnership. Much of the impetus for this arose from persistent problems with crime, disorder and anti-social behaviour in local authority estates, much of which was drug-related (McAuliffe and Fahey 1999). As a consequence, local authorities became more involved in estate management through such measures as the establishment of area housing offices to provide local on-the-ground services in specific estates. One local authority official[8] described these as evidence of its more hands-on and consultative approach: 'We really adopted the whole concept of consultation with residents ... I think the results of that or the outcome of that are probably not measurable in financial terms, but certainly we have much less problems in our estates than we had years ago.' The most significant development in the process of extending the council's role was the 1997 Housing (Miscellaneous Provisions) Act which provided for 'exclusion orders' to be made against 'illegal occupiers' and tenants engaged in illegal or anti-social behaviour. This gave local authorities enhanced powers to sanction their tenants and ultimately evict them. One council official described this as 'the year that we took our role seriously in relation to getting rid of drug dealers out of our flat complexes', and contrasted this with the council's previous 'lack of role'.

Since the 1997 Act was introduced, the number of evictions for anti-social behaviour has dropped steadily: from 44 in 1998 to 30 in 1999, 12 in 2000, 10 in 2001, 8 in 2002 and 15 in 2003 (figures supplied by Dublin City Council). The council carried out a higher number of evictions of 'illegal occupiers' allegedly involved in anti-social behaviour, although this figure too has dropped since the introduction of the Act (from 97 in 1998 to 23 in 2003). While these powers can become an important resource for the police, one senior Garda officer nevertheless spoke of his concern at the 'massive powers' involved, wondering whether they were 'draconian'. As one housing official stated, 'About five years ago we were very inactive in relation to dealing with these problems. Five years on, we're very proactive and that brings its own problems.'[9] This greater involvement of local authorities in estate management and with it the greater availability of the sanction of eviction gave added weight to allocation decisions. Away from the glare of publicity and the procedural requirements of the formal criminal justice process, these hugely consequential decisions become a quasi-policing environment in which the resource of accommodation (and its potential removal) is dependent first and foremost on a contract with a landlord, with the potential input of residents' representatives (see also Crawford 2003). Because of the impact that drug-related issues have had on local authority housing estates generally, residents' groups have sought to become more involved in allocation decisions, raising questions in turn about the boundaries of 'consultation' and community involvement in official decision-making (Bissett 1999; see also McAuliffe and Fahey 1999). Moreover, the fact that police have been in attendance at some meetings adds a further dimension to this process. As one resident noted: 'If, you know, the guards need to be involved in, you know, in assessing somebody's right to live in a particular area, it's like, there's a worrying aspect about it as well.'

The Act outlines a number of specific ways in which local authority involvement in crime prevention may occur, such as the provision of closed circuit television schemes, but the most prominent mechanism of local authority involvement is in relation to the establishment of 'joint policing committees' (JPCs) in each local authority area (with the cooperation of the Garda Commissioner). The stated function of JPCs is 'to serve as a forum for consultations, discussions and recommendations on matters affecting the policing of the local authority's administrative area' (s. 36.2). The Act specifies that JPCs are obliged to keep under review the 'levels and patterns of crime, disorder and antisocial behaviour in the area' and 'the factors underlying and contributing to' these; and to 'advise the local authority concerned and the Garda Síochána on how they might best perform their functions having regard to the need to do everything feasible to improve the safety and quality of life and to prevent crime, disorder and anti-social behaviour within the area'. The Act also notes that JPCs may, in consultation with the local Garda Superintendent, establish local policing fora within specific neighbourhoods in the area, and coordinate the activities of such fora.

The guidelines for JPCs were published by the Ministers for Justice and for Local Government on 28 June 2006, nearly a year after the Act came into force. As its authors noted: 'Great care has been taken in drawing up the guidelines to ensure that all those involved will have the opportunity to play a constructive role in making the committees a success' (Department of Justice 2006: 1). Notwithstanding this 'great care' in their design, it is apparent that the guidelines are viewed as rather provisional in nature, and despite the importance attached to the Act generally and the JPCs in particular, the guidelines appear little more than a holding pattern until 'practical experience' identifies how these committees might be structured in future. For instance, initially a pilot scheme of JPCs was established, comprising 22 local authority areas spread throughout Ireland.[10] The guidelines specified that this pilot phase would run for several months, and in 2007 would be evaluated with a view to establishing JPCs across the 114 local authority areas nationwide. As the guidelines stated: 'These new committees represent a radical new departure. As such, it is only through practical experience gained through their operation that we will discover how best they should be structured and should operate. The pilots will be evaluated on an ongoing basis and in the light of the experience gained these guidelines will be amended as necessary' (Department of Justice 2006: 1). The legislation, however, specifies that the Minister for Justice may – after consultation with cabinet colleagues – 'revise' the guidelines or withdraw them and issue new ones. It does not specify any grounds on which this might occur, nor does it impose any requirement to consult with the joint policing committees themselves.

Although discussion of local consultative mechanisms in other jurisdictions has often highlighted the capacity of such entities to serve as a means of securing local accountability and oversight (Crawford 1997; Jones 2003; Wood and Dupont 2006), the focus of JPCs is firmly on consultation surrounding crime prevention measures. The nature of such consultation, however, remains unclear. While the membership of JPCs generally includes local councillors, members of parliament, the city/county manager (effectively the local authority's executive officer) and another local authority official, and at least two local Garda officers of appropriately senior rank, this effectively amounts to providing a formal context for local authorities' expanded role in crime prevention. Only two or three seats in a JPC's membership of 25 will be reserved for representatives of the community and voluntary sector. The guidelines place a strong emphasis on informality, and mention no fewer than four times that procedures should be as informal as possible. For instance, it notes that: 'Procedures should have a minimum of formality and should reflect the cooperative nature of the committees and subcommittees. It is envisaged that decisions would be taken by agreement rather than by voting' (p. 16). The guidelines also envisage that two meetings per annum for each committee 'would prove adequate in most circumstances' (p. 10), specifying that JPCs should not inhibit ongoing police–public contact and consultation: 'The establishment of the committees should not detract from, or substitute for, either regular day-to-day contact and consultation at ground level which is a feature of ordinary policing or the maintenance and development of suitable local liaison between local authority and Garda representatives not requiring a formal structure' (p. 3). Informalism, it appears, has a future in Irish policing.

## Conclusion

The changing prominence and role of 'community' within the landscape of Irish policing stands as one dimension of wider social change unfolding across Irish society. Given the short period of time in which these developments have been in place, their full trajectory has yet to unfold and further research is required to consider their impact. Nevertheless, the establishment of formal mechanisms for police–community consultation does seem to suggest that Ireland is at last moving from a framework of policing modelled on informalism, to one based on formal structures. Such an assessment might seem to support the view that conditions of globalisation have overcome local resistance to technological developments and that, in the marketplace of policies, good ones travel until, eventually, best practice asserts itself worldwide.

To consider 'best practice' in this way – as an innocent policy application suitable for all contexts – fails to appreciate the complex issues involved in transferring policies from one jurisdiction to another. In this respect, it is interesting to consider some of the range of factors shaping the Garda Síochána Act 2005. Many of its provisions are, for instance, closely modelled on England and Wales' 1998 Crime and Disorder Act. However, in the intervening period the Patten Commission's (1999) report on policing in Northern Ireland was quickly acclaimed as an authoritative statement of international best practice in policing (Mulcahy 2006). It is no small irony that the Garda Act should be so ambivalent towards these developments in Northern Ireland. For example, in 2004 the Minister for Justice rejected calls for an oversight body equivalent to the Northern Ireland Policing Board, stating that such a structure 'would diminish if not remove the supervisory role of Dáil Éireann' (the Irish parliament) – despite the fact that the Dáil's traditional and ill-defined role in performing this function had been roundly criticised as ineffective (Walsh 1998). As the Minister stated in evidence to a Dáil committee: 'What is good for Northern Ireland is not necessarily good for a sovereign state' (Joint Committee on Justice, Equality, Defence and Women's Rights 2005: 28). It appears that the 'strong' model of community involvement in policing elaborated in the Patten Report[11] was deemed incompatible with existing structures of Irish policing and, perhaps, unnecessary in light of traditional Garda claims concerning the strength of police–community relations in Ireland.

It is clear, then, that the spread of policies and practices from one jurisdiction to another does not follow a simple global pattern oblivious to local conditions (Deflem 2002; Newburn and Sparks 2004).[12] This review of developments in Ireland confirms that policing is, at heart, a cultural enterprise, and the symbolism invested in policing in any society has profound implications for the range of policy interventions that may be implemented, or even considered (Loader and Mulcahy 2003). In the Irish case, the development of policing reflected the key tenets of cultural nationalism, and informal understandings of community trumped any broad-based move towards more formal and uniform structures. While the system of joint policing committees established under the provisions of the Garda Síochána Act 2005 adds a structured format to police–public consultation, the guidelines governing their operation bear the indelible mark of the informalism that characterised police–community initiatives since the force's creation. However, as these new institutions of police–community consultation are rolled out across Ireland, what is most important is not where they are situated along the continuum of formalism–informalism, but rather whether such structures enhance local capacity, further the cause of democratic oversight and provide innovative responses to problems of crime, disorder and insecurity. In terms of promoting these goals, the impact of joint policing committees remains to be seen.

## Notes

1 This chapter forms part of a larger research project on 'policing and social change in Ireland' funded through a Government of Ireland Research Fellowship and includes some data from Mulcahy and O'Mahony (2005). I am grateful to the editor and to the participants of the GERN 'Justice and Community' seminars, and to the audiences at a number of conferences and seminars at which earlier versions of this chapter were presented, for their feedback and support.

2 This gives rise to the term *garda* to describe individual officers (*gardaí* in the plural), and to the colloquial term 'the guards'.

3 Each contributed 5.6 per cent of Garda recruits during this period. Thus, although Dublin accounted for 17 per cent (or one in six) of the population, it yielded only one in 20 recruits.

4 For an extended discussion of the links between Gaelic sports and Irish nationalism, see Cronin (1999).

5 The outbreak of widespread violence in Northern Ireland in the late 1960s and the subsequent development there of a sustained armed conflict also brought very specific pressures to bear on the police. The conflict absorbed enormous amounts of resources, led to dramatic increases in the number of armed robberies (among other crimes) and greatly increased the risks officers faced.

6 It also operates a system of 'community gardaí' who are assigned to particular geographical areas and are encouraged to adopt a problem-solving approach to matters of concern in those areas. Since 1963 the force has operated a highly regarded diversion system for young offenders, largely operating through programmes established by juvenile liaison officers. More recently the force has established a system of restorative justice conferences under the provisions of the Children's Act 2001. The force also operates a number of 'Special Projects' which function as crime prevention measures in what typically are socially deprived areas (Bowden and Higgins 2000).

7 For a discussion of the deployment of 'community support officers' in London, an initiative not dissimilar to the Garda Reserve, see Johnston (2005).

8 This and subsequent quotations are taken from Mulcahy and O'Mahony (2005).

9 Some of the difficulties associated with the application of these enhanced powers were crystallised by the case of Noel Cahill, who died in January 2003 after developing hypothermia while sleeping rough outside the local authority flat from which he had been evicted in October 2002, following allegations that some of his acquaintances had been engaged in anti-social behaviour in his flat (*Irish Times* 2 and 3 February 2003).

10 The selection of the pilot areas was determined by the desire to include a cross-section of various local authority areas (cities and large towns, and rural and urbanised counties), as well as by the requirement that local authorities that had recently obtained funding for CCTV schemes could only implement these once they had been ratified by the local JPC.

11 For a preliminary assessment of the Patten Report and its reform programme, see Mulcahy (2006). For a further elaboration of the 'nodal governance' logic underpinning its recommendations concerning 'policing with the community', see Johnston and Shearing (2003), Shearing (2005) and Wood and Dupont (2006).

12 For example, in relation to developments across Europe to target organised crime, Den Boer suggests that while greater European integration has not produced a convergence of criminal justice system responses, it 'has increased the transparency and knowledge of one another's systems', a process she characterises as 'horizontal cross-pollination' rather than the centralised imposition of specific initiatives (Den Boer 2001: 272).

## References

Allen, G. (1999) *The Garda Síochána: Policing Independent Ireland 1922–82.* Dublin: Gill & Macmillan.

Association of Garda Sergeants and Inspectors (1982) *A Discussion Paper Concerning Proposals for a Scheme of Community Policing.* Dublin: AGSI.

Barr Tribunal (2006) *Report of The Tribunal of Inquiry into the Facts and Circumstances Surrounding the Fatal Shooting of John Carthy at Abbeylara, Co Longford on 20th April 2000.* Dublin: Stationery Office.

Bennett, D. (1988) 'Are they always right? Investigation and proof in a citizen anti-heroin movement', in M. Tomlinson, T. Varley and C. McCullagh (eds), *Whose Law and Order?* Belfast: Sociological Association of Ireland, 21–40.

Bissett, J. (1999) *Not Waiting for a Revolution: Negotiating Policing Through the Rialto Community Policing Forum.* Dublin: Rialto Community Policing Forum.

Bowden, M. and Higgins, L. (2000) *The Impact and Effectiveness of the Garda Special Projects.* Dublin: Stationery Office.

Brady, C. (2000) *Guardians of the Peace.* London: Prendeville.

Brewer, J., Lockhart, B. and Rodgers, P. (1997) *Crime in Ireland*. Oxford: Clarendon Press.

Connolly, J. (2002) *Community Policing and Drugs in Dublin: The North Inner City Community Policing Forum*. Dublin: North Inner City Drugs Task Force.

Crawford, A. (1997) *The Local Governance of Crime*. Oxford: Clarendon Press.

Crawford, A. (2003) 'Contractual governance of deviant behaviour', *Journal of Law and Society*, 30: 479–505.

Cronin, M. (1999) *Sport and Nationalism in Ireland*. Dublin: Four Courts Press.

Deflem, M. (2002) *Policing World Society*. Oxford: Clarendon Press.

Den Boer, M. (2001) 'The fight against organised crime in Europe: a comparative perspective', *European Journal on Criminal Policy and Research*, 9 (3): 259–72.

Department of Justice (2006) *Garda Síochána Act 2005: Joint Policing Committees –Guidelines*. Dublin: Stationery Office.

Garda SMI Implementation Steering Group (2004) *Final Report of the Garda SMI Implementation Steering Group*. Dublin: Stationery Office.

Hughes, G., McLaughlin, E. and Muncie, J. (eds) (2002) *Crime Prevention and Community Safety*. London: Sage.

Inglis, T. (1998) *Moral Monopoly: The Rise and Fall of the Catholic Church in Modern Ireland*, 2nd edn. Dublin: University College Dublin Press.

Inglis, T. (2003) *Truth, Power and Lies: Irish Society and the Case of the Kerry Babies*. Dublin: University College Dublin Press.

Interdepartmental Group on Urban Crime and Disorder (1992) *Urban Crime and Disorder: Report of the Interdepartmental Group*. Dublin: Stationery Office.

Johnston, L. (2005) 'From "community" to "neighbourhood" policing: police community support officers and the "police extended family" in London', *Journal of Community and Applied Social Psychology*, 15 (3): 241–54.

Johnston, L., and C. Shearing (2003) *Governing Security: Explorations in Policing and Justice*. London: Routledge.

Joint Committee on Justice, Equality, Defence and Women's Rights (2005) *Report on Community Policing*. Dublin: Stationery Office.

Jones, T. (2003) 'The governance and accountability of policing', in T. Newburn (ed.), *Handbook of Policing*. Cullompton: Willan, pp. 603–27.

Keogh, D. (1997) *Illegal Drug Use and Related Criminal Activity in the Dublin Metropolitan Area*. Templemore: Garda Research Unit.

Kilcommins, S., O'Donnell, I., O'Sullivan, E. and Vaughan, B. (2004) *Crime, Punishment and the Search for Order in Ireland*. Dublin: Institute of Public Administration.

Loader, I. and Mulcahy, A. (2003) *Policing and the Condition of England*. Oxford: Oxford University Press.

Mac Greil, M. (1996) *Prejudice and Tolerance in Ireland Revisited*. Maynooth: St Patrick's College.

McAuliffe, R. and Fahey, T. (1999) 'Responses to social order problems', in T. Fahey (ed.), *Social Housing in Ireland*. Dublin: Oak Tree Press, 173–90.

McKeown, K. and Brosnan, M. (1998) *Police and Community: An Evaluation of Neighbourhood Watch and Community Alert in Ireland*. Dublin: An Garda Síochána.

McNiffe, L. (1997) *A History of the Garda Síochána*. Dublin: Wolfhound.

Minister of Justice (2004) *Address by Minister McDowell at the 26th Annual Delegate Conference of the Association of Garda Sergeants and Inspectors*. See: www.justice.ie/80256E01003A02CF/vWeb/pcJUSQ5YYCUV-ga (accessed on 1 August 2006).

Mulcahy, A. (2006) *Policing Northern Ireland: Conflict, Legitimacy and Reform*. Cullompton: Willan.

Mulcahy, A. and O'Mahony, E. (2005) *Policing and Social Marginalisation in Ireland*. Dublin: Combat Poverty Agency.

National Crime Council (2003) *A Crime Prevention Strategy for Ireland: Tackling the Concerns of Local Communities*. Dublin: National Crime Council.

Newburn, T. and Sparks, R. (eds) (2004) *Criminal Justice and Political Cultures: National and International Dimensions of Crime Control*. Cullompton: Willan.

O'Donnell, I. (2005) 'Crime and justice in the Republic of Ireland', *European Journal of Criminology*, 2 (1): 99–131.

O'Donnell, I. and O'Sullivan, E. (2003) 'The politics of intolerance – Irish style', *British Journal of Criminology*, 43 (1): 41–62.

O'Donnell, T. (2004) 'Building public confidence through the deliberation of police strategy', *Communiqué: An Garda Síochána Management Journal*, December, 17–29.

O'Dwyer, K., Kennedy, P. and Ryan, W. (2005) *Garda Public Attitudes Survey 2005*, Research Report No. 1/05. Templemore: Garda Research Unit.

Patten Commission (1999) *A New Beginning: Policing in Northern Ireland*. Belfast: Stationery Office.

Shearing, C. (2005) 'Nodal security', *Police Quarterly*, 8 (1): 57–63.

Vaughan, B. (2004) 'Accounting for the diversity of policing in Ireland', *Irish Journal of Sociology*, 13 (1): 49–70.

Walsh, D. (1998) *The Irish Police*. Dublin: Round Hall/Sweet & Maxwell.

Whittaker Committee (1985) *Report of the Committee of Inquiry into the Penal System*. Dublin: Stationery Office.

Wood, J. and Dupont, B. (eds) (2006) *Democracy, Society and the Governance of Security*. Cambridge: Cambridge University Press.

**Chapter 10**

# New directions in Canadian justice: from state workers to community 'representatives'

*Isabelle Bartkowiak and Mylène Jaccoud*

Since the 1970s, the concept of 'community' has become a much discussed topic which researchers in criminal justice and socio-legal studies have been trying to define (Crawford 1997; Clear and Karp 1999). At first, and primarily related to ideas of culture and ethnicity, communities' prerogatives and identities became more prominent when the state (at least in Western countries) decided to withdraw to some extent from its role as a service provider and first port of call for citizens. Neo-liberal ideologies, decentralisation movements and the crisis linked with state agencies' loss of legitimacy have contributed to an increase in the potency of the idea of community in several domains.

Though socio-economic issues have often been an essential focus for the state (welfare, employment, housing, etc.), justice and especially criminal justice had become the *champ privilégié* of state-based agencies. The state had established itself as the tenant of social norms, deciding what was right or wrong and providing apparently appropriate responses to social deviance. Over time, the Canadian justice system became the one and only agency or body responsible for the management of criminal justice and for decision-making. Justice became focused on systemic responses to crime, especially at a time when extensive punitiveness was being recommended[1] as a sign of firmness and political stability. Very much centralised and considered a 'Euro-based' justice system, it was increasingly accused of ignoring issues such as individual differences, the community environment, social context and cultural background or, from a quite different opposite perspective, of accentuating these issues, by clearly focusing on ethnicity (Hazlehurst 1995), socio-economic backgrounds, etc. (Barsh 1995).

Victim and community lobbies were the first to complain about what was considered a 'snapshot way' of dealing with crime. Though their claims extended over a very wide range of issues, they mainly protested either against their being shunned by the justice process or against stigmatisation of their members. From the 1970s onwards, however, a striking parallel can be observed in Canada and in the United States, as justice agencies and bodies increasingly withdrew from the arena. Justice and government officials seemed to progressively value community input and to some extent even restore communities' own decision-making power. Clearly, the state was beginning to realise that it could not deal with all justice matters by itself: individuals and communities could and *would* be of tremendous help. The issue of empowering communities became therefore strongly embedded in the ethos of the Canadian justice system.

In this chapter, we shall consider first what the idea of community means and its involvement in today's justice in Canada, mapping the contribution communities have made to the Canadian justice system. We will also consider the evolution of community-based ideas and initiatives (defined as the involvement of communities in justice issues) from the 1970s onwards, while differentiating the community justice models (seen as a transfer of justice matters into the hands of communities) that have been developed at the same time. After developing a typology of community and state collaboration in justice matters, we shall conclude by looking at the contested assumptions in what seems to be a 'communitarianism' of justice in Canada and particularly in Quebec.[2]

## Communities in the Canadian justice system: a top-down perspective

### Defining communities

While it shares a great deal of resemblance to its European counterpart, the general idea of community in Canada has been very much influenced by the federalisation and colonisation of North American countries. It is usually accepted as an easy way of describing a geographical entity, but also can imply a sense of belonging or a common sharing of interests or concerns with other people. There is, however, something very specific about Canadian communities *per se*, and the meaning of the word becomes much clearer when one sets definite and specific ethnic, cultural and geographical limitations to the notion. The word 'community' in Canada usually refers to Aboriginal peoples and rural areas, and is also used to differentiate between Aboriginal and non-Aboriginal groups. We will briefly describe these usages separately, though remembering that on occasions two or even three meanings may be closely intertwined.

### Aboriginal peoples[3]

When 'community' refers to Aboriginal peoples, it implies a connotation close to the sense of 'minority'. However, it shares some legal and ideological differences from other political minorities and one should be very cautious about conflating the two. Aboriginal peoples have a right to stake territorial claims which other minorities cannot have in Canada, and they have been very dynamic since the 1970s in establishing their specificity not only in relation to Canadian culture and politics but also in respect to the Canadian justice system. The Aboriginal identity of some Canadian communities is what makes the notion quite sensitive from a socio-legal perspective. Since the 1990s (though the movement was initiated in the 1960s), important lobbies have focused their political action on empowerment and self-government, especially in justice matters.[4] These lobbies insist on the need to give powers to Aboriginal communities, in order not only to establish justice initiatives that would be more respectful of aboriginal cultures and traditions, but also to try and address issues of 'over-criminalisation' and the over representation of Aboriginal people in social and penal institutions (Nielsen 1992, 1996). These demands, emphasised by judicial personnel themselves (including judges) have had a tremendous impact. Policing services have been the main area affected by this transfer of powers: Aboriginal communities were provided with specialised police services and a police force. Some *comités de justice* were established in particular communities and enabled to address specific offences. However, we should acknowledge that these transfers of power remain limited, as Canada does not grant the capacity for legislation itself to Aboriginal people. Except for the enactment of some municipal by-laws by local councils, Aboriginal people are not entitled to develop their own statutes. The prevailing Canadian legislative model, as regards substantive criminal law, therefore remains a unified model of justice (the Canadian Criminal Code). It follows that the arena in which there has been most adaptation has been sentencing policies, intended to make the criminal justice system more respectful towards indigenous specificity (Depew 1996; Jaccoud 2006).

### Rural communities in Canada

When considered on a rural-urban dimension, the meaning of 'community' only has geographical associations. It refers to isolated areas, mostly found in Manitoba, Saskatchewan and the Northern Territories.[5] The justice system which operates in these relatively remote geographical areas is very difficult to describe, since it looks more like a colourful patchwork than a definite, unified whole. The main issue at stake for these isolated communities is how to make justice services accessible to local inhabitants, and how to provide appropriate quality justice services in places where two plane connections and a car are sometimes needed to reach a village. This is conceptually very close to the pressures Wyvekens (this volume) describes as leading to a perceived need for geographically localised 'proximity justice':

> Each group is faced with a high demand situation due to the large demographic areas and the isolation of many communities ... many communities are so small and remote that they [contribute] to the fly-in and fly-out policy observed on some court circuits. (Kueneman *et al.* 1992)

### Non-Aboriginal communities

There is a more general sense of the word 'community' which is only rarely used, except when trying to separate native communities from other groups. Some examples may be found in the literature differentiating 'white' communities and Aboriginal peoples. Non-Aboriginal communities are very diverse and not particularly coherent. Therefore the meaning of the word has slowly evolved so that it now also refers to communities of interest or attachment communities (which are also hard to define). Within this latter definition, one would find reference to small neighbourhood entities, as well as the usual informal references to specific and definite communities, like 'the black community' (referring to ethnic groups), 'the French community' (referring to immigration groups) or even the 'English-speaking community' (referring to language differences common in Quebec). This more general sense of the word 'community' certainly has some importance in discussion of justice policies though it carries less definite political meaning in political debates than the two previous ones. Enlarging this already general definition would lead us back to a simpler (yet difficult to firm up) meaning, which would separate 'communities' (capable of self-help in some way) from larger social groups (often dependent on state-run services) represented by the federal or provincial governments.

To conclude this first definitional section, we shall, for the purposes of this chapter, take it that the Canadian notion of community most often relates to Aboriginal peoples,[6] geographically isolated areas or communities of interest. A very basic idea of a Canadian community could thus be a small, isolated group of people sharing the same culture and origins, living in a very limited geographical area (sometimes legally theirs). The term is clearly used as a means to separate groups, and to target people in these groups according to their common sharing of interests, or their attempts at wielding political or social power.

*Efforts to explore new directions for justice: a brief summary*

As mentioned above, there has been growing involvement, from the 1970s onwards, of communities within the Canadian criminal justice system. General agreement on the inappropriateness of a 'fossilised' Euro-Canadian justice system is the main explanation for this ongoing evolution. Alongside this main issue, researchers have identified several other factors influencing the changes in the Canadian justice system (see, for example, Hazlehurst 1995; La Prairie 1995a; Crawford 1997; Jaccoud 1999, 2002; Clear and Karp 1999; Bartkowiak 2003a):

- general popular anxiety about the quality of justice;
- general dissatisfaction (emanating from the administration) related to the cost involved in running the justice system;
- Aboriginal concern about access to justice, over-representation in the criminal justice system as well as in correctional facilities, unequal treatment, the quality of defence provision and the provision of legal advice, all of which has led to a strong distrust of and suspicion towards the Crown and legal representatives;[7]
- a problem of delay (the court process is sometimes very slow);
- the strong presence of victim lobbies claiming recognition for victims within the justice system.

All these concerns address two main issues within the Canadian criminal justice system, which focus on cultural diversity and quality.

Canadians have long been very proud of being part of an important melting pot and of their ability to address some multiple and specific needs generated by socio-economic heterogeneity. The 'One Size Does Not Fit All' motto illustrates this desire to preserve variety and the wish to respect Canadian multiculturalism. One Euro-based justice system could not efficiently attempt to adapt its responses to such social diversity and needs (Canada 1991, 1996). Community partnerships thus became essential to maintain quality and to provide appropriate responses in criminal matters:

> The driving force behind new approaches is that the criminal justice system as it presently operates ignores the social context in which crime and disorder occur and, in doing so, de-contextualizes the offence and marginalizes various players … the expected end result is that communities and individuals are empowered in dealing with their problems and in influencing the directions of the criminal justice process. (La Prairie 1995a)

The crisis in government legitimacy and various lobbies' claims (with victims' rights associations and pan-Canadian Aboriginal movements among the most influential) helped transform the relationships between Canadian citizens and Federal/provincial government, so aiding the disinvestment of the 'welfare state' in justice matters. After much criticism of the Indian Act[8] and of the inefficiency of a rigid state justice which had lost legitimacy, the overall movement showed more determination in promoting citizen participation and community representation outside and within the criminal justice system. Through the appointment of prominent community members, better access to legal aid and the development of what is called 'portable bureaucracy' (reaching out to isolated territories: Canada 1997, 2002), improved community representation seemed to be being achieved:

> Whereas the movement towards finding alternatives to the existing system seems to have begun within First Nations communities, it seems to have grown to a search for an alternative for all Canadians. (Point 2001)

The Aboriginal component of community participation in justice issues provides further insight as to how social-legal transformations started to occur in Canada (Griffiths and Hamilton 1996). Back in the 1960s,

Aboriginal communities were effectively ignored in justice matters. This was indicated in the comments of Kim Campbell, as Minister of Justice (1963), when she stated that there was no room for a separate Aboriginal justice system in Canada. That point was reinforced in 1969, when the White Paper of the Trudeau government suggested the abolition of all special status provisions which Aboriginal peoples might have had in the past. This major political statement precipitated the creation of a pan-Canadian Indian movement (Jaccoud 2002) and increased dissatisfaction among Native peoples. With time, however, Aboriginal peoples were officially granted more rights by the same Prime Minister Trudeau in 1973, when the Supreme Court of Canada, in the *Calder* case,[9] established that Aboriginal peoples actually had a right to land. It is none the less difficult (and debate continues to rage on the matter) to simply refer to Aboriginal peoples as a 'community'. Although it may seem to greatly simplify discussion, it reduces the spectrum of their rights, culture and history, which is why the main native leaders insist on the use of the 'Prime' or 'First Nations' reference. The expression 'Aboriginal community' is seen to imply minority status and is also considered politically and historically incorrect.

When considering Aboriginal peoples, the government's socio-legal efforts have tended to include native traditions and culture within justice processes and to appoint members of native communities to enforce law and order in an attempt to pacify relations between Aboriginal and non-Aboriginal communities (Jaccoud 2002 refers to a 'peacemaking policy'). It is also a way to solve the problem of legitimacy of a state justice system within Aboriginal jurisdictions, as well as attempting to reduce crime, lower Aboriginal incarceration rates and enhance access to justice services. When Chester Cunningham (third appointee of a Canadian justice-related agency: the Canadian Native Friendship Centre) founded the Native Counseling Services of Alberta (NCSA)[10] in 1970, Aboriginal people became more familiar with legal culture and education. The services provided by NCSA first focused on giving assistance in relation to drink-related offences, but the services rapidly broadened to offer assistance to Native people charged with virtually all types of offences. Throughout the following 30 years, because of an ever growing demand for service and legal assistance, Cunningham developed a successful province-wide non-profit organisation dedicated to Aboriginal people. This resulted in better access to legal information and services to First Nations peoples, who were considered almost totally ignorant of their rights when the experiment began.

As a result of these political pressures, courts now travel out to sit on reserves. The rise in community participation in justice matters has consisted mainly of the appointment of paid or lay community representatives within governmental agencies (probation or correctional agencies, special Aboriginal justices of the peace) or non-governmental agencies (victim associations or alternative justice organisations, *boutiques de droit*, etc.). They are entrusted with a huge task: to bring a new perspective to justice issues and to deal with almost every flaw within the justice system. It is important to keep in mind that these workers are, supposedly, not judges (Green 1998). Yet they are the ones who have to bring quality to the system, apparently through empathy with the parties at stake in a dispute. This perspective seems to differ from a purely professional approach, since community representatives have been less subservient to procedures and judicial practices. The cases are not only dealt with according to institutionalised legal criteria and main justice mechanisms, but also according to the general cultural context within which the dispute occurred. What is meant here is that community representatives have tended to refer to more global (though still normalised) frameworks: essentially a combination of good common sense, tradition, morals and human rights. They take counsel from their grasp and understanding of the community they are believed to represent and they have access to local knowledge which allows them to deal with conflict in a more understanding and sympathetic way.

In this context and in order to maintain a certain level of quality and legitimacy, it was decided to appoint prominent and respected members of communities to these positions and to give them enough decision-making power to deal with everyday life needs. Though these reforms are clearly noticeable, these transfers of power to handle legal issues remain limited, as the most important and serious criminal-related cases are left in the hands of state justice representatives who travel around rural communities to provide decisions when needed. Power transfer into Aboriginal hands also corresponds to a 'communitarianism of justice', a context which is currently generalised at all levels of the socio-legal domain.

Before analysing the collaboration of communities with the justice system, it has to be pointed out that the current justice trends we have just discussed seem to be evolving in a way that closely resembles Bottoms' (1977) twin-track tendency. Governmental institutions keep their prerogatives to deal with serious crimes (providing those crimes have not first been dealt with by community justice committees), leaving extra-judicial measures to focus on minor offences. The most usual extra-judicial measures which keep the offence within a community context are mediation practices, family conferences, *groupes consultatifs* or *comités de justice*, etc., most of which relate to restorative justice principles.

We have described two tendencies in the way the Canadian criminal justice system has been relinquishing some authority into the hands of the community: a cautious transfer of power towards community-based justice agencies or community 'representatives', and greater inclusion of the community within government agencies. We will now explore both trends and the ambiguities which are at the heart of their operationalisation.

## A typology of collaboration within the Canadian criminal justice system

It would be long and tedious for the reader to describe every judicial collaboration programme in Canada, not only because there are many of them, as shown in Table 10.1, but also because specific programmes can be different in structure, ideology and implementation from one province to another. Rather than describing the programmes, we have decided to analyse how collaboration is articulated between the Canadian criminal justice system and communities.

We shall consider two elements in setting out our argument. First, we shall postulate that there are two definite theoretical entities in Canadian justice: on the one hand the criminal justice system and on the other hand the community. We assume that both entities may work together. We also assume that both might theoretically work single-handedly and in total autonomy. It follows that in respect of governance and self-help, some pseudo-judicial matters might be dealt with in the community itself, without anything ever transpiring outside community limits. An example of this would be neighbours resolving a dispute by themselves without calling the police. Another (more questionable yet possible in theory) example would be an Aboriginal community dealing with a problem *intra muros* without mentioning this problem to state justice representatives.

Figure 10.1 hence provides a provisional theoretical description of professional justice and community collaboration. The criminal justice system and the community might work together within a collaboration zone. The vertical dotted line in the middle of the figure symbolises the perfect and balanced role of each actor in justice matters. Within the collaboration zone, the more central an element is, the more

**Table 10.1** Types of programmes which include collaboration between the state and Canadian communities in justice matters

| Programme | Other possible names for the programme | Number of provinces implementing the programme |
|---|---|---|
| Arbitration | | 8 |
| Community courts | Sentencing circles *Cercles de détermination de la peine* *Cercles judiciaires de détermination de la peine* | 9 |
| Community probation | | 10 |
| Community service | | 10 |
| Community supervision | | 10 |
| Conferencing | Community forum | 10 |
| Mediation | | 10 |
| Mentoring | | 9 |
| Reparative boards | Healing circles *Cercles de conciliation communautaire* Community circles | 5 (especially among indigenous communities) |
| Restitution | | 10 |
| Victim impact panels | | 4 |
| Victim impact statement | | 3 |
| Victim services | | 10 |
| Work crews | | 4 |

*Source*: Statistics Canada Database (2005), Bartkowiak (2003b).

balanced is the collaboration. On the left, the criminal justice system remains the predominant actor in the judicial process. On the right, the community has more autonomy in justice decision-making. When considering state and community collaboration in justice issues, this produces a model with four different types of cooperation.

### Extension of governmental control into communities

In this type, elements of the criminal justice system are transferred locally to the community and establish more efficient and community-based law enforcement. This type of collaboration is embodied in activity related to community policing and has been characterised by the decentralisation of crime control agencies, allowing the widening

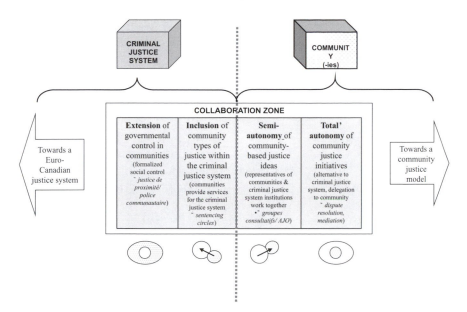

Figure 10.1 Justice and community collaboration

and amplification of social control. In non-Aboriginal communities, a community police or district police presence in large urban centres is the best example of this extension. In Aboriginal communities, it takes the form of a transfer of social control authority to these communities. For instance, in Quebec, itinerant courts have been set up to make justice services more accessible to isolated Aboriginal communities. This type of cooperation is an extension of community policing, largely justified by a concern for equity and efficiency (in relation to the administration of justice, it also tends to mean producing better results in crime detection, case handling and real-time processing).

### Inclusion of communities in the criminal justice system

Communities provide services to the justice system, although the criminal justice system still mainly steers judicial processes. The Canadian Aboriginal sentencing circles (in which members of the community work with victim, offender and judge to consider what might be done about the offence) are the main example of this type of collaboration. There seems to be a real effort from the state to include the community within the justice system in this way, but this

219

participation is considered a mere add-on, since the state retains the power to give final clearance to community action. In this model, the community (symbolically reconstructed by a selection of members said to be representatives of the community) is called upon to take part in the administration of justice, but is still constricted by processes and structures of the state judicial system. In such a case we can refer to a 'participative justice' model. Another example is the policy of hiring target groups to represent their respective communities: what has been called 'indigenisation of the criminal justice system' (such as Aboriginals specifically hired to fulfil particular functions). These indigenisation policies and equal access programmes mainly affect police services. Hiring police officers from specific ethnic and cultural groups, or hiring women, are ways by which the government can at least be seen to be inclusive of communities.

Obviously, this raises the question of the extent to which those hired can be seen as true representatives of their communities. From a holistic perspective, this model fits well alongside our first category, that of the movement of state-based structures towards communities. These structures have often been accompanied by policies of inclusion of community members in the same structures, either by hiring representatives of the community for specific functions (such as an Aboriginal constabulary) or by an incentive for community members to take part in justice decisions (as in sentencing circles or by having an elder sit by the judge during court sessions).

### Semi-autonomy of community-based justice ideas

In this model, representatives of the community are granted an official role within the Euro-based justice system. In North America, this orientation appears to have been a mandatory one. The criminal justice system has found itself helpless in many situations, because of the geographical isolation of some communities or due to Aboriginal claims of autonomy. In this context, community-based actions provide immediate solutions and services to the criminal justice system. This model is a practical example of Bottoms' (1977) twin-track policy: semi-autonomous structures allow for management of specific crimes to deal with situations from which the state has withdrawn. The justice system actually appeals to prominent community members (Aboriginal people, women, gay people, etc.) in order to appear closer to and more representative of the community at stake. Once again, the extent to which these people are still regarded as true community members, clearly perceived as such, or whether they start to become perceived as government and justice agents remains to be seen, as we shall discuss below. The real problem of status these workers have comes from their belonging to the community and also being hired by the state. Examples of such structures can be found in Aboriginal communities' *comités de justice*. Alternative justice organisations (AJOs: Charbonneau and Beliveau, 1999) in Quebec are also part of this model. What defines these authorities is their relative freedom to act independently of the state, although their survival is closely linked to the judicial system, which set up the structures and decides which situations will be referred to the local authorities.

### Autonomous criminal justice initiatives

The autonomy of community justice initiatives still remains very relative. Even though, in this model, there is a real attempt by the criminal justice system not to interfere in community decision-making, community initiatives are directly linked to the criminal justice system and the government through funding, judicial and legal training, etc. We will include in this model any initiative created by citizens and supported by community bodies to set up a neighbourhood mediation programme (*programmes de médiation de quartier*). These initiatives are autonomous because they act without support or control from the official judicial system, although governmental guidelines are very often relied upon (in relation to youth policy, availability of legal advice, etc.). Such categories are often models of non-professional justice and highlight the importance of volunteer involvement. One of them, through the *Regroupement des Organismes de Justice Alternative du Québec* (ROJAQ) is in the process of being implemented in Trois Rivières (Quebec).

Another way to describe these four types of collaboration is shown in Table 10.2.

## Community representation in Canadian justice: actual reality or mere illusion?

We have established in the previous section that AJOs belong to a 'type 3' model of collaboration (semi-autonomy). However, when interviewed by the authors, the professionals within an AJO claimed they were the most community-representative organisation in the whole justice system and therefore a type 4 in our typology. It is important, then, to explore the idea that, in some cases,

**Table 10.2** Community and justice in Canada: a typology of collaboration

| | Type 1:<br>State extension | Type 2:<br>Inclusion | Type 3:<br>Semi-autonomy | Type 4:<br>Autonomy |
|---|---|---|---|---|
| Connection between state institution and community | Extension of state justice structures and representatives to a community | Inclusion of community representatives and principles within state and systemic types of justice | Collaboration of state and community justice representatives | Alternative to formal justice practices |
| Principles | The state establishes formal social control over community groups by delocalising structures and personnel | Community references are included within the system; they are used as a link or as an anchor for the offender with the 'outside world' | Decision-making power is delegated or mandated to community members. Community members or neighbourhood groups are used as 'systemic' appendices to state and criminal justice system | Multiple services are provided to and from the community. Relations with state and justice representatives are avoided. Extra-judicial way of dealing with minor offences, dispute resolution, etc. |

|  | Community policing, circuit court | Victim-offender mediation in prisons, sentencing circles… | *Comité de justice, groupe consultatif,* family conference, AJO | *Boutiques de droit,* social and neighbourhood mediation |
|---|---|---|---|---|
| Examples |  |  |  |  |
| Further comments | Despite proximity of community, state-based agencies and ideologies remain prominent. Community organisations are not delegated any power but are sometimes consulted | The community is nothing but an addition to the criminal justice system. Any 'community' decision has to be accepted and ratified by a Canadian justice system representative | Normally no investment of the Canadian criminal justice system. These community-based ideas are often found within Aboriginal communities. Very often found in Northern provinces (cf. scarcity of resources in isolated areas) | Corresponds to Walgrave's minimalist perspective of restorative justice. Appeals to community. Attempts to recreate a coherent social fabric. 'Autonomy' is sometimes very relative (cf. grants and funds) |

organisations belonging to types 2 and 3 (like an AJO for example) might be a true example of autonomy in criminal justice. We need, therefore, to question the notions of autonomy and of community representativeness supposedly embodied in an AJO by addressing the issues of professional ideologies and training.

## The constitution of AJOs

The AJOs are the main non-governmental justice organisations throughout Quebec and English-speaking Canadian provinces. Not being directly linked with any governmental justice office, they claim to have the most objective and community-oriented perspectives in dispute resolution and mediation. An important difference appears here between Quebec and the other Canadian provinces. In Quebec, 38 AJOs are linked and administered through ROJAQ (*Regroupement des Organismes de Justice Alternative du Québec*). Though each AJO remains independent, ROJAQ allows each entity to be structurally organised and linked to the other entities, and even for the organisation of joint initiatives (training, exhibitions, information campaigns, etc.). In the other Canadian provinces, each AJO remains a strictly independent and separate entity. Their diversity makes a thorough study impossible, since implementation techniques, processes and outcomes vary considerably, though all in practice seem to share the same principles (AJOs in English-speaking provinces actually do not have the same administration and professional ideologies). We will then focus on AJOs in Quebec, since the existence of ROJAQ provides sufficient similar material to explore community representativeness in such an organization.

Figure 10.2 is a synthetic summary of community participation and representativeness in alternative justice organisations. Although this figure deals particularly with Quebec (only partially with other provinces), it may be used as a general schema for a more global and theoretical point of view.

Two elements are portrayed in Figure 10.2. On the left side of the figure is the AJO. The voluntary or paid workers of the AJO have to undertake mandatory training in all types of dispute resolution (from victim-offender mediation to conciliation) and administrative paperwork. They have a thorough knowledge of juvenile law and judicial procedure, which is swiftly updated whenever legislative changes occur. In Quebec, their professional ideology is embodied in a mediation protocol, the latest version of which was revised in June 2003 (the protocol insists on victim-offender mediation, which is directly linked with state-based judicial processes).

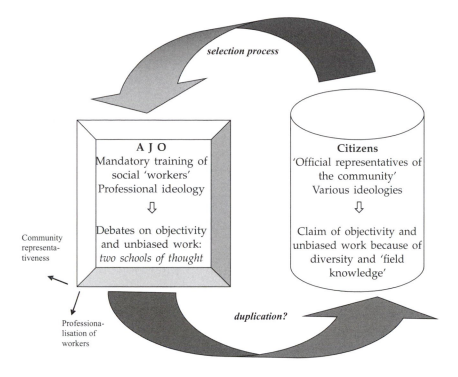

**Figure 10.2** Community representativeness: community participation in Quebec AJOs.

In order to be, as AJOs claim, 'representative of the community', the AJO has to acquire members from the broader community (the box on the right side) to act in its name and to perform a range of activities (from answering telephone calls to organising and facilitating mediation meetings and monitoring their results). As shown in the figure, representativeness of the community is expected to be achieved through the appointment of citizens who embody various ideologies, cultures, ethnicities, etc. Objectivity and unbiased work are supposed to be achieved through diversity in its members in terms of their individual social backgrounds and field knowledge.

It is the issue of professional ideology that generates much debate on community representativeness and objectivity in AJOs. Are training and professional ideologies an obstacle to community representativeness and objectivity? Is community bonding lost with training and professionalism? Two schools of thought may be observed.

The first school of thought remains confident about community representativeness despite training and professionalism. The workers, coming from within the community, share the same values and knowledge. Even if they have to treat a case from a professional point of view, this model simply gives them an ongoing guarantee of unbiased work.

The second school of thought suggests a loss of community representation and bonding as a result of the training process. It concludes that any professional ideology kills diversity and provides a system-biased point of view which echoes the philosophy of mainstream justice treatment. To counteract this, one should therefore deliberately keep seeking more diversity and objectivity through the participation of more citizens in the AJO.

Both approaches have a point. But each forgets to stress another very important issue: the pre-selection of community members within an AJO. The workers seem indeed to come from the communities at stake in a dispute resolution case. However, they have previously been chosen by an AJO, through a specific selection process that tends not to select people who do not fit specific criteria (no extreme points of view, no tendency to violence, etc.). Surely these criteria and selection processes will tend to duplicate a pre-existing professional and preconceived normalised ideology during the selection process? It would also be prudent to evaluate both the quantitative and qualitative angles of how AJOs are formed and how they see themselves as representing the community for which they are supposed to work.

### Assumptions at stake in community representativeness

As mentioned above, local knowledge and holistic frameworks are supposed to be the main assets of community members. However, with the growing participation of community representatives in justice matters, justice professionals have become distrustful of the latter's ability to show quality and equity in the field. Scholars have also referred to some possible drawbacks in the appointment of lay workers (Crawford 1997): particularly that empathy and exaggerated sympathy might occur and favour one side or another in a dispute resolution case. Diversity can actually generate difficulties when community representatives have to remain objective in justice matters. Neutrality in community initiatives is sometimes undermined by political, ethnic or racial bias one might naturally find in a community. This is a paradox in the implementation of community justice. One wants necessary objectivity in dispute resolution and in the facilitation of mediation, yet it must be combined with the subjective approach of local knowledge. The point is to avoid the duplication of the professionalised 'snapshot' model in addressing crime.

Much of the debate focuses today on the training or non-training of community appointees. The debate rages between 'training' and 'coaching' approaches. Training advocates doubt community impartiality and fairness. They stress the danger of letting community representatives steer justice processes without specific precautions being taken. Coaching advocates, on the other hand, have deep trust in the socio-cultural diversity that is embodied in community appointees and which, furthermore, matches the Canadian 'One Size Does Not Fit All' motto. Some also advocate that miscellaneous representation from within the community is in itself a safeguard in relation to radicalism and extreme views, as the pre-set cohesiveness of the community ensures a sufficient and reliable cluster for opinions to be freely exchanged and debated. Here again, many points of deliberation could be raised (among them the extent of cohesiveness and the nature of the community itself). Table 10.3 compares the

**Table 10.3** The debate between coaching and training

| Coaching | Training |
| --- | --- |
| Formal training is avoided, yet general knowledge of criminal legislation is valued | Diversity slows processes and prevents real objectivity and equity |
| Trust in diversity and 'common good sense' | Active training and evaluation in judicial processes, mediation protocols, dispute-resolution facilitation and administrative tasks |
| Community representatives bring several different perspectives to dispute resolution, thus implying objectivity | Training ensures objectivity and unbiased handling of cases |
| Supervision of cases and community members by 'justice professionals' remains passive. Influence of institutions and professional entities are avoided when possible | Regular assessments and updates on legal knowledge, legal and/or civil procedures |
| Evaluations of quality are regularly conducted | Evaluations of quality are regularly conducted |

different points of contention which arise when advocating coaching or training practices.

Whatever the term used, judicial and legal training (in mediation, facilitation, etc.) remains an easy way for state-based institutions to harness individual abilities in dealing with justice matters. It also appears to 'legitimate' community members in their judicial tasks within governmental or non-governmental institutions. The question of legitimacy remains important in the debate and needs to be further addressed, particularly because legitimacy and status have been a problem in the administration of justice since the inclusion of community members in Canadian justice administration. The first part of the problem lies in several questions that need to be explored in further research (we can only raise them here):

- What kind of legitimacy is needed?
- Who should grant legitimacy – the state, the community or both?
- How can this legitimacy be attained?

Since training is mainly focused on judicial training and proficiency in legal matters, the question of the imposition of a judicial framework seems important. Are community members changed into new justice representatives through training? Do they lose their community representativeness? If that is the case, the circle in Figure 10.2 needs to be endlessly reproduced in a vain effort to maintain community representativeness. If so, what other means could be found to ensure community representativeness?

The second part of the problem lies in the double status community representatives are faced with. When the government actually decided to appoint prominent members of the community within the administration of justice, the appointees never seemed to fit either side (their community or the justice system). It was a problem faced by community police officers (Native constables for example) and justices of the peace and it is still met by probation or justice workers nowadays. On the one hand, community representatives have always been cast by justice professionals as ill-trained and non-efficient performers.[11] On the other hand, the community appointees seemed to be regarded in their community as traitors or government spies. That attitude led into their being shunned by their communities (some of them, feeling rejected and misunderstood, eventually moved away).

*Community participation: the cautious reinvention of Canadian justice*

Being either an Aboriginal or a more ill-defined non-Aboriginal entity, the very notion of *community*, in Canada, can sometimes be totally different from the European one, mainly because of a different course in history and of a different type of government. It has for some years been reappropriated by the state and has experienced strong institutionalisation.[12] After a long period of state monopoly, the Canadian criminal justice system has experienced a policy of withdrawal, apparently giving plenty of room for the growing development of community-based ideas. However, the evolution of community justice in Canada is very ambiguous, and entails that we ask ourselves four questions. They show the complexities of the Canadian justice system dealing with Aboriginal peoples' existing rights, its legitimacy, the involvement of community in justice issues and the direct accusations the government has received with regard to its efficiency. We will try to give hints as to the answers to these questions, considering our description of several types of collaboration and of the history of community participation in justice matters:

1 Does the movement towards communitarianism in Canadian justice actually involve transferring power to the community and is it a way to increase citizen participation in justice issues?

2 Is this just an illusion in order to allow more social control and a way for governmental institutions to regain lost legitimacy and justification?

3 Do community representatives lose their community legitimacy when 'officially' trained?

4 Are we dealing with a sound transformation of the Canadian criminal justice system or are we looking at a mere duplicate of a formal justice system within communities?

Several elements have to be taken into account in answering these questions. First, it is not obvious that the criminal justice system has been officially modified over the years. It has been *adapted* to specific cultures (as is the case for Aboriginal peoples), rather than modified in essence. We might also highlight the perspective of a paternalistic system (some communities have a right to a somehow lighter or more specialised justice considering their past suffering) which tries not only to buffer cultural discrepancies, but also to make amends for the mistreatment and past ill-treatment of Aboriginal communities, which are then once again refused full sovereignty in justice matters. It seems that the Euro-based justice system, while recognising past mistakes, attempts to reach out to previously ignored or vulnerable communities by hiring some of their members and 'integrating them' into the Canadian justice system. It gives the impression that the transfer of actual judicial power remains cautious, some might even say calculated. According to the peace-making policies of the governments, some community representatives (police officers, judges, justices of the peace, a court) have indeed enough room to manoeuvre in their decisions, providing they belong to a formal entity within the justice system.

This system, we will concede, while at the same time preserving its judicial boundaries, looks more representative of its communities than it did in the past and seems to be making a real effort to mirror Canadian social and geographical diversity. However, training community representatives in legal practices seems to undermine not only their inclusion in their communities, but also to weaken or dismiss their individual local knowledge by the imposition of legal frameworks, codes and procedures. Although the *communitarianism* of justice seems to address the systemic problems generally met by state-based agencies, the issue of actual empowerment of communities remains questionable. Jaccoud (2002) refers to a *particularisation* of legal processes regarding Aboriginal communities. Considering also La Prairie (1995b), we would like to re-emphasise that comment by referring to the *culturalisation* of specific statements and provisions within the justice system. Nonetheless, if legal training is actually found to weaken community representativeness, it would seem that the pseudo-communitarianism of justice in Canada would in reality be nothing but the duplication of the Euro-Canadian justice system, yet on a smaller community-based scale. The communitarianism of justice would thus merely be a way to increase social control in Canadian provinces and to enable it to cross the geographic or symbolic threshold of previously isolated and possibly untouched gated communities.

## Notes

1 A significant expansion in prison places and facilities is to be observed throughout the 1970s, 1980s and 1990s, following 'Just Say No!', 'Three

Strikes and You're Out' and zero tolerance campaigns in the USA and in Canada, especially in English-speaking provinces of Canada.

2 The notion of community remains stronger in English-speaking provinces in Canada than in Quebec, which is why we tend to separate the two. This difference is mainly due to the influence of the Crown and to the strength of the common law in English-speaking provinces. Quebec has experienced both French and British influences. One example is the prominence of religious associations – which gave potential to community organisations – in English-speaking Canadian provinces, while in Quebec, increasing secularisation has occurred rapidly and has had a major influence on what could be referred to as 'community disinvestment' in the province.

3 The expression 'Aboriginal peoples' refers to Inuit, Metis and Indian populations.

4 The Federation of Saskatchewan Indian Nations (FSIN), for example, is debating Indian justice rights established in treaties going back to the 1850s (FSIN 1994). Considering these 150-year-old documents set the political and administrative arrangements between Indians and the Federal Crown, Aboriginal peoples would like them to be understood as a manifestation of their inherent rights to self-government. Some treaties not only contain provisions that give First Nations the authority to maintain peace and order in their own community (-ies), but Treaties 6 and 8 also recognise the Aboriginal right to develop and enforce law in the same locations. Although all Aboriginal communities have claimed local governance in justice matters, this example allows an insight into what was and still is an ongoing debate in Canadian justice and politics. It is important to keep such an example in mind, since much of our thoughts will show the issues at stake in justice collaboration models.

5 Linking this meaning of community to an Aboriginal meaning brings us on to deal with entities such as Indian reserves.

6 And more specifically to Aboriginal people settled in reserves. More precisely, linking Aboriginal peoples with the use of the word community is also understood as a direct historical reference to the way in which First Nations peoples have suffered relative deprivation.

7 It is said that in some isolated Aboriginal communities, only reachable by air, community members have been strongly suspicious of justice professionals who came to their community to provide services. To reduce costs in a criminal case, for example, the prosecutor and the defence attorney often had to travel on the same plane. It thus appeared that the case had already been discussed and settled during the flight, without community members ever being able to participate in the hearing of the case (see, for example, Clark 1992; Crnkovich 1993).

8 The 1876 Indian Act is said to have taken away all the self-governing powers of the First Nations and replaced them with a Euro-Canadian system of government. Its 1951 revision empowered the Canadian government to regulate all aspects of Native life (Adkins, in Hazlehurst 1995).

9 In 1968, Chief Frank Calder led the Nisga'a tribal council on the land question to court. After lengthy deliberations, the Supreme Court was evenly split on the decision on the *Calder* case, with one judge voting on a technicality of whether or not the Nisga'a could actually sue the government. Even though the decision was not a clear victory, Aboriginal title was recognised and Prime Minister Trudeau reversed his policy on the land question. In 1973 he announced a comprehensive land claims policy. Later, in 1982, a constitutional law established the ancestral or treaty-based rights of Indian nations. However, some provisions within the law need to be clarified, since the issue of sovereignty still seems to be avoided.

10 For more details on the NCSA and Chester Cunningham see Adkins, in Hazlehurst (1995).

11 Research has, however, stated that some quality in their work was indeed attained (Hazlehurst 1995).

12 The YCJA (Youth Criminal Justice Act 2002) recently replaced the Young Offender Act 1984 (see, for example, Leschield and Gendreau 1994) and is seen by some justice professionals and scholars as a toughening of juvenile legislation in some ways. It includes several provisions for alternative modes of dispute resolution inside communities for young offenders.

## References

Barsh, R. L. (1995) 'Evaluating the quality of justice', *Justice as Healing*. Lethbridge: University of Lethbridge.

Bartkowiak, I. (2003a) 'Justice réparatrice: étude comparative de son élaboration et de son application selon les réprésentations sociales et les contextes politico-historiques de la France, du Royaume-Uni, des Etats-Unis et du Canada', in *Justice en Perspectives*. Paris: Ecole Nationale de la Magistrature.

Bartkowiak, I. (2003b) 'Bénévolat, initiative citoyennes et participation communautaire: à la recherche d'une meilleure justice?', *Congrès annuel du ROJAQ*. Montréal: ROJAQ.

Bottoms, A. (1977) 'Reflection on the renaissance of dangerousness', *Howard Journal of Penology and Crime Prevention*, 16 (2): 70–95.

Canada (1991) *Les Peuples Autochtones et la Justice Pénale*. Ottawa: Commission de réforme du Droit.

Canada (1996) *Par Delà les Divisions Culturelles: un Rapport sur les Autochtones et la Justice Pénale au Canada*. Ottawa: Ministère des Approvisionnements et Services.

Canada (1997) *Les Quatre Cercles de Hollow Water*, Groupe de la Politique Correctionnelle Autochtone. Ottawa: Solliciteur Général & Ministère des Approvisionnements et Services.

Canada (2002) *Elargir nos Horizons: Redéfinir l'Accès à la Justice au Canada.* Ottawa: Ministère de la Justice.

Charbonneau, S. and Beliveau, D. (1999) 'Un exemple de justice réparatrice au Québec: la médiation et les organismes de justice alternative', *Criminologie,* 32 (1): 57–78.

Clark, S. (1992) 'Crime and community: issues and directions in aboriginal justice', *Canadian Journal of Criminology,* 34, 513–16.

Clear, T. R. and Karp, D. R. (1999) *The Community Justice Ideal: Preventing Crime and Achieving Justice.* Boulder, CO: Westview Press.

Commission Royale sur les Peuples Autochtones. (1996) *Par-delà les Divisions Culturelles: un Rapport sur les Autochtones et la Justice Pénale au Canada.* Ottawa: Ministère des Approvisionnements et Services.

Crawford, A. (1997) *The Local Governance of Crime: Appeals to Partnerships.* London: Clarendon Press.

Crnkovich, M. (1993) 'Rapport sur le Cercle de Concertation tenu à Kangiqsujuaqq'. Unpublished MS, Pauktuuit/Inuit Women's Association and Ministère de la Justice du Canada.

Depew, R. (1996) 'Popular justice and Aboriginal communities', *Journal of Legal Pluralism and Unofficial Law,* 36: 21–67.

FSIN (April 1994) *It's Time for Action.* Federation of Saskatchewan Indian Nations Tribal Justice System Symposium, 23 (3).

Green, R. G. (1998) 'Aboriginal community sentencing and mediation: with and without the circle', *Manitoba Law Journal,* 25 (1): 77–125.

Griffiths, C. T. and Hamilton, R. (1996) 'Sanctioning and healing: restorative justice in Canadian Aboriginal communities', in B. Galway and J. Hudson (eds), *Restorative Justice: International Perspectives.* Monsey, NY: Criminal Justice Press, pp. 175–92.

Hazlehurst, K. M. (ed.) (1995) *Popular Justice and Community Regeneration: Pathways of Indigenous Reform.* Westport, CT: Praeger.

Jaccoud, M. (1999) 'Les cercles de guérison et les cercles de sentence autochtones au Canada', *Criminologie,* 32 (1): 79–106.

Jaccoud, M. (2002) 'La justice pénale et les autochtones: d'une justice imposée au transfert de pouvoirs', *Canadian Journal of Law and Society,* 17 (2): 107–21.

Jaccoud, M. (2006) 'Aboriginal criminal justice: from imposed justice to power transfer', in G. Christie (ed.), *Aboriginality and Governance: A Multidisciplinary Perspective from Quebec.* Penticton: Theytus Books, 203–15.

Kueneman, R., Linden, R. and Kosmick, R. (1992) 'Juvenile justice in rural and Northern Manitoba', *Canadian Journal of Criminology,* 34, 435–60.

La Prairie, C. (1995a) 'Altering course: new directions in criminal justice: sentencing circles and family group conferences', *Australian and New Zealand Journal of Criminology,* December, 77–99.

La Prairie, C. (1995b) 'Community justice or just communities? Aboriginal communities in search of justice', *Canadian Journal of Criminology,* 37, 521–45.

Leschield, A. W. and Gendreau, P. (1994) 'Doing justice in Canada: YOA policies that promote community safety', *Canadian Journal of Criminology*, 291–303.

Nielsen, M. O. (1992) 'Criminal justice and native self-government', in R. A. Silverman and M. O. Nielsen (eds), *Aboriginal Peoples and Canadian Criminal Justice*. Vancouver: Butterworth, 243–57.

Nielsen, M. O. (1996) 'A comparison of developmental ideologies: Navajo peacemaker courts and Canadian native justice committees', in B. Galway and J. Hudson (eds), *Restorative Justice: International Perspectives*. Monsey, NY: Criminal Justice Press, 207–25.

Point, S. (2001) *Alternative Justice, Testing the Waters*. Lecture series, University of Saskatchewan, 29 January.

Umbreit, M. S. (1996) 'Restorative justice through mediation: the impact of programs in four Canadian provinces', in B. Galway and J. Hudson (eds), *Restorative Justice: International Perspectives*. Monsey, NY: Criminal Justice Press, 373–86.

# Index

Added to the page number 'n'
denotes a footnote and 't'
denotes a table